The Best Of Fine WoodWorking

Bench Tools

W9-BSR-469

The Best Of Fine WoodWorking®

Bench Tools

The Taunton Press

Cover photo by Irving Sloane

BOOKS & VIDEOS

for fellow enthusiasts

First printing: September 1990
Second printing: April 1995
Printed in the United States of America

A FINE WOODWORKING Book

FINE WOODWORKING® is a trademark of The Taunton Press, Inc.,
registered in the U.S. Patent and Trademark Office.

The Taunton Press, Inc.
63 South Main Street
PO Box 5506
Newtown, Connecticut 06470-5506

Library of Congress Cataloging-in-Publication Data

The Best of Fine woodworking. Bench tools : 34 articles / selected
   by the editors of Fine woodworking magazine.
     p. cm.
   "A Fine woodworking book" — T.p. verso.
   Includes index.
   ISBN 0-942391-84-5
   1. Woodworking tools.   2. Benches.   I. Fine woodworking.
II. Title: Bench tools.
TT186.B474   1990
684'.082 — dc20   90-39639
                              CIP

Contents

Introduction

Stationary power tools may be the muscle of the modern shop, but the bench and hand tools continue to be its heart and soul. The workbench embodies the genius of efficiency that's been evolved by generations of thoughtful woodworkers; bench work is the finest craftsmanship.

The bench is, first of all, a work table sturdy enough to withstand the most energetic planing and pounding. Its vises and dogs offer countless clamping combinations to hold the workpiece securely, at just the right height and orientation. And, if something goes wrong, these same vises can provide the power to pull pieces apart.

The real beauty of the bench, however, becomes apparent when it is teamed up with traditional hand tools. Whether you are laying out stock, planing drawer fronts, sawing tenon cheeks, paring dovetails or chopping mortises, the bench and bench tools make the most of your skills. Sure, it's possible to rig a machine for most of these jobs, but the machine will not imprint the work with your own special touch.

This collection of 34 articles from *Fine Woodworking* magazine shows the potential of well-designed benches, from a classic European-style heavyweight to the simple and ingenious systems of the Japanese. In addition, skilled craftsmen share their experience in such essential operations as squaring up stock and marking out joints, in choosing and using hand planes, paring chisels and scrapers, and in sharpening these basic bench tools.

—Dick Burrows, editor

The *Best of Fine Woodworking* series spans issues 46 through 80 of *Fine Woodworking* magazine, originally published between mid-1984 and the end of 1989. There is no duplication between these books and the popular *Fine Woodworking on...* series. A footnote with each article gives the date of first publication; product availability, suppliers' addresses and prices may have changed since then.

Frank Klausz created his ideal work area in a small space by pairing a hefty workbench with a utility table. The bench provides lots of clamping power and the table contains storage bins and drawers.

A Classic Bench

Workstation's center is worth building right

by Frank Klausz

I f you are a serious woodworker who prefers handtools, one of your first investments should be a hefty, well-designed workbench. My joiner's workbench, shown in the photo above, is the heart of the ideal workstation. Based on a traditional design, my bench is outfitted with shoulder and tail vises and steel dogs that can clamp a workpiece in a variety of positions. And it's built solidly enough to be stable under any kind of sawing, planing, scraping, or pounding.

Near my workbench is a wooden chest with my chisels and other handtools, all sharpened and ready to use. To make it easier to use the chest I built a small platform that raises the box

10 in. to 15 in. off the floor. If your bench is near a wall, you might prefer a wall-hung cabinet, as workmen in Europe often do. A 27-in.-high utility or helping table with a 40-in. by 60-in. work surface is located about 4 ft. behind the bench. This table, shown in figure 1 on the facing page, houses 12 plastic drawers (available from W.W. Grainger, Inc., 5959 W. Howard St., Chicago, Ill. 60648): small ones for dowel pins or screws, larger ones for chisels and other tools. Larger planes and portable power tools fit on its bottom shelf. Don't try to save steps by putting the drawers in your main workbench—if you clamp a large piece in the shoulder vise, you can't open the drawers. You could build drawers

From *Fine Woodworking* magazine (July 1985) 53:62-67

Frank Klausz

Assemble the 27-in. high utility table with mortise-and-tenon joints. Locate shelves to fit standard plastic drawers for small tools and odds and ends. Larger tools go on the bottom shelf. Make the 40-in. by 60-in. top from particleboard and ¼-in. maple plywood. To plane long boards, right, Klausz uses a bench slave with the shoulder vise.

that open from both sides of the bench, but putting them in the utility table is much handier.

By arranging my workspace like this, I have plenty of room to work comfortably and can easily step over to get a chisel or a handful of screws. Everything is at my fingertips. The workbench and table also work well together. I do all of my planing, sawing and joint cutting on the bench, then assemble the pieces on the table. The table, being several inches lower than the bench, is perfect for holding a chair or a chest of drawers at a comfortable work height. When I'm assembling on the table, I still have a clear workbench for trimming joints and other last minute touches.

Apart from the knots in the base, my workbench looks pretty much like any other traditional cabinetmaker's bench. Our ancestors invested more than 1,000 years in developing its design and they left very little for us to change. When I worked in Europe, I visited many different shops and the workbenches were always the same design and about the same size—7 ft. by 3 ft.—although the bench height was tailored to the height of the cabinetmaker who used it. Apart from little touches like the stops and oil dish shown in figure 2, the only difference I found was that some craftsmen treat their benches with loving care and some don't.

All the European cabinetmakers I visited used similar shoulder and tail vises to hold their work. The bench screw (available from Garrett Wade Co. in New York City and Woodcraft Supply Inc., Woburn, Mass.) on my shoulder vise gives it about a 7-in. capacity. It can hold a short piece by itself or, working with a bench slave (see figure 2), hold a long piece in an efficient work position. The slave is a notched 1½-in. by 2-in. piece of hardwood tenoned into a cross-lapped base. A wooden block hanging from two wooden ears connected with a dowel supports the work.

The tail vise can hold wood in the same manner as the shoulder vise, but it's most often used with the bench dogs to lock pieces down flat on the benchtop. I use traditional square metal dogs (I ordered mine from Garrett Wade). It's crazy to try to use dowels for bench dogs. They might work if the dogs just kept the wood from sliding on the benchtop, but they must also clamp the work tightly against the top. Square dogs have slightly angled faces so you can pinch the board between the jaws, then drive the dogs down to snug the piece against the top. A workpiece suspended in midair between the dogs will chatter when you work on it.

A good bench should be built of hardwood, heavy enough so that you can't move the bench with a stroke of your handplane. Hardwood is expensive, so I cut costs by buying green wood and drying it myself or scavenging rejects at local sawmills. The bench legs and base are cut from second- or third-class chunks of red oak, white ash and beech—any hardwood will do. It's not scrap, but it's not good enough for furniture.

Though each workbench is a little different, depending on the material you have to work with, don't drastically alter the basic dimensions shown on the drawings. You could go a little wider or longer without creating a monster, but scaling the bench down and using much thinner stock eliminates the weight essential to a good bench. The correct height of the bench is easy to determine. Stand up, put your hands next to your pockets and your palms parallel to the floor. The distance between your

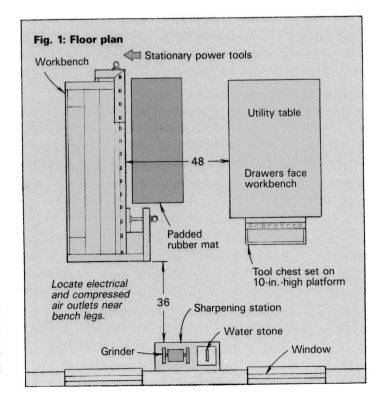

Fig. 1: Floor plan

Workbench

⟸ Stationary power tools

Utility table

48

Drawers face workbench

Padded rubber mat

Locate electrical and compressed air outlets near bench legs.

36

Tool chest set on 10-in.-high platform

Sharpening station

Water stone

Grinder

Window

palms and the floor equals the bench's height. If you make the bench higher, you can't take advantage of your body weight when handplaning. Using your body weight, not just your arm muscles, will give you hours of easy planing while the other guy is pushing and shoving.

Construction of the base—My bench is supported by a sturdy base: two heavy uprights joined by a pair of wide stretchers. The pieces for the uprights are mortise and tenoned; the leg-to-top-brace joints are through-wedged; the others blind. So the bench can be broken down to be moved, the stretchers are fastened to the legs with bolts and captured nuts. To position the top, bullet-shaped dowel pins in the top braces of the uprights fit into holes

bored in heavy bearers screwed to the underside of the bench top. The weight of the top holds it on the base.

Begin base construction by determining the height of your bench, as discussed above. I'm 6-ft. tall and my bench is 33-in. high. Adjust the leg length, up or down, in the area between the stretchers and feet, then cut all the parts as shown in the plan. I cut the mortises with a hollow-chisel mortiser, but you could chop them by hand or mill them with a router. Drill a bolt hole through each stretcher mortise from the inside of the mortise. Insert the stretcher tenon and use the hole in the leg as a guide to bore into the end of the stretcher. Remove the stretcher and deepen the hole to accept a 6-in. hex-head bolt. I rout a slot at the end of the bolt hole to house the captured nut.

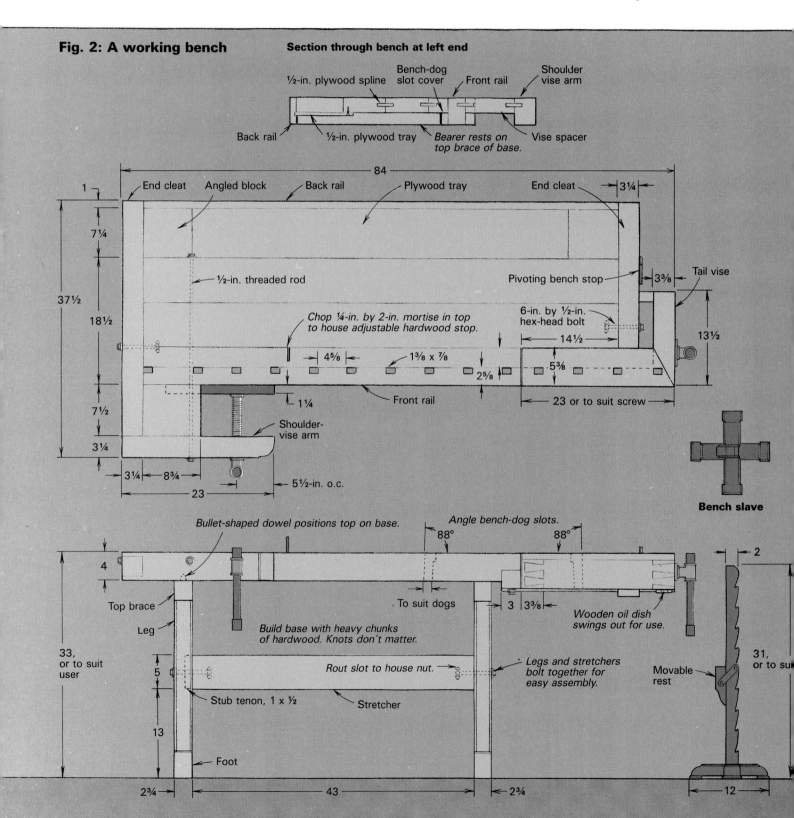

Fig. 2: A working bench

Section through bench at left end

½-in. plywood spline • Bench-dog slot cover • Front rail • Shoulder vise arm
Back rail • ½-in. plywood tray • Bearer rests on top brace of base. • Vise spacer

End cleat • Angled block • Back rail • Plywood tray • End cleat • 3¼
84
1 • 7¼ • 37½ • 18½ • 7½ • 3¼

½-in. threaded rod
Chop ¼-in. by 2-in. mortise in top to house adjustable hardwood stop.
4⅝ • 1⅜ x ⅞ • 2⅝
Pivoting bench stop • 3⅜ • Tail vise
6-in. by ½-in. hex-head bolt • 14½ • 13½
5⅜
1¼ • Front rail
23 or to suit screw
Shoulder-vise arm
3¼ • 8¾ • 5½-in. o.c.
23

Bench slave

Bullet-shaped dowel positions top on base.
Angle bench-dog slots. • 88° • 88°
4 • Top brace • Leg
To suit dogs • 3 • 3⅜
2
Build base with heavy chunks of hardwood. Knots don't matter.
Wooden oil dish swings out for use.
33, or to suit user
5
Rout slot to house nut.
Legs and stretchers bolt together for easy assembly.
Movable rest
31, or to suit
Stub tenon, 1 x ½ • Stretcher
13
Foot
2¾ • 43 • 2¾ • 12

Assembling the top—The benchtop, with its tool tray and two vises, is the most complicated part of the bench so you must measure very carefully when making the parts. It consists of 2½-in. thick boards sandwiched between a thick front rail, which is mortised for the dog slots, and the tray and back rail assembly in back. Both ends are capped by heavy cleats. All pieces are splined and glued. The vises themselves are constructed separately and then fitted to the top.

For the 2½-in. stock, I used quartersawn maple, but you might want to jazz up your top by using several different woods. That's OK if the different species are about the same density and will move with the seasons and wear at similar rates. Lay out the glue joints so that the notch for the tail vise is created in gluing up—

this avoids a lot of sawing and awkward cleaning up later. Since you want to reinforce the shoulder vise with a threaded rod through the top, as shown in the drawing, remember to bore a ½-in. diameter hole through each component before assembly. You can take care of the splines and minor alignment problems when you attach the vise. Glue the 2½-in. pieces together with 1½-in. by ½-in. plywood splines, trim the assembly to size, then cut the grooves for the end cleats, as shown in the drawings. Although the glued-up top is big and heavy, you can cut the grooves by standing the top on end and passing it over your tablesaw's dado head. If this sounds too nerve-racking, use a router. Always reference the top surfaces of the benchtop and cleats against the fence or router base so the grooves will line up. Next,

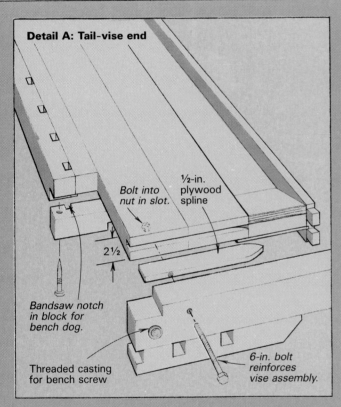

Detail A: Tail-vise end

½-in. plywood spline

Bolt into nut in slot.

2½

Bandsaw notch in block for bench dog.

Threaded casting for bench screw

6-in. bolt reinforces vise assembly.

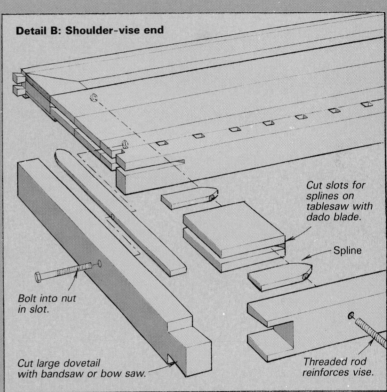

Detail B: Shoulder-vise end

Cut slots for splines on tablesaw with dado blade.

Spline

Bolt into nut in slot.

Cut large dovetail with bandsaw or bow saw.

Threaded rod reinforces vise.

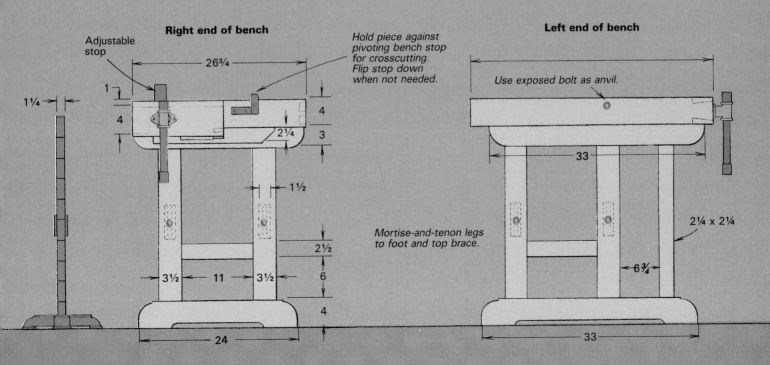

Right end of bench

Adjustable stop

Hold piece against pivoting bench stop for crosscutting. Flip stop down when not needed.

1¼

1

4

26¾

2¼

4

3

1½

2½

3½   11   3½   6

24

4

Left end of bench

Use exposed bolt as anvil.

33

Mortise-and-tenon legs to foot and top brace.

2¼ x 2¼

6¾

33

Benchtop is positioned on the base by bullet-shaped dowels, left. The base itself is low-grade hardwood. Before assembling the top, above, chisel out dadoed slots so L-shaped dogs fit flush with top.

mill the front rail and the bench-dog slots in it. Note that the front rail and tail-vise face must be the same thickness so the bench-dog slots line up. I cut the slots with a dado head on my radial-arm saw, then chisel the L-shaped notch for the dog's head by hand. After assembly, I glue a backing piece to the front rail to enclose the notches. Test the fit of each dog before you glue up. If they are too tight, it will be hard to trim the slots after the rail is glued to the top. I set the dogs into the bench at an 88° angle, nearly perpendicular to the surface. A greater angle might increase the dog's down-clamping pressure, but you'd lose the ability to reverse the dogs and use them to pull something apart—the dogs would slide out of the angled slots. I use the dog's pulling ability in my restoration work. If I have to disassemble a chair that's too fragile to withstand much hammering, for example, I reverse the dogs, fit the chair parts between the padded dogs, then crank the tail vise out until the joints separate. This technique also works on other kinds of furniture.

The tool tray is a piece of ½-in. plywood screwed to the underside of the 2⅜-in. top and housed in a groove in the back rail, which is in turn dovetailed to the end cleats. I glued two angled blocks in each end of the tray to make it easier to clean.

The end cleats support the two vises. Six-inch by ½-in. hex-head bolts and captured nuts reinforce the splined glue joints. The holes are not too long to bore with standard hand or power auger bits. Chisel or rout the blind notches for the nuts in the underside of the top. I leave the bolt heads exposed. That good-looking hex head makes a handy little anvil for blunting nails so they won't split wood, or for tapping out hinges or other hardware. Before you glue on the cleats, however, make the vise parts and assemble everything dry to make sure it works okay.

Design of vises—I prefer 2-in. dia. wooden bench screws for vises, but they are so rare that most people use metal screws, even though they don't have as nice an action. Tailor your vise to fit the length of the screws you have. The shoulder-vise screw in the drawing is 1¼ in. in diameter by 13 in. long. The tail-vise screw is 1¼ in. by 17 in. Be sure to have the screw (and all other hardware) before you build the vise.

The tail vise has two parts—a jaw assembly and guides fixed to the benchtop. The jaw assembly consists of a heavy jaw and face piece dovetailed together. The jaw houses the screw, the face piece is the same thickness as the front benchtop rail and is likewise slotted for bench dogs. A guide rail, parallel to the jaw, is dovetailed to the face piece and a runner connects it and the jaw. This assembly is further held together by two top caps, whose top surfaces will be flush with the benchtop. Two guide blocks bolted under the bench are notched for the runners that guide the jaw assembly. The vise-screw nut is housed in the end cleat.

I cut the large dovetails on the bandsaw or with a bowsaw. The dovetails are very strong, beautiful and show craftsmanship. Finger joints would work, too. You can cut these on the tablesaw. The dog slots are cut using the same method as on the front rails. Close off the open side of the slots by gluing on a piece of ¼-in. plywood after the jaw assembly is glued up.

To ensure proper alignment, bore the holes for both vise screws on a drill press before assembly. I first bored a 1⅞-in. dia. hole for the depth of the embedded nut, then, using the same center point, bored a 1¼-in. dia. hole through the piece for the screw. After boring the end cleat, I clamp the tail vise to the bench and use the drill bit to mark the center of the screw hole. Unclamp, transfer the center point to the outside of the piece and bore a 1¼-in. dia. hole. Make fine adjustments with a rasp.

After assembling the tail vise on the bench, I close it and, to make sure its faces are parallel, saw through where the end of the vise meets the bench with a sharp, fine-point backsaw, being careful to keep the saw between the two pieces. Then I glue top-grain cowhide to each face.

The shoulder vise is much more straightforward, but you may have a little trouble with the treaded rod running through the top to reinforce the dovetail joining the end cleat and vise arm.

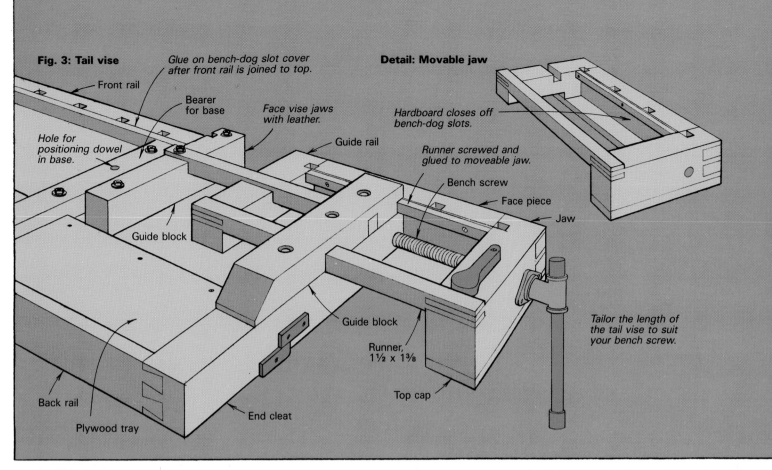

Fig. 3: Tail vise

Glue on bench-dog slot cover after front rail is joined to top.

Front rail

Bearer for base

Face vise jaws with leather.

Hole for positioning dowel in base.

Guide rail

Guide block

Back rail

Plywood tray

End cleat

Guide block

Runner, 1½ x 1⅜

Top cap

Detail: Movable jaw

Hardboard closes off bench-dog slots.

Runner screwed and glued to moveable jaw.

Bench screw

Face piece

Jaw

Tailor the length of the tail vise to suit your bench screw.

Flip-up bench stop is handy for crosscutting near tail vise, top left. Carved oil cup under vise swings out when you need to lubricate plane sole or saw, left. Underside of bench near shoulder vise, above, shows hardwood bench stop and the track that guides vise jaw.

Since you drilled the top pieces before assembly, you should be able to clear the splines and any misalignments by running a bit on a 12-in. extension in from the front and back. Then bore the vise block and arm separately before attaching the unit to the top.

To finish the bench, level the top with a sharp jointer plane, checking by eye, straightedge or winding sticks, then sand with a large vibrator-type finish sander. I put two coats of Waterlox (available at large building supply houses) on every wood surface, then add several more coats to the top. Next rub on paste wax for a beautiful shine that will protect the top from glue or stain. Wax your bench regularly and resurface it every year. I believe lots of people, including customers, look at your bench as an indication of your craftsmanship. Besides, I am spending about 10 hours a day looking at and working at the thing, and it should be beautiful. ☐

Frank Klausz makes furniture and restores antiques in Plucke-min, N.J. Klausz's two videotape workshops, Dovetail a Drawer *and* Wood Finishing, *are available from The Taunton Press. For more on building workbenches, see pp. 14-17 and 18-21.*

18th-Century Workbench

A key to understanding joiners past

by Scott Landis

Accustomed as we are to today's benches, with their complex vises and involved construction, it's easy to forget they didn't start out that way. Like the automobile, the modern-day workbench evolved from a much simpler design. Yet unlike many other mechanical objects, one can make a case that much of the bench's evolution since the mid-18th century has been icing on the cake—perhaps even superfluous.

In his classic four-volume treatise on woodworking, *L'Art du Menuisier* (Paris, 1769-1775), joiner/historian Jacques-André Roubo wrote, "The bench is the first and most necessary of the woodworker's tools." The bench Roubo describes is so simple it's tempting to dwell on what it lacks. There's no tail vise, no regimental line of benchdogs marching across the top, no quick-action front vise, no sled-foot trestle base. A massive single-plank top supported by four stout legs, Roubo's bench is equipped only with a large bench stop, a wooden hook screwed to the left front edge of the bench and an optional leg vise.

How, you may wonder, could such a primitive contraption serve for work on the refined furniture of Roubo's day? How would delicate moldings be held or drawers be dovetailed? The

answer lies in the division of woodworking trades at the time, as depicted in Roubo's engravings (see facing page). The workers shown are architectural joiners, not furniture- or cabinetmakers. Leaning against the wall of the shop are the fruits of their labor: windows, paneling, stair stringers and the like. These men would have spent their time efficiently performing a few operations. The ability to trap short or irregular bits of wood in a vise, while critical for a cabinetmaker, would have been superfluous for the joiner. In looking at Roubo's bench, it becomes clear that the type of work being done was a major determinant of the bench's design.

Discovering Roubo's workbench was, for me, a rare treat—akin to unearthing in some long-lost voyageur's journal a description of my favorite canoe route. Finding a reproduction of the bench was even better. Its owner and builder, timber-framer and erstwhile medieval scholar, Rob Tarule, enjoys the bench at least as much for what it tells him about the 18th century as for what it enables him to do. Perhaps most of all, Tarule enjoys the bench's simplicity, observing, "That's one of the things I like about it: four legs, four rails, twelve joints. It couldn't be any simpler."

Drawings: Mark Kara

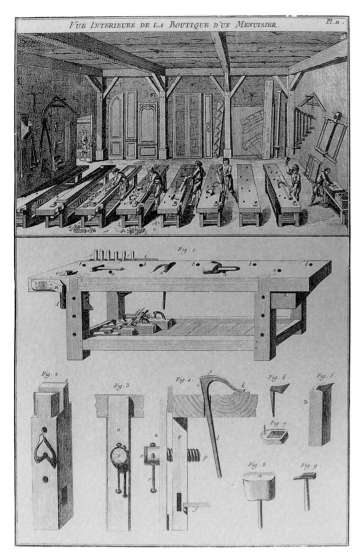

Fig. 1.

Fig. 2.   Fig. 3.   Fig. 4.   Fig. 6.   Fig. 5.

Fig. 7.

Fig. 8.   Fig. 9.

An 18th-century joiners' bench might look underequipped, but it's as capable as modern benches. Tarule removes the leg vise for edge planing, using a long 2x4 to support the board instead. The 2x4 is held in place with iron holdfasts, while the board to be jointed is wedged into the wooden hook. Above, engravings from L'Art du Menuisier *show how joiners worked and provide a close-up look at the bench, its holding mechanisms and typical joiners' tools.*

The Roubo bench is so simple, in fact, that I couldn't help wondering if Tarule was making a virtue of necessity. After all, the workholding system is the guts of a workbench. Wouldn't woodworkers of the period have been the first to adopt more secure methods of holding the work if any had been available?

In answer, Tarule refers to Roubo's plates—for the type of work shown, vises may not have been as efficient as simple stops and holdfasts. Roubo's holdfasts are one-piece iron bars, hand-forged in the shape of an L. The long leg, or shank, of the L is inserted in a hole bored through the benchtop. The bent corner, or head, is struck with a mallet or hammer, securing the work beneath the pad at the end of the neck. In the process, the shank is wedged firmly across the hole in the bench. The time spent engaging and disengaging the screw of a vise would have slowed down a joiner. One or two blows on the head of a good holdfast, on the other hand, will hold a board securely in almost any position; one quick shot on the side of the shank frees the work just as quickly.

Having decided to build a reproduction of the Roubo bench, Tarule first began searching for a top, described by Roubo as a

single plank of hardwood, 5 to 6 in. thick, 20 to 24 in. wide and between 6 and 12 ft. long. "When I copy something," Tarule notes, "I try to copy it as accurately as possible." By the time he was through, however, Tarule had departed from the original Roubo bench several times in building his interpretation.

In the first place, nobody stocks dry wood that large, so Tarule knew he'd have to compromise on the top's dimensions. (Roubo mentions that the benchtop tends to cup until it's fully seasoned, suggesting the use of at least partially green wood.) After almost a year of picking over lumber piles at local Vermont sawmills, Tarule found a mammoth maple plank, which he was able to dress down to almost 5 in. thick, 18 in. wide and 98 in. long.

After handplaning the top flat, Tarule set it aside and turned his attention to other projects. Two years passed, and Tarule took a job as Curator of Mechanick Arts at Plimouth Plantation, a restored 1627 Pilgrim village in Plymouth, Mass. In need of a bench, he decided to resurrect the Roubo project.

With a few minor exceptions, all joinery and surface preparation was done by hand—to leave the appropriate tool marks. Tarule flattened the underside only in the area of the joints. Legs were cut from scraps of 4x6 red-oak floor joist material. Although the top was still relatively green, Tarule reasoned that this would allow the top to shrink and seat itself more tightly around the double tenon at the top of each leg. Roubo doesn't mention glue, so Tarule assumed that none was used. Besides, joints that aren't glued can be disassembled—no small blessing for Tarule, who's had to move his bench several times over the years.

In the same spirit, Tarule decided not to reinforce the double tenons with wedges, as Roubo recommended. He planned to add them later if the legs loosened up, but wanted to be able to remove the legs to transport the bench. In the process, Tarule discovered that, by orienting the heartwood in the top up (as instructed by Roubo), the massive plank seated itself more firmly on the legs as it dried and cupped slightly.

Tarule made stretchers for the bench's base of maple and cut a full-width tenon on each end. The tenon layout was not specified by Roubo, presumably because such construction details were understood by craftsmen of the period. The leg-to-stretcher mortise and tenons are pinned with two dry white-oak pegs driven into the marginally wetter red-oak legs, so the legs shrink tight around the pins as the drier pins expand slightly.

For strength, it was critical that the tenon shoulders fit tight to the mortised leg. Shrinkage across the width of the leg would open a gap at the shoulders, so less wood between pin and shoulder should mean less potential shrinkage and a tighter joint. But if the pin were placed too close to the shoulder, Tarule ran the risk of weakening the mortise. Thus, he placed the pins about $\frac{5}{8}$ in. from the edge of the leg (they can be safely placed as close as $\frac{1}{2}$ in.). He then strengthened the joint with drawboring— an old technique whereby the corresponding holes in the tenons are offset by about $\frac{3}{32}$ in. toward the shoulder. Driving a slightly tapered pin through the holes in the assembled joint pulls the shoulders tight to the leg.

To store tools, Tarule filled the base of the bench with short lengths of 1-in.-thick pine boards, resting on a ledger nailed to the inside of the long stretchers. The boards are positioned to allow the ends of planes to rest on the stretcher while keeping their blades just off the shelf.

Today, Tarule's completed workbench is a testament to strength and simplicity. Because of the top's shrinkage and the stable construction of the base frame, Tarule guessed that gaps would form at the bottoms of the short stretcher tenons where they entered

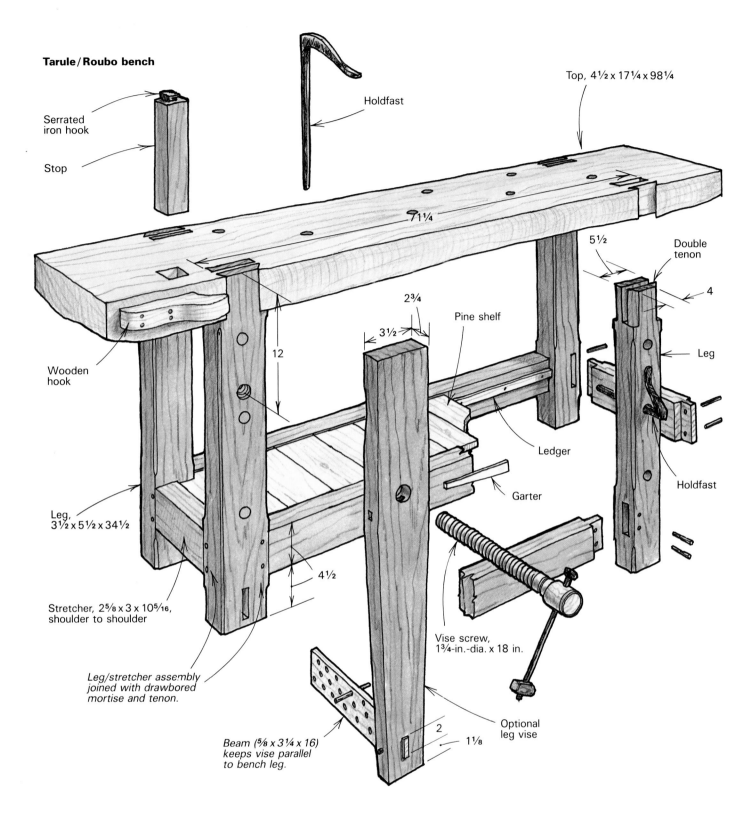

Tarule/Roubo bench

Serrated iron hook

Stop

Holdfast

Top, 4½ x 17¼ x 98¼

7 1¼

5½

Double tenon

2¾

3½

Pine shelf

4

Leg

12

Wooden hook

Ledger

Holdfast

Garter

Leg, 3½ x 5½ x 34½

4½

Vise screw, 1¾-in.-dia. x 18 in.

Stretcher, 2⅝ x 3 x 10⁵⁄₁₆, shoulder to shoulder

Leg/stretcher assembly joined with drawbored mortise and tenon.

Beam (⅝ x 3¼ x 16) keeps vise parallel to bench leg.

2

1⅛

Optional leg vise

the legs. Sure enough, they've all opened up a little, giving the bench a slight A-frame-like structure. Tarule speculates that this angularity might contribute to the bench's overall rigidity.

After being resurfaced several times, the top measures 4½ in. thick, 17¼ in. wide and 98 in. long. It's been given a protective coat of all-purpose "miracle finish"—a mixture of turpentine, beeswax and boiled linseed oil used at Plimouth. This homespun recipe calls for about 2-oz. of melted beeswax (roughly an egg-size chunk) cut with a pint of turpentine. The linseed oil is added in equal measure to the combined beeswax and turpentine.

The bench is 34½ in. high, several inches taller than Roubo's specified 31¾. Tarule points out that recommended bench

heights vary considerably among historians and practitioners. He agrees that a low bench allows for greater pressure in handplaning, but still finds a relatively high bench more comfortable. (Tarule is 5 ft. 8 in. tall, so the benchtop falls a bit below his elbows.)

The stop and holdfasts transform this heavy table into a work-bench. The 12-in.-long stop is made from a single chunk of white oak. It fits snugly in a square hole in the benchtop, and is adjusted by tapping it with a mallet.

In the block's top, Tarule installed a serrated iron hook (a flea-market find) similar to the one drawn by Roubo. Although Roubo specifies the hook's position in the block (see drawing, p. 15), Tarule has experimented with different placements. If the hook

Drawings: Mark Kara

Stops and holdfasts

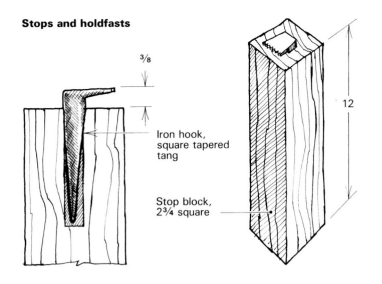

3/8

Iron hook, square tapered tang

Stop block, 2¾ square

12

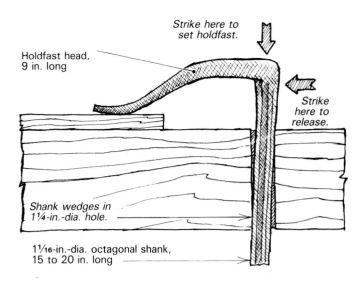

Strike here to set holdfast.

Holdfast head, 9 in. long

Strike here to release.

Shank wedges in 1¼-in.-dia. hole.

1¹⁄₁₆-in.-dia. octagonal shank, 15 to 20 in. long

protrudes beyond the front edge of the block as described by Roubo, the block cannot be hammered below the benchtop for an unobstructed work surface. And, due to the size of the hook's square tang, it's easy to split out the front of the block if the hook is installed too close to that edge. Tarule's hook head is thicker than the one illustrated by Roubo, so he's found it convenient to install it in the middle of the block, allowing the head to protrude about ⅜ in. above the block. In this position, the iron hook can't be engaged if the top of the stop is extended above the bench. To date, this hasn't presented much of a problem since most work requires only a slight grip of the teeth at the bottom, or can be pushed against the wooden side of the stop.

After struggling unsuccessfully to get small, commercially made holdfasts (⅝-in.-dia. shank, 8 in. long, with a 4-in. reach) to grip, Tarule recently had a pair of hefty iron holdfasts custom-made according to Roubo's description. One is 20 in. long, the other 15 in. long. Both have 1¹⁄₁₆-in.-dia. octagonal shanks, which hold securely in 1¼-in.-dia. holes bored through the top of the bench and the front legs. The longer holdfast is used in the top, and the shorter one is used in the legs—at 15 in. long, it's short enough not to hit the rear leg of the bench when set. Hand-forged by a local blacksmith, the pair cost Tarule $130.

A wooden hook screwed to the front edge of the benchtop holds the end of boards during edge planing. Shaped out of a piece of white oak, the hook accepts stock up to 2 in. thick.

Tarule also built a modified version of Roubo's optional leg vise. Where Roubo's vise had no garter, Tarule added one. A slim, tapered oak wedge, the garter fits in a mortise in the side of the vise and engages a groove turned just below the screw's head. It allows the jaw to retract as the screw is withdrawn. In hindsight, Tarule concedes a simpler solution would have been to bore a round hole in the side of the vise, then tap a dowel into the groove.

To keep the vise jaw parallel to the leg of the bench, Tarule installed a horizontal beam near the bottom of the vise. To stop the bottom of the leg from moving as the vise is closed, a peg is placed in front of the leg in one of a series of holes bored through the beam. To determine hole placement, Tarule laid out a grid of three parallel lines along the length of the beam, then drilled ½-in.-dia. holes at 1½-in. intervals along each line. The holes are staggered by ½ in. on each line to provide maximum flexibility of adjustment. For the screw, Tarule turned a hard-maple cylinder on the lathe and borrowed a friend's screwbox to cut the 1¾-in.-dia. threads.

Battens—thin scraps of wood used in a wedging action with holdfasts and stops to provide additional grip—play a major role

in Tarule's workholding system. To gain flexibility, or to plane diagonally across a board, Tarule fastens a batten to the bench with a holdfast. The end of the batten pushes against an edge of the board, which is wedged between it and the stop. This process secures the work and enables Tarule to plane the entire board from one position. For quicker setups, the holdfast can also ride loosely in a hole, just touching one edge of the stock for slight lateral support.

Most modern workbenches have two main operational areas—the tail vise and the front vise. On Tarule's bench, the focal point is where the stop, hook and holdfasts convene. To plane the edge of a board, one end is jammed in the wooden hook on the bench's front edge. Short boards are clamped to the left leg with a holdfast.

To support a board that's too long to be supported by one holdfast, but too short to span both legs, Tarule attaches a 2x4 to both legs (see photo, p. 14), using holdfasts. The 2x4 serves as a platform for a board of almost any length. Stock can be jammed in the hook, flipped end-for-end quickly as it's worked and re-placed with another piece of stock—all without adjusting the support platform.

The ease and speed provided by Tarule's workbench is a convincing argument on behalf of the simple bench. But is it really appropriate for the modern woodworker, who works with a variety of materials and tools? I know of only a few woodworkers who reject the tail vise and prefer to work on a bench as simple as Roubo's. "I've done a lot of work on the bench," Tarule says. "For my purposes, it needs to be adaptable to a variety of methods."

Before adding the workholding devices to the Roubo bench, Tarule kept a Record vise mounted on one end—to handle the miscellaneous small holding tasks of a modern workshop. After unbolting it in honor of my research, he discovered that he missed it on several occasions.

Clearly, the insights Tarule has gained into 18th-century woodworking won't be his last. "I see myself quite seriously tinkering on this kind of stuff—spending the next ten years figuring out how Roubo used the bench." Tapping the benchtop, he adds: "If I didn't have to make money, I'd do it all the time." □

Scott Landis is an associate book editor at The Taunton Press. This article is adapted from his book The Workbench Book, *available from The Taunton Press (Box 5506, Newtown, Conn. 06470).* L'Art du Menuisier en Meubles *(1982) was published by Leonce Laget, Paris, France. A facsimile edition of Roubo's original treatise, the book is now out of print.*

Body Mechanics and the Trestle Workbench

Some appealing virtues, with nary a vise

by Drew Langsner

Fig. 1: Trestle bench

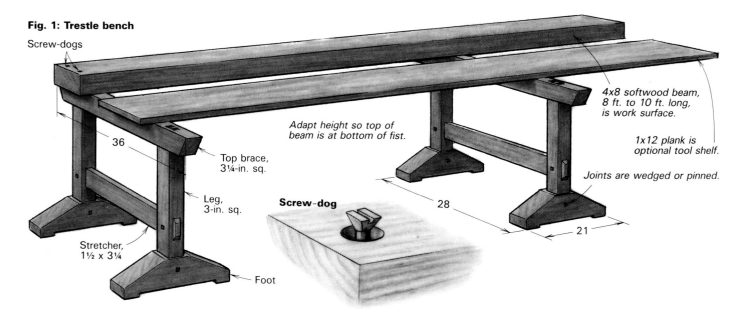

Screw-dogs

36

Top brace, 3¼-in. sq.

Leg, 3-in. sq.

Stretcher, 1½ x 3¼

Foot

Adapt height so top of beam is at bottom of fist.

Screw-dog

4x8 softwood beam, 8 ft. to 10 ft. long, is work surface.

1x12 plank is optional tool shelf.

Joints are wedged or pinned.

28

21

For the past two summers Carl Swensson has been teaching a five-day course in Japanese woodworking at Country Workshops, the series of hands-on seminars I offer at my home in the North Carolina mountains. Up to that time, Country Workshops had specialized in my own main interests—traditional American crafts and the European roots they sprang from.

For several years I had also been attracted to Japanese woodworking but was reluctant to get involved. It seemed an exclusive realm for specialists, craftsmen who dedicated years to perfecting their skills. Western-style woodworking, to me, had been providing enough challenges, and I wasn't sure I was ready for further complications. But I also had a strong intuition that Japanese woodworking had much to offer. The opportunity for a hands-on introduction came when I learned about a Baltimore-area woodworker named Carl Swensson. After working for several years in a conventional cabinet shop, Swensson began to look for a more challenging and personal way of working wood. His initiation in Japanese woodworking began with eight months of work with Kieth Mesirow. Swensson then came under the tutelage of master tea house builder Makoto Imai, for one-and-a-half years. Makoto's students learn by observation and personal trial—the master discourages questions. As a result, Swensson had to translate traditional ideas and methods into western concepts that he could identify with.

Although many Japanese woodworkers work on the floor at very low horses (5 in. to 8 in. high), Makoto uses a trestle bench almost as high as a western workbench. It consists of two horses crossed by a heavy bench beam (the work surface) and an optional plank (the tool shelf), both about 8 ft. to 10 ft. long.

One prominent aspect of traditional Japanese woodworking is the absence of bench vises and dogs. During this century, Japanese craftsmen have adopted lightweight bar clamps, mostly for marking out or sawing multiple units of stock, such as *shoji* rails. But in general, Japanese woodworkers regularly accomplish very complicated tasks using only the body, the force of gravity and a pair of simple trestles to support the work. With practice, Japanese holding methods can be a lot faster than using vises and clamps. At a western workbench, you waste a lot of time loosening and tightening vises and repositioning dogs. At the trestle, you simply flip a board over or change your body position.

The trestles, shown in figure 1, are of straightforward construction. Joints are through mortise-and-tenon, and are wedged or pinned as appropriate. The beam is typically a surfaced 4x8, but can be smaller. It's usually fir or another softwood, which doesn't become as slick as the hardwood top of a typical western bench. This aids the craftsman in holding the material with his body because the material is less liable to slip. A trestle bench is usually sized so that the beam is at the height of the standing woodworker's fist. Swensson's beam is 30 in. above the floor.

Woodworkers who work flat materials with hand tools will

From *Fine Woodworking* magazine (September 1985) 54:82-85

probably benefit from the trestle bench, especially when using Japanese tools. If you're tempted, you can make up a quick version using a pair of cut-down sawhorses. The beam's weight and mass are important. If a 4-in.-thick beam isn't available, laminate one to the approximate thickness.

During his workshop, Swensson demonstrated the use of the trestle bench for chiseling, planing and sawing. The first thing that struck me was the variety of body positions he employed. He doesn't maintain any working stance long enough for it to become tiring. What I didn't fully realize at the time was that all the movement had two more important and interrelated purposes—first, to direct the tool so that it would cut most effectively; second, to combine the tool's cutting action with the most efficient way to hold the work.

Japanese craftsmen use gravity as a work aid. The Japanese believe that one's center of gravity is just below the belly button. As you extend arms or tools away from this center, control becomes more difficult. One reason for pulling a saw or plane to your body is that each stroke becomes more controlled as you finish it. Also, any body (or structure) loses stability with increased height. This is partially why Japanese craftsmen often sit on the floor, and why many Japanese tools tend to be low or short.

Many tools, western as well as Japanese, are easier to use if you keep in mind some of the following rules of gravity and balance. When you can, situate your body with a wide, low base, such as by kneeling on the floor or sitting on the bench with legs forward and spread well apart. When you need control and accuracy, position the tools and the wood close to your body.

Learn to limit movements to the required joints and muscles. Large, more stable lower-body muscles are suited for comparatively slow and powerful movements, such as hogging wood with a plane. Small muscles of the upper body, arms and hands are best suited for detail work, which requires accuracy and subtle adjustments, or speed with less power (i.e. fast sawing).

Whichever set of muscles and joints you use, the other parts of your body should be immobile, but relaxed. Your work stance does not have to be tense if your center of gravity is well within a stable base. Extraneous tension is tiring and a waste of energy. Facial grimacing is a good example of this. Hanging over a workbench with a bent back is tiring and can lead to injuries. If you need to get over your work, extend one leg forward to support the shift in the center of gravity. When bending from the waist, support the weight of your upper body with an arm, thus taking strain off your back and also widening your support.

Chiseling—The cross-trestle leg should be directly under the chiseling area of the work beam, so that chiseling force goes directly to the floor instead of being wasted in bending or vibration. To immobilize the stock, Swensson usually sits on the piece, generally side-saddle, with at least one foot well based on the floor. The idea is to maintain at least a three-point base. You can vary the amount of weight taken by any one of these points. A simple shift in weight will dramatically increase "clamping pressure" on the work. Shorter boards are sometimes secured by folding a leg across the bench, with the piece under one's shin. Problems with very short pieces can often be avoided by chiseling before sawing a board to final size.

I was surprised to learn that Japanese woodworkers use steel hammers instead of wooden mallets. After trying this, I became a convert. A mallet absorbs striking shock that could be transferred to the chisel. The compact hammer head allows better visibility. There's also a greater range of balance adjustments since the

Swensson clamps the work with his thigh and shin (top photo) as he begins to tap out the waste from a dovetail. Heavy paring cuts can be driven by chin pressure (photo above), using the strong muscles of the upper body. This provides good control.

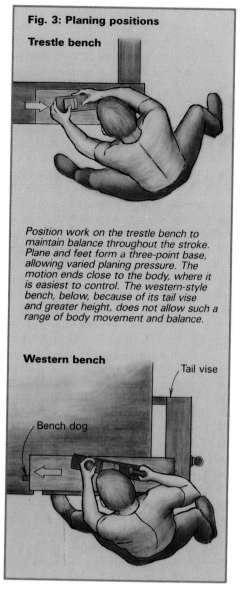

Fast, flattening or hogging work is done with the large muscles of the legs and back, while the rest of the body remains relaxed. Balance is ensured by keeping the body's center of gravity inside the broad stance of the feet.

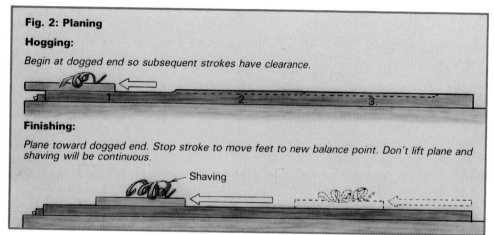

Fig. 2: Planing

Hogging:

Begin at dogged end so subsequent strokes have clearance.

Finishing:

Plane toward dogged end. Stop stroke to move feet to new balance point. Don't lift plane and shaving will be continuous.

Shaving

weight ratio of the head to the handle is much greater than with a wooden mallet. Learn to grasp chisels lightly. A tight grip absorbs the hammer blow and wastes energy. If a chisel is sharp, it will go where it is pointed without your having to choke it.

Planing—Most planing is done with the work pulled toward two adjustable bench stops. Swensson's bench stops are a pair of ordinary countersunk wood screws, located about 6 in. apart, about 1 in. from an end of the bench beam. He has filed their heads to sharpen the circular edge, so it will bite into the wood. Height adjustment is by screwdriver. A small cleat of scrap wood is often set between the bench stops and the work to prevent marring.

During the workshop, Carl likened planing to playing a violin. There are countless methods and nuances dictated by grain and shape of the board. There is no *best way* to plane, but there are general methods that can be used as starters. I'll describe the motions for pulling a Japanese plane. In general, the same ideas work in reverse for pushing a western one.

Fast, flattening or hogging work is generally done with strong leg movements and a locked torso and arm position. Each stroke begins with the forward (left) leg bent and the rear leg extended. The stroke ends with the forward leg extended and the rear leg bent. Long boards are flattened with a series of leg and lower body passes as shown in figure 3, working forward from the dogged end of the board so the plane has clearance.

For finish planing, the legs and body are held steady. The plane is pulled by the arms. To finish plane long boards, you can walk the plane with distinct, controlled steps. Unlike hogging, start at the far end of the board and work backward. Each planing stroke is taken with both legs well based. At the end of the stroke, the plane is held flat on the board, hands and lower arms frozen in place. From this position, take a "two-step" backward, so that arms re-extend for the next plane pass. Because the plane is not lifted from the board, it will take a continuous shaving.

Very thin boards that can't be dogged at the bench stops require a different planing technique. The near end of the board is held flat with downward pressure from the left hand, while the right hand begins the planing stroke. At mid-stroke the plane is frozen, not lifted. The left hand is then repositioned at the far end of the board so that the right hand can finish.

For edge work use a narrower plane, which is easier to steady on a narrow surface. Set the board on the other edge, with the near end pushed against a cleat and the bench stops. To guide and steady the plane, wrap your fingers far enough around the plane block so they can touch the sides of the board being planed. Boards to be edge-jointed can often be positioned side-by-side, so that common edges are planed simultaneously. This will cancel variations in angle; straightness requires care and practice.

When crosscutting, as in the photo at left and the drawing below, rotate the work so the saw's pull is down against the beam, helping to clamp the work. As shown above, rip cuts are best started by resting the work at an angle against the trestle. The left hand, gripping the work, is part of the basic three-point stance. With the body in balance, the arm is free to saw with easy, rapid strokes.

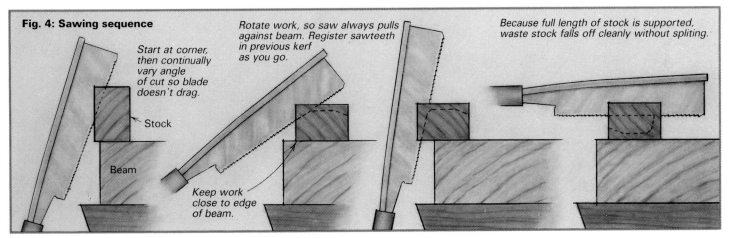

Fig. 4: Sawing sequence

Start at corner, then continually vary angle of cut so blade doesn't drag.

Stock

Beam

Rotate work, so saw always pulls against beam. Register sawteeth in previous kerf as you go.

Keep work close to edge of beam.

Because full length of stock is supported, waste stock falls off cleanly without spliting.

Sawing—Most sawing is done from a kneeling position, as shown in the photos above, with the left hand used as a body support and to hold the work. Locate your body in a position where you won't need to move your head or shoulders during the cut. Your eyesight should align with the saw and the layout lines on the edge and face of the board simultaneously, creating a single, flat plane. This method works well with western-style saws as long as they are sharp and the cut is straight. There will be no need for a tightly clenched hand or the use of force. With a light grasp you'll feel telling vibrations and, therefore, develop subtle control. A light grasp also minimizes physical fatigue. Rapid, light cuts are preferable to slower, heavier sawing. Swensson changes the angle of attack every few strokes, as shown in figure 4, so that he is constantly cutting at a "corner" inside the kerf, not dragging the sawteeth along a flat, full-length cut.

For long timber rips, rest one end of the board across the bench or trestle, and the opposite end on the floor. The prop angle can range from 30° to 90°. If the timber is light, steady it with one foot. Swensson works barefoot or in socks, as shoes may force grit into the wood. Long power rips are usually made holding the saw with two hands. In my experience, kneeling with straight back posture is much less stressful than standing in a bent-over position. You can finish up a rip cut by standing the board on one of the trestles.

Summing up—In my opinion, the Japanese trestle bench is not a substitute for, or necessarily superior to, a western workbench. Both are tools available to the contemporary woodworker. The trestle bench has become my choice for hand work such as mortise-and-tenon joinery and planing. It's fine for sawing, especially with a Japanese saw, if the stock isn't too short. I definitely prefer it for most architectural scale work.

For me, the trestle bench does have its shortcomings. It's too low for doing layout work without bending over at an awkward angle, unless you want to kneel or sit on a stool. Also, the 8-in.-wide beam is too narrow for some assembly work, but you can easily add other pieces up to the full width of 36 in. When I'm building a Windsor chair, or working on very small stock, I prefer the western bench with its extra height and built-in vises.

Working at a trestle bench can become an excellent introduction to the principles of how body mechanics and tool design affect each other. Swensson is quick to point out that there are innumerable sound ways to apply the ideas. Some techniques come quickly, but learning to get the most from the trestle bench is like peeling an onion—many layers and some tears. □

Carl Swensson teaches Japanese woodworking at Drew Langsner's Country Workshops in Marshall, N.C. For information on Swensson's course and other courses offered there, call (704) 656-2280.

Tools for the Making
Recapturing yesterday's standards

by Irving Sloane

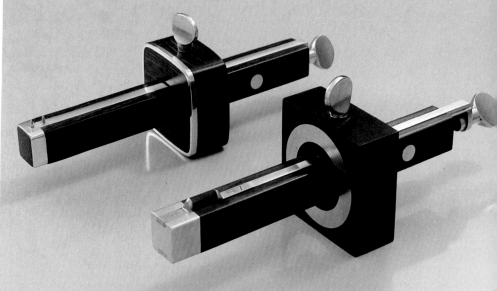

The author makes tools for several reasons—to recapture the quality of days gone by, to meet the demands of special applications, and to improve on the designs available from mass-producers. The objects shown on the facing page recapture the combined elegance of function and appearance that every first-rate cabinetmaker once expected from his tools.

I am probably the only active woodworker with both a Norris and Primus smoothing plane gathering dust on a shelf. The reason for this curious circumstance is that I have built replacements that come much closer to my personal vision of what a plane should be.

I make guitars, working almost entirely with hand tools: a comprehensive collection of planes, saws, chisels, scraper blades and miscellany accumulated over 30 years. The scale of my instrument building does not call for heavy power tools, with their concentration-shattering din. Making musical instruments is essentially a quiet activity, a calming ambiance in which I draw great physical and metaphysical pleasure from planing, sawing, scraping and otherwise working wood by hand.

My idea of a good tool is a solid, well-made object that does the job it was designed to do. It should be comfortable to use and, I hope, look attractive. Finding hand tools that fit these particulars is not as easy as it once was. Power tools have pushed out many hand tools, and manufacturers have dropped others because turnover is too small by today's high-volume standards. Lightweight plastics are fast replacing wooden handles (to the detriment of a handsaw's balance), and high labor costs in industrialized countries will increasingly shift manufacture to low-wage countries, where price will be more important than quality.

The whole ethos of merchandising has changed since the days when tools of durable excellence streamed from the factories of Victorian Britain. Tool manufacturers then shared the universal assumption that having a good product was the high road to competitive success. Skilled journeymen, the "marketplace" back then, demanded fine quality; lesser tools made for dilettantes were whimsically described as "Gent's" tools.

Today, competitive pressures focus on that end of the market where the preemptive word is not so much "good," but "right"—the right tool, the right price, and the right merchandising. The appeal is aimed at the great mass of basically unskilled buyers who are building shelves in their garages. The choice of color for a plastic handle (involving market research and color consultants) is counted a weightier matter than the alloy in the blade. For these and other reasons, I came to understand that if I wanted my dream plane, I would have to make it myself.

I wanted tools that would not only function better than those on the market, but look beautiful too. Using planes as much as I do, I soon realized their shortcomings. The Norris smoothing plane, a famous example from the golden age of British tool manufacture, has deficiencies that make it less than wonderful today. The front grip is a brief stub of wood offering a restricted hand-hold, and the closed handle is designed for the three-finger grip favored by British woodworkers but alien to me. The screw-adjusted cap is inefficient—a half-turn too little can affect the plane's functioning. The cutting edge is concealed from view and can easily strike the bottom of the fixed screw cap or the top of the mouth, and the mouth is not adjustable. The things I really like about the Norris are its heft, coffin-sided shape, thick blade and the configuration of the wooden frog. My own design for a metal bench smoother was based on these Norris features.

The wood-bodied Primus plane is a well-made German tool with a cumbersome adjusting mechanism. Removing the blade for sharpening is an above average bother, and replacing it involves complete repositioning of the blade using two knobs. I find the Primus' horn-style tote unsatisfying in terms of comfort and control. As a plus, the mouth opening can be changed by simple adjustment of a wooden insert. I wanted my plane to have an adjustable throat, depth-adjustment without slack, lever-action blade cap for fast blade removal, and a lateral adjustment by means of a concealed device that could not be knocked askew.

I made many sketches, and tried different styles of tote and handle before constructing the metal bench smoother shown on the facing page. The patterns for the brass lever cap and malleable-iron body casting were made of wood, with the bent sides made of maple veneer laminated over a curved form. Both of these, plus the pattern for the sliding toe piece, were sand castings. The regulating mechanism parts and cap lever were built of boxwood, and cast by a lost-wax foundry using inexpensive silicone molds. Steel regulator shafts and knurled brass knobs were turned by a machine shop. Precise hand-fitting of all the regulator parts eliminated slack motion. Wooden parts are Brazilian rosewood, the handle being a three-piece lamination. The blade is a 2-in. chrome vanadium replacement blade, ⅛ in. thick (available from Woodcraft or Garrett Wade).

For the wood-bodied plane, I used a laminate construction to avoid the difficult job of mortising the throat out of a solid block. Quartersawn teak was chosen for its dimensional stability, and the sole was lined with stainless steel. The metal lining is epoxied to the sole and secured with a "key" mortised into the front and back end of the body. These keys are hard-soldered to the sole plate. Loosening the screw in back of the tote permits movement of an insert in the sole to open or close the mouth. This plane is a joy, comfortable to work with for long periods and has the balance and heft that make it a good all-around plane. It holds a 1¾-in. chrome vanadium blade, ⅛ in. thick.

My total cost for four planes (jack and jointer in process) will average out to about $65 per plane. Not cheap, as planes go, but certainly a worthwhile investment to me. So far, I've built 22 tools—planes, trysquares, mortising gauges, bevels and spokeshaves. Good commercial chisels are not in short supply, so my chiselmaking has been confined to special-purpose kinds. I particularly like the exceptional comfort of a chisel-handle shape based on the handle of an engraver's burin used in conjunction with a square instead of round ferrule. A square ferrule automatically orients the hand in its proper working mode. I plan about 10 more tools, including block plane, instrument-maker's vise, level, hand router, and hand drill of improved design.

The time is not far off when China, India and other developing countries will be shipping basic hand tools of very acceptable quality to world markets. It is interesting to speculate that domestic producers may then abandon the homeowner market and choose to focus on tools for the skilled woodworker. We might see a bench plane that is not a Ford, but a Mercedes. In the meantime, I've found that it's entirely possible to make your own tools using the best materials available, and without the cost constraints manufacturers have to live with. Not the least benefit of surrounding yourself with elegant tools is the constant stimulus to do work that measures up to the tools. □

Irving Sloane makes guitars in Brussels, Belgium. He has written several books on guitar construction, and these, too, focus on the benefits of making special-purpose tools. Making his inlaid bevel gauge is described on pp. 30-31. Photos by the author.

Marking Out

Fig. 1: Anatomy of a marking gauge

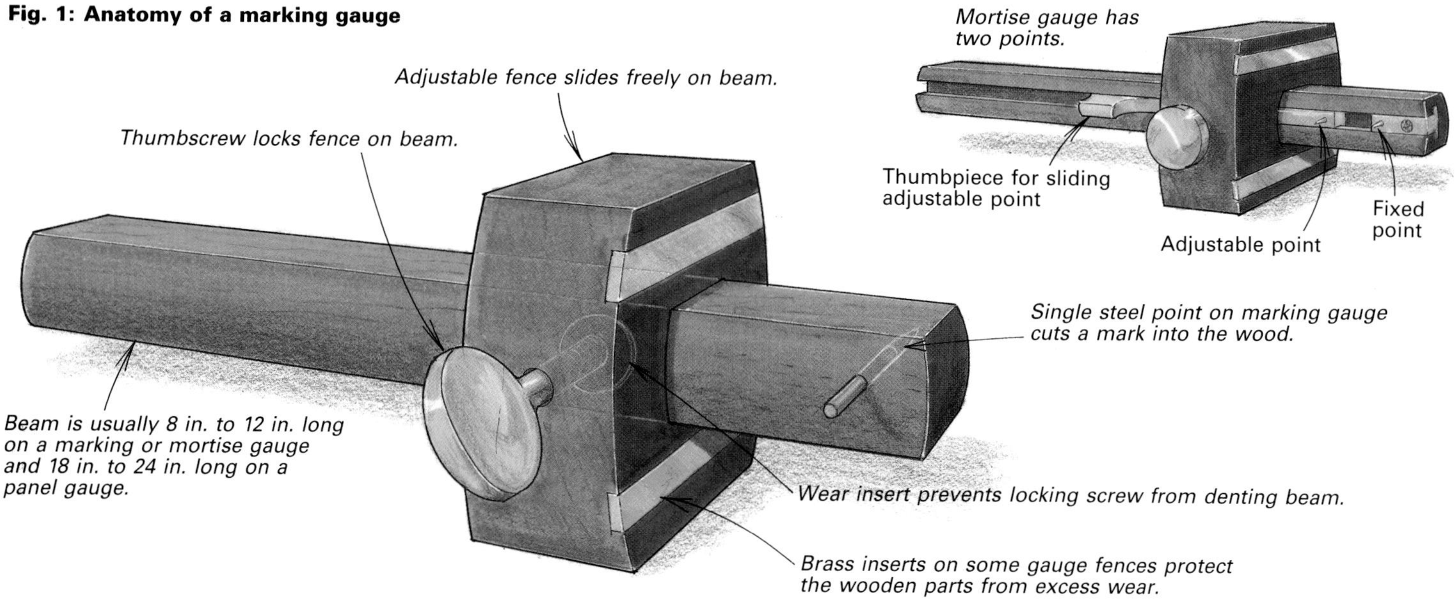

Mortise gauge has two points.

Adjustable fence slides freely on beam.

Thumbscrew locks fence on beam.

Thumbpiece for sliding adjustable point

Adjustable point

Fixed point

Single steel point on marking gauge cuts a mark into the wood.

Beam is usually 8 in. to 12 in. long on a marking or mortise gauge and 18 in. to 24 in. long on a panel gauge.

Wear insert prevents locking screw from denting beam.

Brass inserts on some gauge fences protect the wooden parts from excess wear.

Using the Marking Gauge

by Frank Klausz

When I want to cut some dovetails or make a few mortise-and-tenon joints by hand, the first tool I reach for isn't the saw or the chisel—it's the marking gauge. A marking gauge is the fastest and most accurate way I know to lay out lines for cutting joints and to mark stock to be edged, jointed, thicknessed with a handplane or ripped to width with a handsaw.

A basic marking gauge consists of a sharp steel point set into a stick called a beam. A block with a hole in it, called the fence, slides on the beam and locks firmly to it with a thumbscrew or cam lock (see figure 1 above). In use, the fence rides against the edge of the stock being marked while the point scratches a thin line. The distance from the point to the fence determines how far from the edge the line is scribed. Marking can be done with the grain, across the grain or on the endgrain of a workpiece.

The advantage of using a marking gauge instead of a pencil to mark a layout line is that the scribed line is much thinner than a pencil line, so it can be placed on the workpiece with pinpoint accuracy. This is essential if you want to cut precise joinery. When you saw or pare to the relatively wide pencil line, it's easy to make a mistake and produce a loose or too-tight joint. Further, the marking gauge scribes a consistently thin line, whereas a pencil line changes in thickness depending on whether the pencil point is sharp or dull. A disadvantage to scribing layout lines with a gauge is that if you make a mistake, you can't erase the etched-in line—it has to be scraped or sanded out.

Types of gauges—I keep several kinds of marking gauges handy in my shop: a regular marking gauge, a mortise gauge and a panel gauge. Each has a specific use. The marking gauge has a single point and a beam that's 8 in. to 12 in. long. It's used for many layout jobs, from marking stock that's to be dressed to locating the position of a row of holes to marking the depth of dovetails. The panel gauge is also single pointed, with an 18-in.-long to 24-in.-long beam. It looks like a longer, bigger version of the marking gauge. It's great for marking boards or panels to be ripped to exact width or for doing marking jobs on boards too wide for a regular marking gauge. The mortise gauge also looks like the marking gauge and has a 8-in. beam, but it has two points and can mark out two parallel lines at once. This is essential for good mortise-and-tenon joints.

Marking and mortise gauges are readily available from tool shops, or you can make a gauge yourself (see accompanying article on p. 26). Panel gauges are uncommon, because most people do their ripping on the tablesaw instead of by hand. You'll have to find a panel gauge either at an antique tool sale or make one. Regardless of type, most gauges have nail-like points, which scratch the surface of the workpiece instead of cut it cleanly. A nail point that just scratches will make a fuzzy line when used across the grain and is likely to follow the grain and veer off when working along the grain. For best results, the point of a gauge should be refiled to a knife-like profile. Remove the point from the gauge before filing; otherwise, the beam of the gauge will be scratched. After filing the point to the knife shape, shown in figure 2, reset the point into the beam so the leading edge of the knife points away from the fence about 5° to 10°. When you pull the edge toward yourself during marking, the skewed leading edge will pull the fence tighter against the workpiece. On mortise gauges, both points are filed and set as above. Set the points to protrude from the beam the same amount so they'll make equally deep marks.

The marking gauge—When I use my marking gauge for a layout job, say marking the depth of dovetails on a set of drawer sides, I first set the position of the gauge's adjustable fence. Because the distance from the gauge's fence to the point must match the thickness of the drawer sides, it's easiest to set the position by holding the gauge against a drawer side for direct reference instead of measuring the side with a ruler and then transfering the distance to the gauge. With the gauge's fence in position, tighten the

From *Fine Woodworking* magazine (May 1988) 70:74-79

fence's locking screw enough to secure the fence on the beam. Don't overtighten the screw; otherwise, its point may dent the beam. Before I begin marking, I stack all the pieces to be marked on top of one another with their ends overhanging as shown in the photo at right. Holding the top drawer side firmly with one hand, I bring the fence of the marking gauge against the edge of the drawer side and, with light pressure, score a line across the end. I apply pressure at a 45° angle as I pull the gauge toward me—to press the fence firmly against the stock and engage the point so it'll scribe a light line. When I finish all the pieces, I flip the stack over and do the other sides. Then, I turn the stack end for end and repeat the process. This way there's no wasted motion and less chance that an end will miss getting marked.

A marking gauge will score endgrain as cleanly as it scores across the grain. When cutting half-blind dovetails on a drawer front for instance, the dovetails' depth must be marked on the endgrain as well as on the sidegrain of the drawer front. If you have trouble holding the piece steady while you mark the end, support it in a vise or hold it firmly under your armpit. Also, the scored line may be harder to see on the endgrain, so highlight it with a pencil if necessary.

You have to be a bit more careful when marking along the grain, because the grain may cause the gauge's point to veer off. To prevent this, refile the point as described on the previous page and keep the fence firmly against the work. Also, it's best to take a couple of light passes with the gauge rather than one heavy one, especially on an unplaned surface. I often use my gauge along the grain to size and thickness a square chair or table leg by hand. I first square two adjacent sides of a piece wider and thicker than the finished leg with a jack plane and try square. These two sides provide reference surfaces for marking and planing the other two. I then set my marking gauge to the final size and scribe a line down the length of one squared-up side and the unplaned side parallel to it, with the fence bearing on the second squared side. With the leg clamped down on the bench, second squared side down, I use a jack plane to chamfer the top edges at about 45° down to the scribed lines. Then, with a smooth plane, I plane down the leg's thickness until the chamfers are gone—a sign that I've reached the scribes. Repeat this process to square the remaining unplaned side.

The panel gauge—The panel gauge works just like the marking gauge, except you must use two hands—one to hold the fence against the edge of the workpiece and the other to press the scribing point to the stock. Square one edge of a board and use it as a reference surface to mark the board's width on both sides with the panel gauge. The board can then be ripped (or trimmed by the chamfer method above) to the same width from one end to the other. This is especially important if you're gluing up several boards for a large rectangular tabletop and want the top's final dimensions even.

Although marking gauges are best for scribing straight lines, I occasionally need to mark around the top of a round table for edgebanding or scribe along the length of a serpentine leg or table apron. Since the fence of a regular marking gauge is straight, the gauge will wobble as you try to work around a curve. On a single radius concave edge, you can keep both ends of the fence firmly seated as you scribe. A convex edge gives the fence only one point of contact in the middle, so you must wrap your fingers around the ends to act as shims and keep the gauge's beam pointed toward the radius center. This is very difficult if you try to scribe more than 1 in. to 2 in. from the edge. A better method is to shape an auxiliary fence to fit the curved edge and

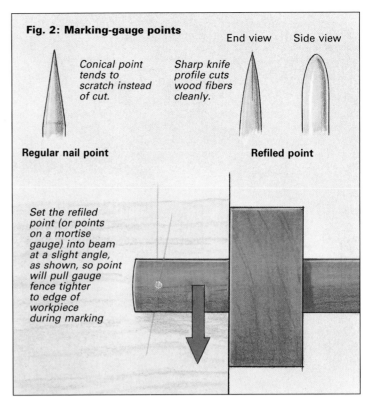

Fig. 2: Marking-gauge points

End view   Side view

Conical point tends to scratch instead of cut.

Sharp knife profile cuts wood fibers cleanly.

Regular nail point

Refiled point

Set the refiled point (or points on a mortise gauge) into beam at a slight angle, as shown, so point will pull gauge fence tighter to edge of workpiece during marking

To make marking a set of drawer sides quick and orderly, stack the sides and mark your way down through the pile. Mark each set of ends in sequence to minimize the risk of mismarking similar pieces or skipping a piece.

Although it's an uncommon marking tool, the panel gauge is handy for marking a panel or a wide board to be handsawn to consistant width. Two hands hold the long-beamed gauge for stability and to get a clean scribe line.

The mortise gauge scribes two parallel lines for marking mortise-and-tenon joints or grooves to be plowed out with a multiplane. The distance between the points is adjustable, as is the position of the fence on the beam.

Using a tightly held pencil as a marking gauge, Klausz marks the board's edge from both sides to find its center.

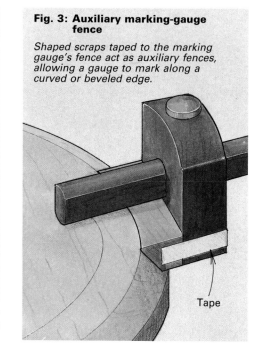

Fig. 3: Auxiliary marking-gauge fence

Shaped scraps taped to the marking gauge's fence act as auxiliary fences, allowing a gauge to mark along a curved or beveled edge.

Tape

tape it to your gauge. This can also be the solution if the edge you want to scribe is mitered or beveled and the gauge's fence can't contact it solidly.

The mortise gauge – Mostly used for laying out mortise-and-tenon joints, as shown in the photo above, left, the double-pointed mortise gauge can be used to mark grooves and slots as well. One of the two points is fixed and the other can be moved up and down on the beam. Before marking out a mortise-and-tenon joint, I set the distance between the two points to match the width of the chisel I'll use to chop the mortise. I hold one edge of the chisel's blade against the fixed point's tip, then slide the other point until it just touches the blade's other edge. Then the fence is set so the two points will scribe at a set distance from the stock's edge. Locking the fence also locks the movable point on many gauges.

Mark the mortise first, then use the same gauge adjustment to mark the tenons (if the faces of the two frame members will be flush). Remember to saw to the outside of the scribed line; otherwise, your tenon will fit too loosely in the mortise. I start at the tenon's base and mark with the grain, moving the gauge around

the end and then finishing at the base on the other side, marking all three sides in one motion. If you have several sets of mortises and tenons to mark, lay the pieces side by side and mark them in order. Just as with the dovetail depth marking, this makes the layout process faster and more orderly.

Marking without a gauge – If you don't have a marking gauge, you can easily mark lines with a sharp pencil, as long as the lines aren't more than an inch or two from an edge. Grasp the pencil firmly with your thumb, middle and index fingers and use the middle finger's nail as a fence, as shown in the photo above. Be sure to mark with your fingers pointing away from the direction you move your hand, lest you get a splinter under your fingernail. You can find the center of a board's thickness by grasping the pencil and marking a line you estimate to be centered along the edge of the board from one side. Then, without changing your grasp on the pencil, mark the edge from the other side. The difference between the two lines will be the exact center. □

Frank Klausz makes furniture and restores antiques at his shop in Pluckemin, N.J.

Shopmade Marking Gauges

by Fred Palmer

I got the idea for this two-dowel marking gauge while trying to simplify a more complex gauge. The tool couldn't be much easier to make: It's nothing more than two short lengths of dowel and a piece of scrap for the fence block. Unlike traditional gauges, the locking mechanism requires no thumbscrews or clumsy wedges, just the two dowels sliding in intersecting holes. The larger of the dowels, the beam, carries the pin or blade that does the marking. The smaller locking dowel has a wedge cut into it, which presses against a flat on the beam, locking the gauge setting.

Figure 1 shows the sequence of construction. I prefer maple for the fence because it's cheap and durable, but any tight-grained hardwood will do. For the beam and pin, you can turn

your own hardwood dowels or buy them at your local hardware store. I recommend making several fences at once from a single piece of stock – it'll be easier to clamp the stock for hole boring, preferably with a drill press. After boring, bandsaw the fences to shape and sand their edges smooth.

The dowels for the beam and locking pin should be turned or sanded slightly undersized so they'll slide smoothly in their holes without binding or sticking. The beams shown here are 7¾ in. long, but this dimension can be altered to suit. I handplaned the flat on each beam by clamping the dowel between dogs on my bench. The flat should be about ⅝ in. wide and uniform from end to end. The low-angle wedge cut into the locking pin is the

Fig. 1: Two-dowel marking gauge

Step 1: Fences

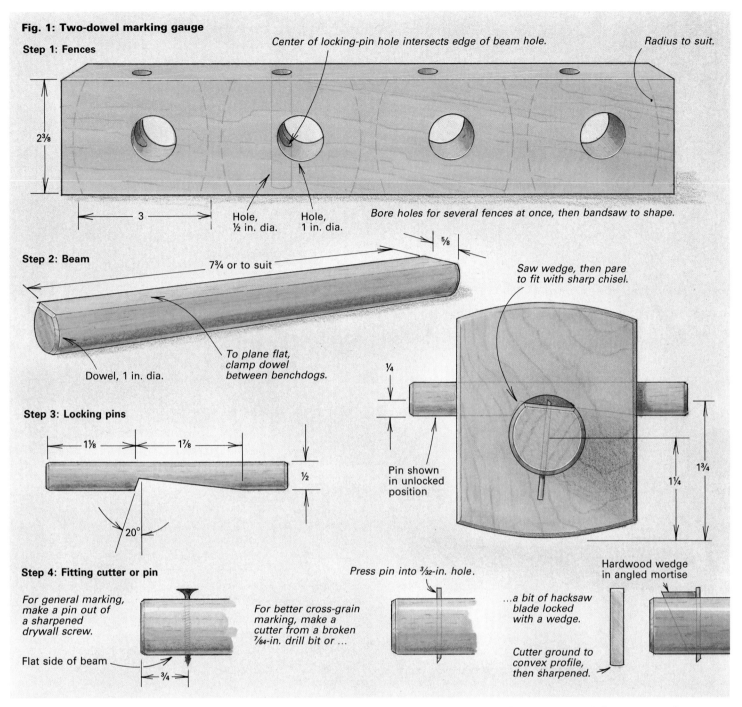

Center of locking-pin hole intersects edge of beam hole.

Radius to suit.

$2^{3}/_{8}$

3

Hole, ½ in. dia.

Hole, 1 in. dia.

Bore holes for several fences at once, then bandsaw to shape.

Step 2: Beam

$7^{3}/_{4}$ or to suit

$5/_{8}$

Dowel, 1 in. dia.

To plane flat, clamp dowel between benchdogs.

Saw wedge, then pare to fit with sharp chisel.

¼

Pin shown in unlocked position

$1^{3}/_{4}$

$1^{1}/_{4}$

Step 3: Locking pins

$1^{1}/_{8}$

$1^{7}/_{8}$

½

20°

Step 4: Fitting cutter or pin

For general marking, make a pin out of a sharpened drywall screw.

Flat side of beam

¾

For better cross-grain marking, make a cutter from a broken $^{7}/_{64}$-in. drill bit or ...

Press pin into $^{3}/_{32}$-in. hole.

...a bit of hacksaw blade locked with a wedge.

Cutter ground to convex profile, then sharpened.

Hardwood wedge in angled mortise

Made from a pair of dowels and a scrapwood fence, each of these gauges is fitted with a different type of cutter. At left, a hardwood wedge holds a cutter made from a hacksaw blade.

A broken drill bit sharpened and fitted into the center gauge's beam is good for general marking, and the drywall screw in the gauge at right works well for most applications.

secret of the gauge's quick adjusting action. To fit the pin, saw the deep end of the notch with a backsaw, then pare out the notch with a chisel until the beam slides easily through its hole with the pin fully unlocked. A tad of looseness is okay, but too much play will allow the beam to rotate, making the gauge cantankerous to adjust. To lock the gauge, simply press the pin with your thumb. The pin should travel less than ¼ in. before firmly engaging the beam's flat.

If the locking action works to your satisfaction, mount a pin or blade in the beam, as shown in step 4. With a drywall screw or a drill point as a scribing pin, the gauge is excellent for general marking work; but for cleaner cross-grain cuts, say for tenon shoulders or dovetail layouts, file the point to a knife edge to serve as a cutting gauge. Although the three cutters shown in the drawing work well, the cutter made from a hacksaw blade held in place by a hardwood wedge is easiest to remove and sharpen, even if it is more work to make. A couple of coats of oil or wax will make the beam slide smoothly and protect the gauge against dirt. □

Fred Palmer is the managing editor of the Pensacola News Journal *and is an amateur woodworker. He lives in Pensacola, Fla.*

Large-Scale Layout

by Percy Blandford

I've spent a lifetime woodworking, mostly building boats and dealing with large sheets of plywood and other materials. Before a boatbuilder even touches a stick of wood, he must loft the boat's curved lines, that is, draw a full-size layup on the shop floor that serves as the actual template for the boat's parts. The layup is drawn on a precise grid of straight lines, with crossings at exactly 90°. Errors in the basic grid could lead to inaccurate measurements and consequent difficulties in building the boat.

Cabinetmakers too need to mark out large surfaces accurately, yet tool manufacturers haven't provided squares, bevels and straightedges large enough for this sort of work. They seem to assume we never want to mark out or test a right angle greater than 12 in. The solution is to make your own marking tools and refresh yourself on those geometric constructions you did in school with a compass and paper.

For short lines up to 48 in., I use a steel straightedge; for longer lines, I use wooden straightedges. Note the plural. I have two 8-ft.-long straightedges—enough to span a plywood sheet. Having two means one can test the other. Mine are made from straight-grained spruce, but you could just as easily use a hardwood like ash, which would better resist damage along the edges. When I first made them, I had to replane the edges every few weeks until the sticks settled to the shop atmosphere enough to retain their straightness indefinitely. My straightedges have a chamfer on their working edge and a curve planed in their back edge. There are two reasons for the curved back: It gives stiffness and resistance to bending at the center, but just as important, it stops me from using the wrong edge. To get the edge straight, joint the stick on a jointer with at least a 4-ft. bed or simply plane the edge with a try plane, sighting as you go and correcting any quick bends or flat spots.

As with squares, a line longer than 8 ft. is never marked by successive moves of a straightedge. For longer lines, the solution is a chalkline, but not the rather coarse string carpenters use— this leaves a line ¹⁄₁₆ in. wide, much too wide for a cabinetmaker. Instead, use crochet cotton, which is fine, strong and whiskery enough to take up the chalk dust. I keep my line on a reel I turned. The reel has hollows for thumb and finger, so it revolves easily. For the other end of the line, I made a little awl with a point out of a steel knitting pin. For chalking most surfaces, I use ordinary school chalk; for a darker line on a light surface, charcoal will do nicely.

To strike a line, push the awl through a loop in the line and into the wood. Hold the reel so it revolves easily, then walk back from the awl, using the other hand to rub chalk on the line. When you have the distance you want, stretch the line without jerking it and hold it to the surface being marked. If the length is not more than 15 ft., reach out as far as you can and lift the line a few inches while maintaining tension. Let it spring back to deposit a line of chalk. If the line is longer, get an assistant to lift the string near the center to strike it. It is important that the lift be square to the surface; otherwise, the struck line will not be true.

Deposited chalk is not very permanent. If you need a more permanent line, put pencil marks at intervals along the struck line, then use a straightedge and pencil to go over the line between the marks.

There are several geometric methods for drawing one line square to another. At small scale, this is easily done with a compass, but when the measurements involve feet rather than inches, you will need a pair of trammel heads attached to a long stick of wood. If you don't have these tools, you can get by with nails driven through a strip of wood or several strips nailed together. But it is not difficult to make a pair of trammels secured to a bar with wedges, as shown in figure 1. The dimensions are not critical, but if you make the heads to fit a 1-in. by 2-in. bar, use ¼-in. steel rod secured with epoxy for the marking points. At times, a pencil is preferable to a steel point—one can be put through a hole in the trammel head and held with a wedge.

The simple way of using trammels to erect a perpendicular is shown in method 1. If your work demands great accuracy, there are two considerations. It is difficult to be certain of the exact crossing point of the arcs at point D if they meet at a shallow angle, which is the result of too narrow a baseline. Therefore, proportion your trammel settings so the arcs at point D will cross at near 90°. Second, have the arcs at point D crossing farther from the baseline than the final length you want the perpendicular line to be; otherwise, you might introduce error by extending the line past the intersection with a straightedge.

Very often the perpendicular must be marked near a corner and the method just described will not work. In this case, use the technique described in method 2, which relies on the fact that any triangle whose base is the diameter of a circle and whose apex is on the circumference of the same circle must have an apex angle of 90°. As with the first geometric method, choose a size that puts the arc crossings farther from the baseline than the most distant point on the perpendicular.

When you need really large sizes, a trammel becomes rather unwieldy. It is possible to use a steel tape measure, marking the

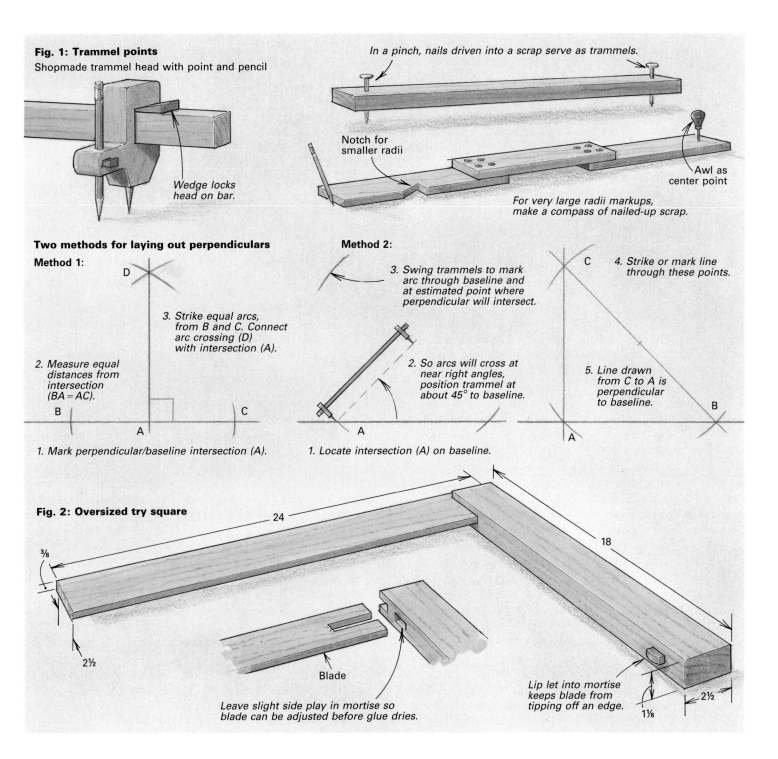

Fig. 1: Trammel points
Shopmade trammel head with point and pencil

Wedge locks head on bar.

In a pinch, nails driven into a scrap serve as trammels.

Notch for smaller radii

Awl as center point

For very large radii markups, make a compass of nailed-up scrap.

Two methods for laying out perpendiculars

Method 1:

3. Strike equal arcs, from B and C. Connect arc crossing (D) with intersection (A).

2. Measure equal distances from intersection (BA = AC).

1. Mark perpendicular/baseline intersection (A).

Method 2:

3. Swing trammels to mark arc through baseline and at estimated point where perpendicular will intersect.

2. So arcs will cross at near right angles, position trammel at about 45° to baseline.

1. Locate intersection (A) on baseline.

4. Strike or mark line through these points.

5. Line drawn from C to A is perpendicular to baseline.

Fig. 2: Oversized try square

24

3/8

2½

18

2½

1⅛

Blade

Leave slight side play in mortise so blade can be adjusted before glue dries.

Lip let into mortise keeps blade from tipping off an edge.

distance with a pencil while the center is held with an awl by an assistant. A more accurate method, however, is to improvise a compass from scrapwood temporarily nailed together. An awl provides the center, and the compass length is cut to the intended radius. If shorter radii are needed, cut notches in the compass, as shown in figure 1.

Geometry takes care of the very large constructions, but it can be unnecessarily tedious when working with pieces 18 in. wide to 48 in. wide. If you often work within these sizes, it is worthwhile to make your own large squares. I have two and would feel lost without them. The first is simple. It is just a giant plywood drafting square cut as large as a standard plywood sheet will allow. It is made of marine-grade mahogany plywood, which is stout enough to be stiff without being very heavy. The square is laid out using the geometric method described above. The center is cut out for lightness.

I also have a wooden try square made of oak, mainly because

that was the wood I had at the time. Any straight-grained species will do just as well. The square is difficult to adjust if the wood warps after you have made the square, so prepare the pieces some time in advance and keep them in the shop for a month or so to give them time to acclimate to the shop's humidity. Construction is straightforward, but sizes and assembly have to be accurate. In particular, edges must be straight, square and perfectly parallel. Give the mortise and tenon very slight sideways clearance, then as you assemble with glue in the joint, set the blade to a line marked square to the edge of a plywood sheet. Try the blade both ways, then leave the glue to harden. The little lip mortised into the handle prevents it from tilting in use. The lip is acceptable, because the square is used mainly for surface work and not for testing over edges—a small square does that. ☐

Percy Blandford is a boatbuilder, draftsman and author. He lives in Stratford-upon-Avon, England.

Building a Wooden Hygrometer

Measuring humidity's dramatic effect on wood

by Warren W. Miller

Most woodworkers are well aware that wood moves with seasonal humidity changes, but few have a convenient way to measure moisture. You can get a rough idea by noting the relative humidity (RH) levels reported on your local weather station or you can buy an instrument called a hygrometer, which measures the amount of moisture in the air. But, since each species of wood expands and contracts at a definite measurable rate, I decided to use this natural relationship between wood movement and moisture as the basis of my own shop-built hygrometer.

My instrument consists of four pieces of wood: a laminated strip that bends with changes in RH, a clamp that anchors one end of the strip, a scale at the free, moving end of the strip, and a strut that connects the clamp and scale, as shown in the drawing on the facing page. The hygrometer looks simple, but it graphically demonstrates how RH causes wood movement by changing wood's moisture content (MC).

Relative humidity's effect on wood—Ignoring the effect of humidity on wood can create problems. Chairs, once tightly joined together in the workshop, become loose and wrack during winter's low RH. Door panels may buckle during damp weather or split during dry weather if they're fit too tightly or inadvertently glued into the door's rails or stiles.

The amount of movement can be significant. Increasing the MC of white oak from 5% to 13%, for example, causes a 2% increase in the width of a flatsawn board; that's ³⁄₁₆ in. in a 10-in. board! Now, that 8% difference in MC happens when RH increases from 30% to 75%, a 45% change that's a common annual occurrence in many locations. A flatsawn piece of redwood, on the other hand, moves less than 1% across its face during the same change in RH. In general, softwoods are more stable than hardwoods. For more on moisture's effect on wood movement, see Bruce Hoadley's book *Understanding Wood* (The Taunton Press, 1980).

Within any one species, movement due to changes in RH is virtually zero along the grain compared to across the grain. Because of these predictable, moisture-related changes, I was able to base my wooden hygrometer on the same principle as some thermometers employing a thin bimetal strip laminated from two metals that move differently when the temperature changes. Instead of a bimetal strip, the wooden hygrometer has what I call a "biaxial" strip: two wafer-thin laminates, one ripped on the longitudinal-grain axis and the other crosscut on the end-grain axis.

How biaxial laminates move—My laminated strip moves as MC levels vary because of the different dimensional changes of the two laminates. The end-grain changes much more than the virtually stable longitudinal-grain that it actually bends the longitudinal-grain strip.

My hygrometer's biaxial strip is cherry, but most domestic hardwoods will do as well. With a 30% change in RH, the end-grain cherry strip will change dimension about 1½%, or about ⁵⁄₃₂ in. in 10 in., making for dramatic strip movement. As previously discussed, softwoods are less affected by moisture changes than hardwoods, so they are a poor choice for a biaxial lamination since strip movement would be so subdued.

You should be sure to saw the end-grain laminate from a flatsawn board, where the annual rings are more or less parallel to its width. A quartersawn board, where the annual rings are more or less perpendicular to the board's width, shrink and expand only one-half as much as a flatsawn board of the same species. This makes quartersawn lumber ideal for woodwork, for which stability is important, but a poor choice for our hygrometer, for which movement is desirable.

Using a thin-kerf ATB carbide blade in the tablesaw and a shop-made narrow-gap saw table insert, I ripped and crosscut the ³⁄₆₄-in.-thick strips of cherry. This proved to be the thinnest section of a cross-grain strip capable of bending freely without breaking.

Laminating the strip—Since the hygrometer's strip should be straight when the RH is near 50%, be sure to laminate it when the RH in the shop is close to 50%, as reported on your local weather forecast. When laminating, avoid filling the open pores of the end-grain strip with glue. The end-grain surface will readily absorb glue, and this could hinder its ability to absorb moisture. To avoid this problem, I use a thick, viscous epoxy and take care to spread a thin coat only on the longitudinal-grain surface before pressing the laminates together. Applied this way the glue acts as a surface treatment and little of it is absorbed by the endgrain. Care should be taken to keep the strip clean and free of moisture-blocking substances, such as oily fingerprints. And, of course, no finish should be applied to the raw wood. After wrapping the laminates in wax paper, clamp the assembly between strips of wood and set it aside to cure overnight.

When the glue has cured, scrape and sand the excess from the edges of the biaxial strip and assemble the hygrometer as shown. The calibration clamp is a 1-in.-long piece of 1-in.-dia. dowel that is inserted into a 1-in.-dia. hole in the bottom of the strut. Kerf the dowel to accept the laminated strip, which is secured with a set screw. The strut also has a thin kerf and a screw tightens the clamp in position after the instrument has been calibrated. The strut, which is longer than the strip, is dadoed for the scale, as deep as the scale is thick, near its top (see the drawing).

The required length of the scale will not only depend on the wood species of the strip, but also its length and thickness and the amount of end-grain glue absorption. For the instrument in the drawing, the free end of the laminated strip moves about 6 in.

From *Fine Woodworking* magazine (March 1990) 81:68-69

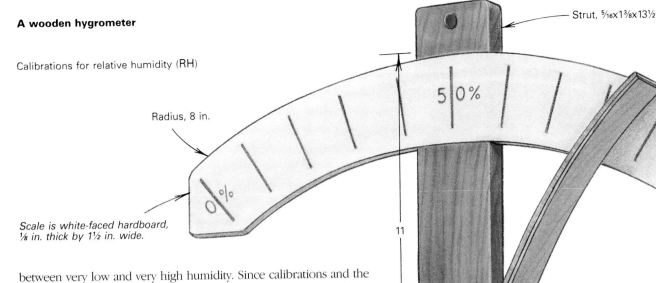

A wooden hygrometer

Calibrations for relative humidity (RH)

Radius, 8 in.

Strut, 5/16x1 3/8x13 1/2

50%

10 0%

0%

*Scale is white-faced hardboard,
1/8 in. thick by 1 1/2 in. wide.*

11

Biaxial strip

Longitudinal grain, 3/64x3/4x11 1/2

Endgrain, 3/64x3/4x11 1/2

Calibration clamp is a dowel,
1 in. long by 1 in. dia., kerfed 3/32 in.

Strut is kerfed to tighten
calibration clamp.

Round-head machine screw,
#8-32 by 1 in.

Round-head machine screw,
#8-32 by 3/4 in.

between very low and very high humidity. Since calibrations and the final size will depend on how much the strip bends, temporarily secure the scale in the strut's dado before making any marks on it or cutting it to size. Tighten the biaxial strip in the calibration clamp and then temporarily tighten the clamp in the strut so the strip points straight up the strut's midline.

Calibrating the hygrometer—The hygrometer is calibrated by subjecting it to a few known, controlled humidity levels in an airtight chamber. The biaxial strip will bend until it stabilizes at each humidity level so you can locate each reading on the scale. Once you've established two or three levels, you can divide the scale into equal increments to establish additional levels.

Accurately controlling humidity requires a shopmade, air-tight chamber and a chemical system that produces a predictable RH level. My chamber was an inverted glass baking dish sealed to the enameled top of my washing machine with tape, although any smooth, shiny surface would have worked.

Begin calibration by placing a dish of plain water in the chamber, along with your wooden hygrometer, and in time the entrapped air will stabilize at 100% RH. As the wood's MC changes, in this instance because it's absorbing moisture, the strip begins to bend with the end-grain side of the strip on the outside of the curve. Leave it until there is no more apparent movement in a six-hour period and then temporarily mark the pointer position on the scale.

To get a second reading, repeat the process, but substitute a calcium chloride chemical solution for the plain water. Anhydrous calcium chloride, such as commercial snow melter, is safe to handle, inexpensive and available in many hardware stores. Since different salts produce different results, be sure you get calcium chloride ($CaCl_2$) and not rock salt (NaCl). In a glass jar, dissolve a handful of the calcium chloride in about half its weight of water. Heat the solution by placing the jar in a pan of hot tap water, and then loosely cover the jar and leave it overnight to cool. A large crop of white crystals of the hydrate ($CaCl_2·6H_2O$) should separate in the dish. If they do not, reheat the solution and add more calcium chloride. Transfer the crystals and some of the solution to the dish in the humidity chamber, add the hygrometer and seal the chamber. The RH of the atmosphere in the chamber will stabilize at 32%. As it does, the strip will bend toward its end-grain side, with the longitudinal grain on the outside of the curve, and establish a new position on your scale. Wait until there is no more movement, as before, and then remove the hygrometer and cover the chamber for final calibration.

Now replace the preliminary calibration marks with permanent ones. I've found that the scale is very nearly linear, meaning each 10% increment is equal. Determine these increments by bending a thin, supple measuring scale along and adjacent to the scale's arc;

be sure to note the length of the arc between the 100% and 32% marks and divide it by 6.8. For instance, if there are 7 in. between the 100% and 32% marks, 10% increments equal 1.03 or one every 1 1/32 in., which is set on a pair of dividers and stepped off on the scale. Now, establish permanent marks at each 10% increment between 0% and 100%, but don't erase the temporary 32% RH mark until after you've fastened the scale and rechecked the calibration.

The next step is to permanently fasten the scale to the instrument's strut. Trim the scale's ends symmetrically, leaving some material beyond 0% and 100%, and permanently glue it in the dado with the 50% calibration mark on the strut's midline. Finally, return the hygrometer to the chamber, which is still set up for 32% RH, let the strip stabilize, turn the calibration clamp until the strip is pointing to 32% and tighten the clamp in the strut. Your instrument is calibrated and ready for use! ☐

Warren Miller is a retired chemistry professor whose woodworking shop is in State College, Pa.

Metal Handplanes
Is a cheap one worth the trouble?

by Richard Starr

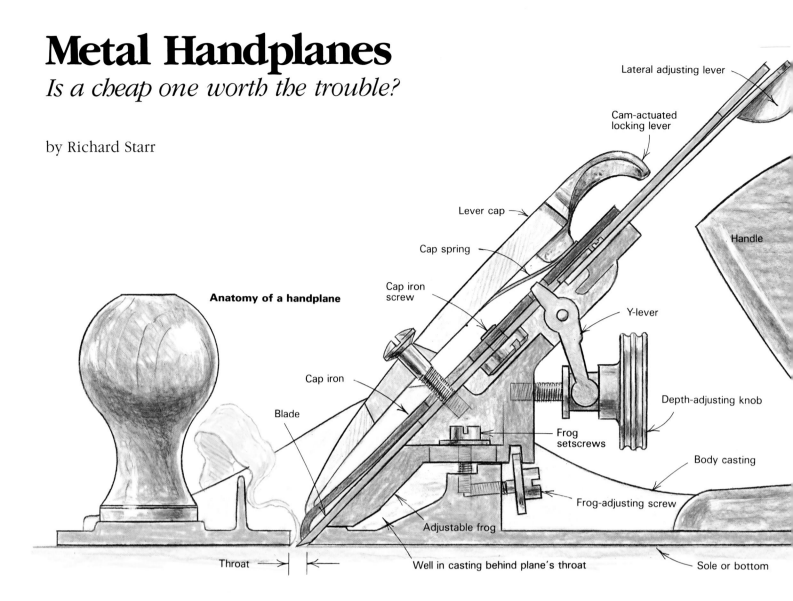

Anatomy of a handplane

Lateral adjusting lever

Cam-actuated locking lever

Handle

Lever cap

Cap spring

Cap iron screw

Y-lever

Cap iron

Depth-adjusting knob

Blade

Frog setscrews

Body casting

Frog-adjusting screw

Adjustable frog

Throat

Well in casting behind plane's throat

Sole or bottom

Some years back, my friend Ken—an excellent woodworker who does almost everything by hand—bought a high-priced, famous-brand metal bench plane and found it too distorted to use. After exchanging it for another plane that was equally as warped, he complained to the manufacturer. The company replied that, these days, making a plane as good as an old one would double the price. Besides, they added, most planes today are purchased as gifts and never used. Instead, they serve as decoration—as symbols of a better time.

Most woodworkers don't rely on handplanes the way Ken does, but nearly everyone likes to keep a plane near the bench for jobs like trimming a door or a drawer. No matter how well-equipped your shop, you'll need a handplane sooner or later—even if only for an occasional odd job.

Today, there are many bench planes on the market, some costing $60 or more. But if you rarely use a plane, do you really need to spend a lot of money on one, or is a $20 cheapie from the corner hardware store good enough? To find out, I bought a selection of inexpensive handplanes, along with two not-so-cheap models to serve as comparison. Then, I tried them all out in my shop.

What I learned surprised me. Some handplanes in the $20 price range could be fine-tuned to perform quite well, although they required more tuning than more expensive planes and weren't as easily adjusted. And while the pricier planes were better-built and easier to operate, they didn't necessarily do better work than a well-tuned cheapie.

Before I get into the specific results of my tests, here's a quick overview of how the various parts of a handplane should work together for best results.

For general planing, the soles on most new planes are flat enough, right out of the box. But for smooth-finishing or jointing, the soles must be really flat. A sole that's hollow along its length will cause the blade to dig in at both ends of the board. Conversely, a plane with a convex sole will take a shaving of varying, unpredictable thickness, skipping over some parts of the stroke while tearing out others.

To take a smooth shaving, the plane's cutting edge must be held rigidly in place by several components working in harmony. The lever cap puts enormous pressure on the arch of the cap iron (see drawing above), which focuses this pressure on the top surface of the blade, right near the cutting edge. To ensure rigidity, there must be something behind the blade to keep it from bending. On the old Stanley planes I own, the frog—a wedge-shaped block that mounts the blade—reaches way down along the blade to give the needed support. But on most new planes, the sole is so thick that the frog can't reach that far down. And on some, the frog stops ½ in. from the end of the blade and is often mounted to the body at only one point—not at two points, as on more expensive planes. Later, I'll explain how you can tune these less well-designed planes to work with minimum chatter.

The only sure way to judge the quality of a plane's blade is to use it, but you can tell if a blade is hard enough by trying to

From *Fine Woodworking* magazine (July 1987) 65:52-56

scratch its bevel with a stainless-steel pocket-knife. If the knife digs into the plane iron, reject it—it's way too soft. Be sure you're not just scratching a varnish coating, and test on the bevel—a spot where the scratch won't show up later when you sharpen the blade. The best blades are ground smooth and flat on both sides, but some cheap blades are ground on only one side. (This small inelegance doesn't affect the quality of cut.)

The blade's depth-adjusting knob (see left) has two functions: it positions the blade and locks it in place. As the knob is turned, it engages a Y-lever that raises and lowers the blade. This adjustment should be easy to make, and without excessive play. After the depth of cut is reduced, the knob's slack must be taken up in the downward direction, effectively locking the blade in place. Since you're likely to spend a lot of time adjusting the blade, a large, easy-to-turn depth knob is desirable.

Y-levers were always made of cast iron on the older planes but, today, many are two pieces of stamped steel held together with a grommet. Cast iron looks nicer, but it's somewhat more brittle. I've seen a lot of broken cast-iron Y-levers, so I don't mind the stamped variety.

The blade's lateral adjusting lever has a small disc that engages a slot in the blade, allowing you to move the blade side-to-side to square it with the sole. The best of these levers consist of three pieces: a disc that fits in the slot of the blade, a shaft and a little tab handle. Cheap planes usually have a single-piece, stamped-steel lateral adjusting lever. In addition to bending out of shape easily, these cheaper levers often engage the blade poorly, which may limit their range of adjustment.

A plane's handles should be strong and comfortable. Wood handles are nice, but unless treated tenderly, they'll break—and they're a pain to repair. I've learned to appreciate the durability of the plastic handles that inevitably come on cheapie planes, even if they aren't as nice-looking or as classy as wood.

A plane sampling—In the school where I teach, I've had good luck showing students how to sharpen and use old Stanley planes and, more recently, English-made Record planes. Since I was curious to learn how some of the cheaper planes on the market might compare, I bought a few and tested them out. The strengths and weaknesses of the bench planes I tested will give you a general idea of what's available, and also help evaluate any plane you're thinking about buying—expensive or inexpensive.

For simplicity's sake, I limited my investigation to 14-in.-long (No. 5) jack planes and 9½-in.-long (No. 4) smoothing planes. (The size numbers of planes were standardized by The Stanley Works years ago, but not all modern manufacturers follow them in identifying their tools.) Number four and five planes seem to be the most popular sizes, and they're also reasonable choices if you're only going to buy one or two planes.

Great Neck is the only brand of bench planes still being made

Starr's sampling of bench planes included four cheap models and two pricier ones—a Craftsman and a Footprint—for comparison. Clockwise, from bottom left, are the six planes Starr tested: Footprint, Craftsman, Menard, Micky, Sears and Great Neck.

in the U.S. (they're manufactured in Mineola, N.Y.). I bought a No. 4 Great Neck—billed as "professional quality"—for about $20 at K-Mart, but I've seen it sold elsewhere under the Master Mechanic label. Overall, Great Neck makes a pretty good plane, with a cleanly cast and machined body and a reasonably flat sole (the one I tested was slightly hollow end-to-end, but so were all the planes in my sampling). Fresh from the store, the hole in the lever cap was too small to fit over the lever screw, but a few minutes with a file fixed that. I'd question the durability of the alloy frog and lever cap if the plane were put to hard use.

The main weakness of this plane lies in its depth-control mechanism. On most planes, the Y-lever pivots on a pin let into holes drilled in the frog. But the Great Neck's Y-lever pivots on a pin set in fragile cast-alloy clips that could easily snap if the plane hit a knot. Of course, you could drill out the frog and press in a new pin, but that would take extra time and trouble.

Also, the Great Neck plane had the worst cap iron of any of the cheapies I tested. The cap had a small arch and practically no spring—a fault that would allow shavings to jam in day-to-day use. But every new cap iron needs a little work, and it wasn't difficult to set this one right.

Some other minor shortcomings of the Great Neck smoothing plane included a heavily varnished sole that needed to be cleaned before use and a blade that was smooth-surfaced on one side only. Despite these gripes, the Great Neck isn't a bad tool for the money—but it wouldn't be my first choice in the price range.

Sears Roebuck's No. 4 smoothing plane—made in England by Stanley—is identical to the cheap line of Stanley planes sold in hardware stores. I got mine for $27 from the Sears catalog (catalog number 9-HT-37168). But while it looked nice and had a pretty paint job, I wasn't too impressed with its performance. Like most of the other planes in my sampling, the bottom of this plane was quite hollow, although flat enough for rough work. It also had a plastic adjusting nut which, besides being small and difficult to use, put durability in question. Surprisingly for such a low-cost tool, the Y-lever was cast, rather than fabricated. Unfortunately, Sears didn't extend the same attention to the lever cap, which had no sheet-metal spring behind the cam. This made it hard to snap the blade assembly closed, and also allowed the cam to dig into the cap iron.

The chief problem with the Sears was its poorly designed, one-step frog that supported the blade too far from the cutting

Not all frogs are made alike: Removed from its plane body, above, the single-step Sears frog (left) has only a single-level mounting surface. The Footprint frog (right) provides a more rigid mounting by seating at two levels. Another important difference is the depth to which a frog reaches to provide blade support. As shown in the photo below, the Record frog (left) supports the blade very close to its edge; the Sears frog (right) leaves about ¼ in. of the blade unsupported and, thus, more prone to chatter.

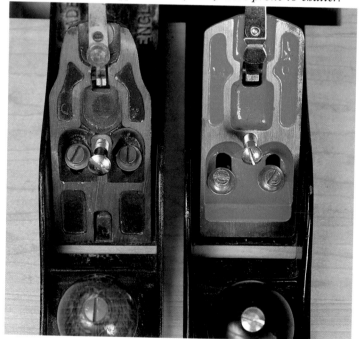

The Footprint plane blade (bottom, photo above) has a highly arched cap iron that tends to make tighter contact and provide better blade support than a flat-arched blade like the one from the Menard (top, photo above). With the Great Neck plane's blade removed (left), you can see the four cast-alloy clips that hold the Y-lever pin in place. The clips seem flimsy, considering the amount of stress they must withstand from the force of the cutting blade.

edge, leaving the plane prone to chatter. You could set the frog so that the back of the throat would support the blade, but the sole is very thin here and could fracture if the plane hit a knot or if the lever cap screw were too tightly set. All in all, don't expect this plane to handle quality work.

The Menard No. 5 jack plane I tested might be called a "handyman special," there were so many peculiar things wrong with it. The plane is sold by Wholesale America (4777 Menard Dr., Eau Claire, WI 54703), a discount tool house that markets a wide range of inexpensive imports. At $18 plus $3 shipping, it's very cheap for its size but, depending on your patience, this Taiwan-made plane might not be much of a bargain in the long

run. Its biggest problem involved its cap iron screw, which ran afoul of the frog long before the blade could be set to take even a shallow cut. To remedy this, you could set the cap iron back about ½ in. from the cutting edge (which would render the cap iron useless as a chip breaker and, worse, leave the blade prone to chatter), or you could excavate a hole in the frog to clear the screw. Fortunately, the Menard has a soft aluminum frog, so drilling out the clearance was easy.

Since the Menard's frog didn't support the blade close enough to the edge, it needed to be adjusted to rest on the thick casting at the throat's back edge. Before I could slide the frog back far enough to make this adjustment, however, I had to file a little

Tuning a plane for better performance

Every woodworking plane you buy—cheap or dear, new or used—will require tuning. Some need more work than others and may have deficits that will forever make them frustrating to use or lead to their premature retirement. Here's how to improve plane performance.

The sole should be checked for flatness with a good steel rule. Hold the ruler on its edge along the plane's bottom, both lengthwise and sideways, and look for light passing underneath it. For rough work, a space the thickness of a human hair along a 14-in. sole may be allowable, but you should detect no light if you expect to do very fine work.

The easiest way to true a plane's bottom is to have a machinist grind the sole flat, but this could more than double the cost of a cheap plane. Be sure the machinist understands the importance of accuracy, and that he or she can figure out a way to clamp the odd-shaped plane to the grinder without distorting the tool's body.

You could save money by truing your planes' soles in your own shop. You'll need a flat surface—one you really trust to be accurate. Use a piece of plate glass that's at least ¼ in. thick, half again as long as your longest plane and 16 in. to 20 in. wide. For abrasives, use coarse wet/dry sandpaper or get a few tubes of automotive valve-grinding compound from an auto-parts shop. If you use the sandpaper, spray-glue or tape the sheets to the glass so the edge of the plane won't tear the seams between them as you grind. If you use the grinding compound, squeeze a dollop on the glass and spread it with the plane until you have a uniform coating. Swirl the plane around in the abrasive for about 30 seconds, then wipe the bottom clean. You'll see a pattern of gray spots that indicate high spots on the sole. Take these down with a belt sander to speed the work along. Grind with a 60-grit belt, and work with just the front roller, focusing the grinding at a single point. Remove just a little metal from the area where the abrasive left gray marks. Now, 30 seconds with the grinding glass will show where the new high spots are. Using this method, I've taken a badly sprung plane down to usable condition in about half an hour.

A few dimples in the sole left by the grinding won't affect the plane's performance, but there must never be a low spot directly in front of the throat. If there is, you won't be able to set the throat small for fine work. The rough gray surface left by the abrasive can be polished out with 220-grit wet/dry paper.

A ding in the edge of the plane's sole will gouge the wood, so bevel the sharp edges around the bottom of the plane lightly with a file or grinder. I like to file huge, barge-prow-shaped chamfers on the ends of my planes so they won't hang up on uneven surfaces.

The throat on most new planes is too small for general work, so you'll need to file the opening larger. Unless you expect to take only very fine shavings, the throat should be at least ⅛ in. wide ahead of the blade, and even more space won't hurt. Occasionally, you'll come across a tool where the sole isn't ground in the same plane as the seat of the frog. To make sure the throat is parallel to the edge of the blade, set the blade to take an even shaving and rest a bevel gauge along its edge. Slide the bevel forward and scribe the line. Then, enlarge the front edge of the throat with a file. To allow shavings to pass through more easily, tip the file back a bit to undercut the throat slightly.

The frog on your plane may not support the blade close enough to its edge to prevent flexing and chattering. To get proper blade support in this case, you must set the frog so that the blade rests on the back edge of the throat, and file that surface smooth and parallel to the blade. Clamp the plane in a vise and use the frog (with the lever screw removed) as a guide to file the seat to the correct angle.

The cap iron needs at least some work on almost every new plane; sometimes, a major reshaping is required. Before unscrewing the cap from the blade, check to see that there's enough "spring" between them. The end of the cap iron should bend down far enough to separate itself from the blade, clear back to the screw. You can add spring by bending the end of the cap iron where it begins to arch. Be careful not to set the lever screw too tight and put undo stress on the adjustment mechanism. Set the screw so the cam on the cap lever snaps firmly—but easily—into place.

Cap irons should contact the blade along a sharp, narrow edge. To shape this edge, clamp a file in a vise and move the cap iron side to side with its tail held about an inch below the file. To check the fit, hold the cap iron and blade together, and point the blade toward a bright light. If you see light leaking through the contact edge, it's back to the file. If you have trouble getting a perfect fit, try using a finer file or an oilstone. Also, file the leading edge of the cap iron until it's smooth and free from burrs.

If you're doing very fine work planing curly wood, set the cap iron ¹⁄₃₂ in. from the edge or closer. Such a setting makes the plane harder to push—it takes more effort to curl the shavings over—so jamming may result. For rougher work, pull the cap back ¼ in. or more.

Lateral adjusting levers often need to be bent up slightly to avoid hitting the rim of the recess on the frog casting. With the cap iron removed, hold the blade in place and move the lever back and forth to see if any part of the lever other than the disc hits the blade. File away any excess metal on the lever or frog until you get maximum freedom of movement. The handle end of the lever may need to be bent down to move freely under the blade, but take care that it still clears the top of the plane's handle.

The depth-adjusting mechanism may need a little tweaking to operate properly. Check the fit between the adjusting nut and the lobes of the Y-lever. If the nut doesn't turn smoothly, unscrew it, clean the threads with a wire brush and oil the nut lightly. A deformed steel Y-lever is easily bent back into shape, and one that has separated at the grommet can be peened together again.

The shape of the plane's blade affects the efficiency of the cut and the quality of surface left behind. The edge should never be hollow (negative camber), i.e. take a thicker shaving along the sides than at the center. A perfectly straight edge is ideal for jointing, when you need a dead-flat surface. For a finishing plane, I prefer an edge with a very slight positive camber, so the corners don't leave sharp tracks along the edge of the cut. A curve just barely visible on a 2-in.-wide blade takes shavings that feather out to almost zero thickness at the edges.

Some plane irons are left with deep grinding marks on their surfaces, and old ones are often pitted with rust. Since the top surface of a plane's blade needn't be as flat as the back of a chisel, you can prevent these pits from eventually showing up on the cutting edge by grinding a very slight bevel on the blade's top edge. As long as it doesn't prevent the cap iron from seating properly, this bevel won't affect the cut.

The handles should be tightened securely to the plane, and be smooth and free from any burrs or roughness. If the handles have loosened (often the case when wooden handles shrink), you can get them to sit tighter by grinding the threaded ends of the mounting screws a bit shorter.

Careful attention to all these details may take some time, but once you've done the job, you're set for smooth, trouble-free planing.

—R.S.

In order for the cap screw to clear the frog casting, allowing the blade to be adjusted, the author had to drill out a small area on the top side of the Menard's frog, as shown above.

Because of the way the adjustment screw on the Micky angles down, the lobes of the Y-lever lose contact with the recess in the adjusting nut when the blade is set for a thick cut.

metal away from the underside of the frog where it hit an obstruction on the body casting.

Instead of a cam-actuated locking lever, the Menard uses a screw to tension the lever cap that was stamped from steel, not cast. This is a minor inconvenience, however, and the Menard's blade assembly is well-made and stiff enough to do the job. You'd probably want to grind the lever cap's front edge a little thinner so you could use it as a screwdriver to disassemble the blade assembly for sharpening.

The best thing about the Menard was its body casting. Heavy and reasonably flat-soled, the body featured reinforcing ribs for added strength. The Menard's blade was slightly harder than the rest in the sampling (judging by the scratch test described previously), but all the blades I tested were hard enough to hold an edge. With all the problems wrung out of it, the Menard would be useful for heavy work. But for a few more bucks, you could get a similarly sized plane that needs a lot less preparation.

Grizzly Imports Inc.—best known for its line of Taiwanese machinery—recently began marketing the Micky, a No. 4-sized plane imported from Japan. At $25.95 (shipping included), the Micky is a nice tool with a good paint job and comfortable red plastic handles. The one I bought had a clean, smoothly ground casting and a reasonably flat sole. The Micky's blade is nearly twice as thick as standard blades, which helps reduce chatter if you slide the frog forward to reduce the width of the plane's exceptionally large throat. Unfortunately, the way the frog is cast limits the amount of forward motion you can take advantage of on this plane.

The cap iron on the Micky was the best of the planes I tested—well-arched and precisely ground where it contacts the blade. Its

surface, however, had a coarse texture that needed to be filed smooth where the lever cap bore upon it at both ends—to prevent friction between the two parts, which must slide smoothly when making adjustments.

On the Grizzly I tried out, the screw upon which the depth-adjustment nut runs was aimed downward, so the Y-lever nearly rode out of the knob's groove at the outer limits of travel. This could probably have been remedied by bending the screw up a little, or by bending the lobes of the Y-lever a bit closer together. Also, the smallish knob makes the plane hard to adjust. And, like the Menard, the forward end of the lever cap had to be filed to serve as a screwdriver for the cap screw.

Despite its problems, I found the Micky to be a sturdily built, substantial tool that worked surprisingly well, right out of the box. It's easily the best of the cheap planes.

Price vs. quality—Having examined the cheap handplanes, I was curious to see how the more expensive tools might compare. You'd think that spending twice as much money would get you a tool that works twice as well, but it ain't necessarily so. Case in point: While Sears' $27 smoothing plane was identical to cheap hardware-store Stanleys, the English-made Craftsman jack plane I bought at Sears for $50 (catalog number 9-HT-37165) wasn't even remotely similar to high-end Stanley tools.

Despite a spiffy appearance, in fact, the Craftsman had a major, irreparable fault that rendered it just about inoperable: Its interior dimension was too narrow to allow proper lateral adjustment of the blade. And since the Craftsman's sole was ground out-of-parallel with the frog seat, it was practically impossible to set the blade to take an even shaving. You'd have to grind the blade's edge off-square to get it to work. On the one I bought, the lever cap was too wide, and its kidney-shaped hole had to be filed almost round before it would slip past the cap screw. And, like the No. 4 Sears I tested, the upper-end Craftsman had an inferior, single-step frog. My sample was also badly concave.

Although the Craftsman costs twice as much as a comparably sized Sears-brand plane, it's basically the same plane. All you get for the extra cash is a large brass depth knob, a spring under the lever cap and some chrome plating—hardly worth twice the price.

The Footprint—a high-quality, English-made jack plane—recently became available through U.S. tool catalogs. I bought mine for $43 from Woodcraft Supply (41 Atlantic Ave., Box 4000, Woburn, Mass. 01888). This plane felt well-made, and it was the only plane in my sampling that boasted wooden handles. But what else did I get for the extra money? The sole was flatter than most, but it still needed some work. The Footprint also had a two-step frog with ground seats, a cast Y-lever and a screw adjustment that moves the frog in precisely controllable increments—handy when setting up the plane. Overall, this plane had a quality feel equal to new, top-of-the-line Stanleys—a bit better feel than the Record planes I own.

I used to be something of a snob about my planes. I loved to restore noble old Stanleys, and I agreed with the Japanese that working with a fine tool is a spiritual experience. But, despite their shortcomings, the cheap planes I tested proved to be a practical alternative to spending top dollar for tools you plan to use only occasionally. It's clear that a little patience and tender tweaking can get these tools humming. Working with them convinced me that any tool that you've carefully tuned can become an extension of your hands and mind—even a $20 cheapie from K-Mart.   □

Richard Starr is a teacher and the author of Woodworking with Kids, *published by The Taunton Press (1982).*

Block Planes

What are they really for?

by Maurice Fraser

The familiar little block plane is something of an enigma. Its origins, function—even the meaning of its name—are a little obscure. The typical block plane has a cast-iron body 6 in. to 7 in. long with an adjustable blade bedded at 20° or, on a low-angle block plane, 12°. Unlike bench planes, the blade cuts bevel up and has no cap iron to add rigidity and serve as a chip-breaker. Some models sport an adjustable mouth that can be set to an ultra-fine opening to reduce tearout. The bulbous lever cap, which gives the plane it's characteristic domed top, clamps down the blade and fits into the palm, making the plane comfortable to use in one hand. The nose of the plane has a dished-out knob or machined dimple as a rest for the index finger.

Small, one-handed planes have been around since medieval times, but the block plane, in the configuration we know, seems to be an American phenomenon a little more than a century old. It wasn't until 1873 that Stanley produced the small Model 9½ block plane, much like the one still being made today. Earlier ''block'' planes were larger, two-handed affairs.

The block plane is an odd jumble of assets and liabilities. Small size and light weight are its greatest assets. It's comfortable to use in one hand, especially on small pieces that would get lost under a large plane. A block plane can be useful for hundreds of small jobs: softening sharp edges, trimming small miters, fitting drawers, trimming excess plywood edging tape or projecting veneer, trimming finger joints or dovetails on small boxes and any time you need to hold work with one hand and plane with the other.

Over the years, Stanley has offered some fifty-odd models of block planes. Today, Stanley and Record, the major manufacturers, make only a handful of models (they differ mostly in the number of possible adjustments) in two basic types: standard (20°) and low-angle (12°). Footprint also makes a few models. Two small German-made wooden planes on the market are in the block plane size category but their blades are bedded at 50° and mounted bevel down like a bench plane.

The No. 9½ made by Stanley, Record and Footprint, is the stan-

Small and light, the block plane is the choice for one-handed planing jobs. Unlike a bench plane, block plane blades cut bevel up. Top of the line models, like these Stanleys, have adjustable blades and mouths. Blade angle on the No. 9½ (right) is 20°. The low-angle No. 60½ has a 12° blade angle.

From *Fine Woodworking* magazine (September 1985) 54:76-78

Entrepreneur Tom Lie-Nielson has brought two vintage Stanley specialty block planes back to life in flashy, manganese-bronze incarnations. Shown here with the cast-iron Stanley originals are (left) the No. 95 edge-trimming block plane and (right) the No. 140 skew-rabbet block plane.

Specialty block planes reincarnated

Flipping through old tool catalogs can make a plane buff long for the good old days when specialty planes abounded. Stanley and Record seem to discontinue another hand plane each year. There's still a market for these tools and, though it may not be large enough to keep the big guys interested, small entrepreneurs may be able to fill the gap by reproducing the plane classics.

Tom Lie-Nielson has been doing just that in West Rockport, Me. He's making reproductions of the pre-World War II Stanley No. 140 low-angle, skew-rabbet block plane and the Stanley No. 95 edge-trimming block plane. Unlike the cast-iron originals, the Lie-Nielson repros are cast in manganese bronze because it's easier to machine and not likely to break if dropped.

The Lie-Nielson No. 140 skew-rabbet block plane is wondrous to behold. Like the originals, one side is removable, allowing the skewed blade to trim a rabbet. The bronze body and lever cap are quite heavy, providing useful damping against chatter. The blade bed offers rather solid support by block-plane standards. In ordinary use it planes well; the optional fence (unique to the Lie-Nielson re-creation) is a fine idea, but not for making rabbets from scratch. For that you would want the cross-grain spurs and depth gauge of a regular rabbet plane. The fence and the skewed blade are useful for smoothing fielded panels that were begun on a tablesaw. The skewed blade cuts nicely across the grain. With the fence, the plane costs nearly $140—no casual purchase (available from Garrett Wade, 161 Avenue of the Americas, N.Y., N.Y. 10013).

The Lie-Nielson version of the Stanley No. 95 edge-trimming block plane holds up well to the original. It is a skewed low-angle block plane with an integral 90° fence. It will trim a straightened edge up to ⅞-in. thick and square it to the face while doing so. But its 6 in. length is inadequate to establish edge-joinable straightness on anything much larger than a bread box. Surely the name implies no such ability. The danger lies in the beholder's eyes: it looks as though it could do anything. It would serve well as a veneer or edging trimmer. At about $125 I would rather receive than give one (available from Garrett Wade and Lee Valley Tools, 2680 Queensview Dr., Ottawa, Ont., K2A 1T4, Canada). —*M.F.*

dard 20° block plane with all the adjustments. I haven't tried the Footprint, but either the Record or Stanley No. 9½ is a good, honest, no messing-around tool for general one-hand planing.

The other conventional block is the low-angle (12°) No. 60½ made by both Record and Stanley. I prefer the Record 60½ to the Stanley because it has a wider blade (1⅝ in. to Stanley's 1⅜ in.) and it's heavier. And, at the time I wrote this, the Record plane cost a bit less than the Stanley. The quality of machining, however, is inconsistent. Sometimes the Record plane seems better made, sometimes the Stanley. Anyway, never buy a tool sight unseen unless you can return it if it's not right.

The textbook myth is that a block plane's low blade angle makes it the best plane for working end grain. Best? Well, they're OK. It isn't that a well-made block plane, perfectly tuned, can't make a decent end-grain cut, it can, if you set the plane for a very light cut, have the blade extra sharp, tighten the hold-down screw (not so tight that the blade can't be adjusted) and use a narrow mouth setting. But more often, my students get chatter on end grain that they wouldn't get with a sharp smooth plane. The low-angle blade doesn't hurt anything, but a low blade angle does not guarantee a low cutting angle. A look at cutting geometry shows that things aren't always what they seem.

As figure 1 shows, with the plane-blade bevel facing up, the 25° bevel angle contributes to the cutting angle. It's common to hone a 5° microbevel which increases the bevel angle to 30°. The standard block plane bed tilts the blade up another 20° for an actual cutting angle of 50° Compare this to the bench plane shown in figure 2. Since the bevel faces down, bevel angle doesn't affect the cutting angle. Standard pitch bench plane blades are seated at 45°, and the cutting angle remains 45° regardless of the bevel angle. So, a 20° block plane really cuts at 50° while a smooth plane cuts at only 45°. The 12° low-angle block plane with a 25° grind and a 5° microbevel has a cutting

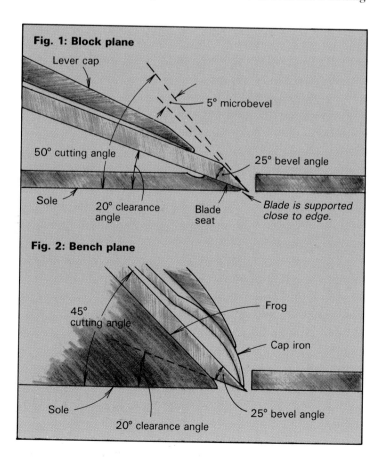

Fig. 1: Block plane

Lever cap

5° microbevel

50° cutting angle

25° bevel angle

Sole

20° clearance angle

Blade seat

Blade is supported close to edge.

Fig. 2: Bench plane

45° cutting angle

Frog

Cap iron

Sole

20° clearance angle

25° bevel angle

The Achilles heel of block-plane design is the skimpy blade support. A small nub on the depth adjuster supports the rear of the blade and a machined flat at the mouth supports the cutting edge. Between these points the blade is unsupported, and likely to chatter.

angle of 42°, only 3° lower than most bench planes but a full 8° lower than the standard block plane.

Any advantage the lower cutting angle may offer on end grain is nullified by a weakness in the block plane's design. The block plane can chatter because it lacks the rigidly-supported blade and substantial body mass of the bench plane. Compare a block plane blade with a smooth plane blade. The frog/bed on the smooth plane supports the blade for several inches underneath, plus a cap iron and a thick lever cap atop the blade. The block plane blade is supported underneath only by a raised nub or two in back and a milled ridge at the mouth, under the blade edge. The bevel-up blade is supported very close to the cutting edge, which could be an advantage if the blade had more support further back, but this skimpy arrangement leaves most of the blade unsupported. This is the Achilles heel in block-plane design and the most significant structural cause of chatter. Other defects—thin blades, improper bevel angles, warped soles—can be corrected by the owner, or manufacturer quality control, but the atrophied blade seat seems inherent in the tool's design as it's now being made. Superior machining in pre-war block planes mitigated this defect somewhat but even they rarely exhibit the rock-solid feel of a good bench plane with it's cap iron and continuous blade bed.

The blade seat problem is exacerbated by feeble lever-cap toggle clamps, a perennial block-plane problem. This design supplies inadequate and uneven clamping pressure on the blade. Much better blade-locking methods—especially the hinged knuckle-joint cap—can be found on some old block planes.

To properly set up the block plane, mount the blade bevel up and advance the adjusting knob until the blade edge can barely be felt along the plane mouth. Clamp on the lever cap handle; if the blade can easily be pressed sideways, tighten the clamping screw by very tiny increments until the blade can only be moved with difficulty. If the blade isn't perfectly parallel to the mouth opening, tilt the blade by means of the lateral adjustment lever. For planes without an adjustment lever, grasp the lever cap and the blade and wrest them left or right a trifle as needed.

If the plane has an adjustable mouth, loosen the finger-rest knob to unlock the mouth adjusting lever. Turn the plane upside down and observe the opening while you slowly shift the lever sideways: a mouth opening of about 1/32 in. is good for most hardwoods and a scant 3/64 in. for mild woods. Avoid zapping the blade's edge with the front portion of the mouth piece when narrowing the mouth. □

Maurice Fraser teaches woodworking at the Craft Students' League in the 53rd St. Y.W.C.A. in New York City. He was woodworking consultant for the book Crafts & Hobbies *(1979, Reader's Digest Press).*

For most cuts, a block plane cuts best when it's skewed to the work. With a low-angle block plane skewed to the work (top photo) Fraser trims tablesaw marks from a miter. Scrap clamped to the board's edge prevents split out of end grain. Author relieves a sharp edge with a low-angle block plane (photo above).

Old Wooden Planes

Reworking brings rewards

by Graham Blackburn

Fig. 1: Parts of a bench plane

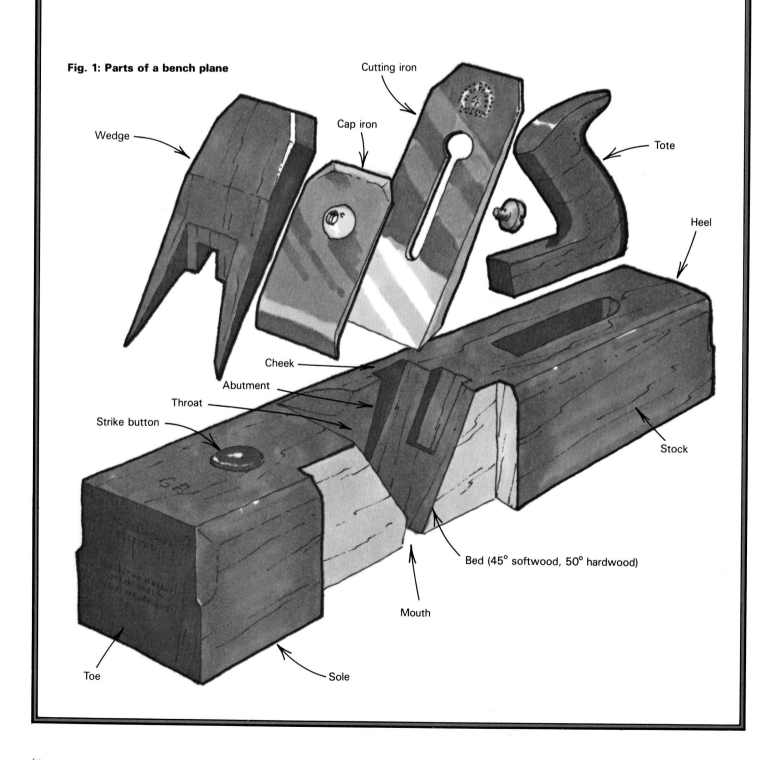

Wedge

Cutting iron

Cap iron

Tote

Heel

Cheek

Abutment

Throat

Strike button

Stock

Bed (45° softwood, 50° hardwood)

Mouth

Toe

Sole

When I was first taught woodworking as a boy in England, metal planes and power saws had long been the order of the day, but we still began with wooden bench planes and the whole array of hand saws. In the years since, the older tools have all but disappeared—not only from the more traditional classroom and tradesman's toolbox, but from circulation in general. Today, many woodworkers don't even know their names, far less their application and the techniques of using them.

Old wooden planes, meaning not only secondhand planes but also planes that may be obsolete and even genuine antiques, can constitute an invaluable workshop resource for today's woodworker. Moreover, these old tools are, in many cases, the last link with an age that saw some of the finest woodworking ever produced. Old wooden planes are usually much cheaper than their modern successors. But they have more to offer than economy, and that has to do with pride, personal satisfaction, and a love of the material. You benefit greatly if you can work with tools and materials that you respect, tools you appreciate for their beauty and their rich history.

Anyone seeking to incorporate a tool from the past into his or her work, for whatever reason, faces the problem of where to find and how to recognize a usable or refurbishable tool. Once you start looking, finding old tools is the easiest part. They crop up all over the place: in antique shops, junk shops, flea markets, yard sales, auctions, and even in modern tool supply houses. What is harder is being able to know if what you have found might be of any use. Buying an old tool isn't like buying your first router, complete in its box with attachments and instructions. Resist the temptation to buy the first old plane you come across until you have studied the matter a little.

Hand in hand with potential utility goes the question of price. Collectors and antique hunters have helped preserve many tools that might otherwise have disappeared, but their interest has often raised the price capriciously, so that utility is no longer commensurate with cost. Collectors frequently look for qualities other than utility, which often means that an eminently worthwhile, but uncollectible tool may be offered for a song. For example, a plane with lots of shiny brass screws but a hopelessly checked wooden stock may be more expensive than a simpler, less-adorned plane in solid condition. The prices of the two are, therefore, in inverse relation to their use to the craftsman. Then again, collectors are often greatly concerned with makers. A perfectly usable plane produced by one manufacturer may cost significantly less than an inferior one made by a more sought-after firm.

In addition to gaining an understanding of how the tool works, you should also remember that its true cost must also include the time you may have to spend refurbishing it. Fixing a tool may seem inconvenient, an extra time-wasting obstacle, but it is, in fact, a very worthwhile process that will give you a more complete knowledge of the tool's functions and capabilities than had you bought the whole marvel complete and pristine in a box. You will make fewer mistakes in learning to use the tool, and be less likely to force it to do something it's not fit for.

At first, the variety of wooden planes may seem endless, but many were made in sets, differing not in function but only in size. You could, in fact, divide all planes into just three basic groups: bench planes, molding planes, and special-purpose planes (figure 2). Bench planes are the long, squarish planes used for smoothing and straightening wood; molding planes are thin upright planes used for molding the edges or faces of boards; and special-purpose planes comprise everything else—

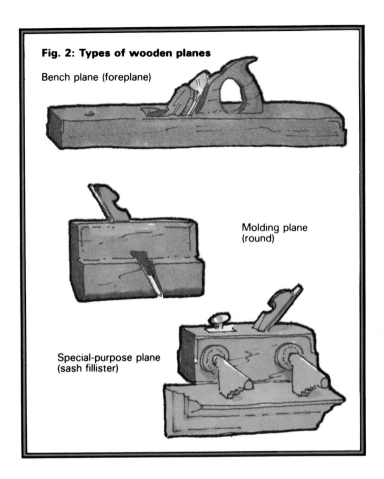

Fig. 2: Types of wooden planes

Bench plane (foreplane)

Molding plane (round)

Special-purpose plane (sash fillister)

they make grooves, rabbets, tongue-and-groove boards, window sash, raised panels, and a host of other things.

Planes that were needed by virtually every woodworker are far more abundant than seldom-used, specialized planes. This means that the planes easiest to find, namely the bench planes, are likely to be of greatest use to you, and, generally, the cheapest to buy. Wooden bench planes exist in a much greater variety of types, sizes, and qualities than modern metal planes and offer niceties not possible with machines or metal planes. For example, it is sometimes difficult to avoid tearout on rowed or curly wood on the jointer, whereas there are bench planes designed specifically for such awkward wood. Remember that much of the following discussion about old bench planes applies to all planes.

There was a time, before the advent of the power planer, when all wood arrived at the bench, or on the site, just as it was sawn from the tree—rough and not necessarily straight or flat, and in varying thicknesses. Before much else could be done to it, it had to be dressed, that is, tried, trued, and made smooth, and it was the bench planes that did this. Most of this work is now done by machine, but for small, individual jobs, as well as for the very best results, most wood must still come under the plane.

The smallest of the bench planes is the smoother, or smooth plane. Its job is to put the final finish on a piece of wood. Wooden smooth planes are 6 in. to 9 in. long, straight-sided or coffin-shaped, and the iron (blade) may be bedded at 45° or 50°—the steeper angle produces a better surface on hard wood.

The jack plane is 12 in. to 18 in. in length and is frequently the first to be used when dressing down the stock. British and American jacks are usually fitted with a handle (called a tote), which is most often of the open type. When the tote is set on a lowered portion of the stock, the plane is called a razee jack in America and a technical jack in Britain. The next size includes planes from 16 in. to 22 in. long. These are variously referred to as panel planes, foreplanes, or trying planes. Their size overlaps not only with some jack planes but also with some jointer planes—the next larger type. In fact, over the last 300 years names have been far from standard; I'll call them foreplanes. Whatever they're called, these planes are used for finer work than the jack: removing the ridges left by the jack, truing the surfaces, and trying (making straight and square) the board's edges.

The fourth, and last, of the bench planes may be anything from 20 in. to 30 in. long, and is known in America as the jointer, in Britain as a trying plane. It is differentiated from foreplanes only by size. Its job, however, is primarily to prepare the edges of boards to be joined to each other—the longer the plane, the easier it is to obtain a perfectly straight edge.

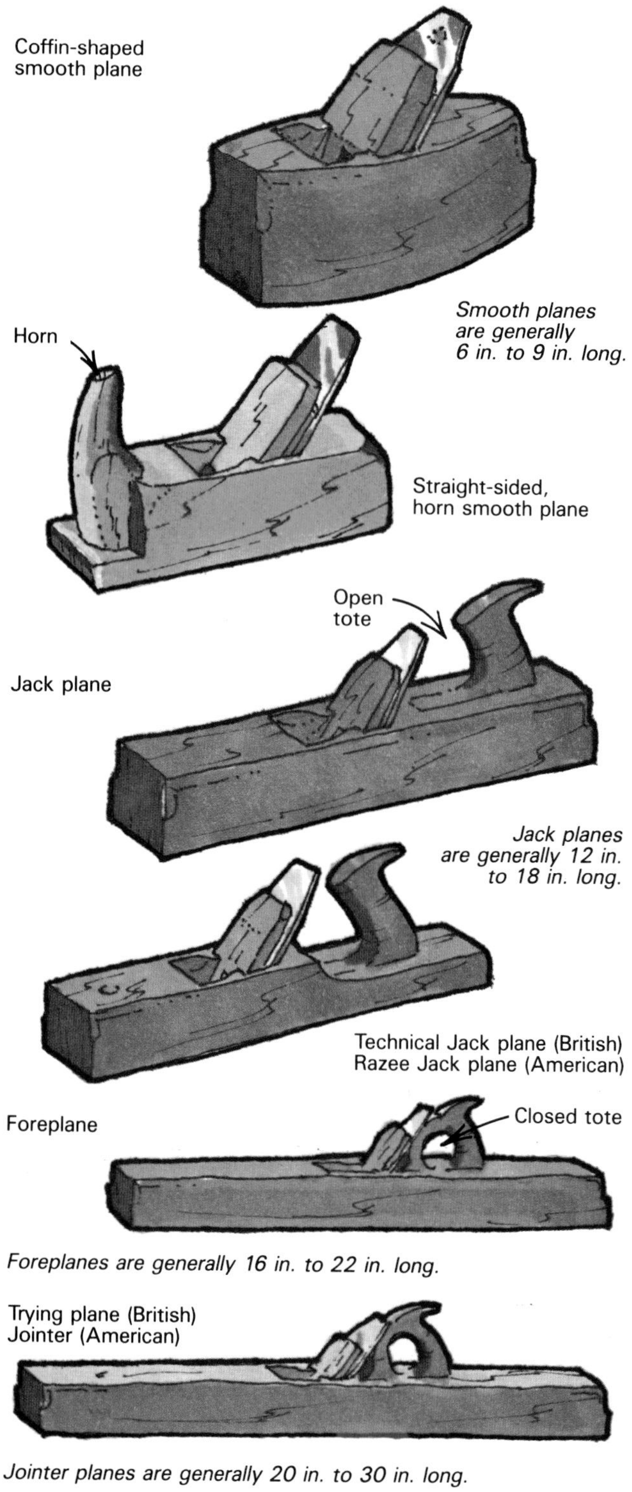

In real life, personal preferences, coupled with a large selection of patterns and sizes, make any absolute rules about the uses of planes ultimately impossible. The jobs to be done remain the same, however, and every woodworker is free to select his or her own slightly different combination of planes to do them.

At first glance, the typical wooden bench plane discovered on a blanket at a flea market might not appear to be capable of anything but the coarsest class of work. However, excepting truly hopeless and unrestorable ones, I think that when refurbished it will probably perform many times better than most contemporary store-bought iron planes.

Several things can render the tool fit for nothing more than decoration or exhibition, and of these the most immediately apparent is the lack of a cutting iron. You might find a replacement iron elsewhere, but it's usually not worth the effort, given the ease with which you could find a plane with its iron. The reverse is true of the iron—that is, the plane might be worth buying for the iron alone, even if the rest of the tool is useless!

Until the 18th century, all planes had only a cutting iron. Thereafter, a second iron, called variously the top iron, the break iron, the back iron, or most commonly the cap iron, was added to stiffen the cutting iron and break the shaving. For this reason, bench planes with double irons are preferable. (Single irons continue to be used for block planes and molding planes.) Cap irons are almost always screwed to the cutting iron, which will have a slot cut in it for this purpose. If your plane has a solid iron there never was a cap iron; if there is a slot but no cap iron, it is missing and you should look for another plane, just as you should if the cap iron isn't the same width as the cutting iron.

Next, examine the back of the cutting iron. It doesn't matter if the edge is in horrible shape, it usually is, but if the back of the iron is deeply pitted with rust, rather than merely rusted on the surface, you should pass it by. To obtain a truly sharp edge, the back of the cutting iron must be perfectly flat. Sooner or later every part of the back will be at the edge, and a pitted back will result in a pitted "saw" edge rather than a smooth "knife" edge.

The most common mystery associated with wooden planes is how to get the iron out of the stock. Jacks and bigger planes must be rapped on the top of the stock near the toe, as shown in figure 4. There is often a strike button inset here for the purpose. Short planes, like smoothers, must be knocked on the back end, and you will usually see the marks of previous hammer blows in this area. A mallet works just as well and damages the wood less.

Resist the temptation to wiggle the wedge as this risks damaging the plane's cheeks and the slot that contains the wedge. If the cheek should already be split or badly checked, there is little you can do to repair it, and the plane will never hold the wedge and iron securely in use. A damaged or missing wedge is another matter; replacement needs to be exact, but isn't difficult.

Look at the body of the plane next. Note the condition of the tote and the areas where the stock has been hit for iron removal. A few moons and dents are to be expected, but beware a plane that has had its toe or back pounded to splinters. A tote can be replaced easily, but, if the stock is too far gone, you must look elsewhere. What consitutes too far gone? Well, it may look worse than it really is. Small checks in the ends are not serious; many can be closed up with liberal applications of linseed oil. Larger checks or

Fig. 3: Types of bench planes

Coffin-shaped smooth plane

Smooth planes are generally 6 in. to 9 in. long.

Horn

Straight-sided, horn smooth plane

Jack plane

Open tote

Jack planes are generally 12 in. to 18 in. long.

Technical Jack plane (British) Razee Jack plane (American)

Foreplane

Closed tote

Foreplanes are generally 16 in. to 22 in. long.

Trying plane (British) Jointer (American)

Jointer planes are generally 20 in. to 30 in. long.

Fig. 4: Removing the cutting iron

Hit short planes here.

Hit long planes here.

A strike button set into the plane's stock prevents damage when removing the iron.

Strike button, smooth plane

Strike button, jack plane

cracks, especially any extending from the corners of the throat where the wedge and iron are seated, are cause for rejection. If the plane has been kept in a damp basement or allowed to dry out over the years, it may appear a deathly gray, but, if the wood isn't spongy, rotted, or riddled with worm holes, you'll be surprised how nice it will look after a sympathetic cleaning and reoiling.

It is unlikely that there will be any checks in the sides, unless these stem from a split throat, since the stock should have been cut so that the annual rings are perpendicular to the sole, thus providing maximum resistance to warping and wear. All other things being equal, ring orientation, as seen on the end of the plane, is a reason for choosing one plane over another.

The ideal sole is perfectly flat and smooth with a narrow mouth—the gap in front of the iron when it is set barely protruding. Here is where you must use some imagination. It has been a long time since most of these tools have been used, and it's extremely unlikely the sole will look anything like it should. First, try to imagine the iron properly sharpened, with the cap iron set right, and everything correctly positioned, and judge how wide the mouth is. If it is wider than the thickest shaving the plane will be expected to take, you must remouth the plane. This might sound like an unpleasant paramedic operation, but it's not too hard, providing the sole is not badly checked or too worn down. (I'll describe the process a little later.) The plane body was originally made square, but use and rejointing—the replaning of the sole to keep it perfectly flat—may have made it somewhat wedge-shaped. It is just possible that there may not be enough body left for more jointing or remouthing. In any event, it is almost certain that you will have to joint the sole, so check it carefully for excessive worm holes (one or two will do little harm) and the odd nail, to be sure you can do this.

If the plane you are considering passes all these tests, and if the asking price is no more than that of a comparably-sized new metal plane, then feel confident about buying it. It will usually cost much less unless the seller believes that he has something "extremely antique" and of interest to collectors.

When you get the plane home, the first thing to do is to disassemble it and clean it. Secondhand planes seem to have an amazing affinity to paint spatters, and these I scrape off with a penknife or razor blade, but if possible, I leave the rest of the patina alone and simply treat the wood with linseed oil. Frequently, however, more is needed. Many people regard removing the finish as a violation of the tool's "antiquity," but unless the tool is a rare or a special example of its class, it is first and foremost a tool, and should be maintained in as good condition as possible,

so that it may function as well as it did when new. Wooden planes were mostly made of beech, oiled or varnished. When the varnish wore off, periodic wipings with linseed oil combined with oil from the user's own hands kept the wood in good condition. If too much grime has accumulated on the plane for oil to penetrate, clean it with paint stripper, soak it in linseed oil, and wax it with a paste wax, such as Butcher's or Johnson's. (If you remouth the plane, oil it after making the new mouth.) Even the grayest plane will respond to this treatment, and with use you will soon rebuild the patina, this time on a healthy body.

For extremely dry planes, and planes with open checks in the ends, you can stand the plane on end in a container of linseed oil to allow more oil to be absorbed, and stuff an oil-soaked rag in the throat (seal the container to prevent spontaneous combustion of the rag), since these end-grain areas get thirsty faster.

The tote is glued into a shallow mortise in the stock; totes sometimes become loose and need to be reglued. The most common damage is to the tip, which gets broken off. It is astonishing how much more comfortable it is to use a plane with a fully-formed tote than one with a piece missing from the end. Depending on the extent of the damage, it will be very worthwhile either to graft on a new tip, or to make a whole new tote. The easiest way to make a new tote is to copy the profile from another one; experience will tell you whether a slightly different shape is more comfortable for you, but be sure to make the tote fit its mortise snugly or it will work loose again.

Damaged or missing wedges are also easy to replace. The new

Planes by post

Not everyone lives in an area well stocked with old tools. Fortunately, a number of old-tool dealers around the country sell through the mail. In addition to collector's items, the four listed here handle large numbers of tools for use. Vern Ward publishes the **Fine Tool Journal** (RD #2, Poultney, Vt. 05764), a combination magazine/catalog that carries ads for his own Iron Horse Antiques, as well as dealers and auctioneers nationwide; $10 buys six issues a year. **The Mechanick's Workbench** (PO Box 544, Front St., Marion, Mass. 02738) publishes a handsome "magalog" several times a year, usually for $10 each. **Bud Steere** (110 Glenwood Dr., North Kingstown, R.I. 02852) puts out six catalogs a year at $5 each. In the midwest, **Tom Witte's Antiques** (PO Box 399, Mattawan, Mich. 49071) will send a catalog and several supplements for $3.50 per year. ☐

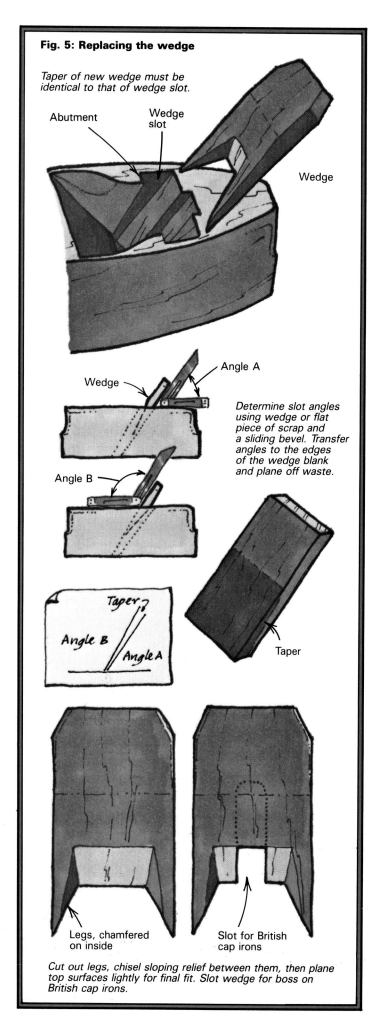

Fig. 5: Replacing the wedge

Taper of new wedge must be identical to that of wedge slot.

Abutment

Wedge slot

Wedge

Angle A

Wedge

Determine slot angles using wedge or flat piece of scrap and a sliding bevel. Transfer angles to the edges of the wedge blank and plane off waste.

Angle B

Taper

Angle B

Angle A

Taper

Legs, chamfered on inside

Slot for British cap irons

Cut out legs, chisel sloping relief between them, then plane top surfaces lightly for final fit. Slot wedge for boss on British cap irons.

wedge, however, must fit its slot exactly or it will not work: either the iron will chatter, you'll damage the abutments, or nothing will ever stay put. The secret is in precisely mating the taper of the wedge to the slot. Cut a wedge blank to width, then plane its back surface flat. Figure 5 shows how to establish the correct taper using a sliding bevel. Transfer the taper to both edges of the wedge blank using carbon paper, then plane away the waste. If you're not copying an existing wedge, you'll need to insert the new wedge and trace the line of the abutments on it to establish the position of the legs. Cut out the legs, and chisel the center slope, which eases the passage of the shavings. Trial-fit the wedge and irons; lightly plane the top surfaces of the legs, where necessary, to give a tight fit against the abutments. (On British planes slot the wedge for the brass boss that holds the cap-iron screw, as shown in figure 5.) Lastly, chamfer the inside edges and tips of the legs and the end of the slope.

Unless the cutting iron rests firmly without rocking on the bed, fine and secure adjustment will be impossible. Check the iron first, for accumulated rust or burrs on the metal. If the bed has warped or moved, careful filing with a flat file, and cautious paring with a chisel, should allow the iron to reseat properly.

Once the stock is clean, the tote and wedge in good shape, and the bed has been checked, all that remains to check is the mouth, but you can't do this until the iron is properly sharpened and the cap iron set. Sharpening is beyond the scope of this article, but make sure the iron is ground to the desired profile—I prefer a slight curve for jack planes and virtually flat for smoothers and foreplanes—and the bevel is ground to the right angle, usually between 25° and 30°, according to the quality of the steel and the hardness of the wood on which you will use this plane. In general, the harder the wood, the greater the angle.

The cap iron must fit perfectly against the back of the iron (figure 6), and, for fine work, exceedingly close to the cutting edge, since not only is it supposed to deflect and break the shaving, but also to put pressure near the cutting edge in order to reduce potential chatter. Furthermore, any gap between the two irons will trap shavings and "choke" the plane. A perfect fit requires that the back of the cutting iron be absolutely flat (if not, work it on a sharpening stone) and the leading edge of the cap iron be straight across its width, and as sharp as possible. You can straighten and square the cap iron with a flat file or diamond plate. A fine sharpening stone will remove file marks and sharpen the edge. It is most important to sharpen so that only the leading edge of the cap iron touches the cutting iron.

Now, slip the iron into the stock so that it barely protrudes from the mouth, to judge whether this gap is too large. It will almost inevitably be so, not only because the sole wears down, and has been possibly rejointed, but also because most irons were themselves wedge-shaped. Being thicker at the cutting end, they were worn to an ever thinner profile by frequent sharpening, thereby increasing the size of the mouth. A wide mouth makes tearout more likely; the remedy is remouthing, which involves inlaying a piece of hard wood into the sole just in front of the iron, as shown in figure 7.

The size of the mouth depends on the type of work expected of the plane—the shavings must be able to pass through. Coarse work producing thick shavings requires a larger mouth than fine work with its thin shavings. For fine work, I prefer a jack plane's mouth to be about 1/16 in. wide, and smooth plane, foreplane or jointer mouths as small as possible. Make the new mouthpiece 1/4 in. to 1/2 in. thick, and wider than the existing mouth to avoid fussy fitting at the corners. Place it on the sole and carefully mark

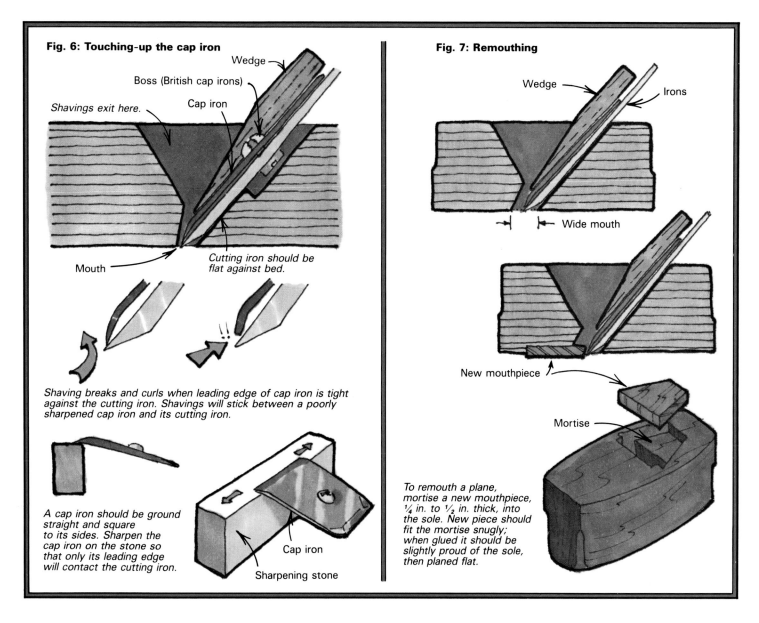

Fig. 6: Touching-up the cap iron

Wedge

Boss (British cap irons)

Shavings exit here.

Cap iron

Mouth

Cutting iron should be flat against bed.

Shaving breaks and curls when leading edge of cap iron is tight against the cutting iron. Shavings will stick between a poorly sharpened cap iron and its cutting iron.

A cap iron should be ground straight and square to its sides. Sharpen the cap iron on the stone so that only its leading edge will contact the cutting iron.

Cap iron

Sharpening stone

Fig. 7: Remouthing

Wedge

Irons

Wide mouth

New mouthpiece

Mortise

To remouth a plane, mortise a new mouthpiece, ¼ in. to ½ in. thick, into the sole. New piece should fit the mortise snugly; when glued it should be slightly proud of the sole, then planed flat.

around it with a sharp scratch awl. Mortise the sole carefully, making the sides square and the bottom level. This is easily done with a light-duty router or Dremel tool, or by hand with a Forstner bit and chisels. The mouthpiece should fit snugly and stand a little proud of the sole—this makes clamping easier. I bevel the edge of the mouth toward the iron, so that subsequent jointing won't widen the mouth unduly.

You can joint the sole of a long plane on a power jointer. But, if yours is a short plane or you don't have a jointer, then secure your longest bench plane upside down in a vise and push the sole over it, the way coopers planed their staves. Sight over the sole by eye and check with a straightedge and square to make sure that it is perfectly flat and square to the sides.

Oil the sole, wipe it dry, then polish it with wax or simply rub a candle over it. Setting the iron is the final step. The theory is simple, but only repeated, patient practice will make you quick and accurate at it. Insert the iron and the wedge so that the iron does not quite protrude, then gently tap the wedge to secure the iron, but only just. To lower the iron, simply tap its top end, then tap the wedge in a little more firmly. Sight along the sole and adjust the iron sideways by tapping its top end to the requisite side. If the iron is protruding too far, simply tap the back of the stock. That's all you need to know: tap the top of the iron to lower it; tap the back of the stock to raise it.

The wedge shape of the blade and the wedge itself are what make the process tricky. As you tap the blade deeper, it necessarily presents a thinner part to the wedge, thereby loosening the latter's grip, causing the iron to slip more deeply than you wanted. The secret is in securing the wedge firmly enough to hold the iron even after you have tapped the iron in some more, but not so firmly that a light tap won't move the iron. This is made a little easier by setting the iron as close to the desired protrusion as possible, before you first secure the wedge.

At this point you should now be in possession of a bench plane that will compare favorably with almost anything you can buy new, and for considerably less outlay. It may take a while before you feel perfectly comfortable with the adjustment process, and, of course, a lot depends on how well you sharpen the iron, which will most likely be of the superior, old-fashioned laminated type. Planing can be taught only partly by words and pictures; experience will teach much more, for the feel of a wooden plane is quite different from that of its metal counterpart. In the long run, I think the potential of wooden planes is far greater, given the wider range of tools making possible a size and shape for almost every job and every hand. □

Graham Blackburn, author of numerous books on woodworking, is a furniture designer and maker in Woodstock, N.Y.

Making a Panel Plane

A tool for the consummate cabinetmaker

by Charles Dolan

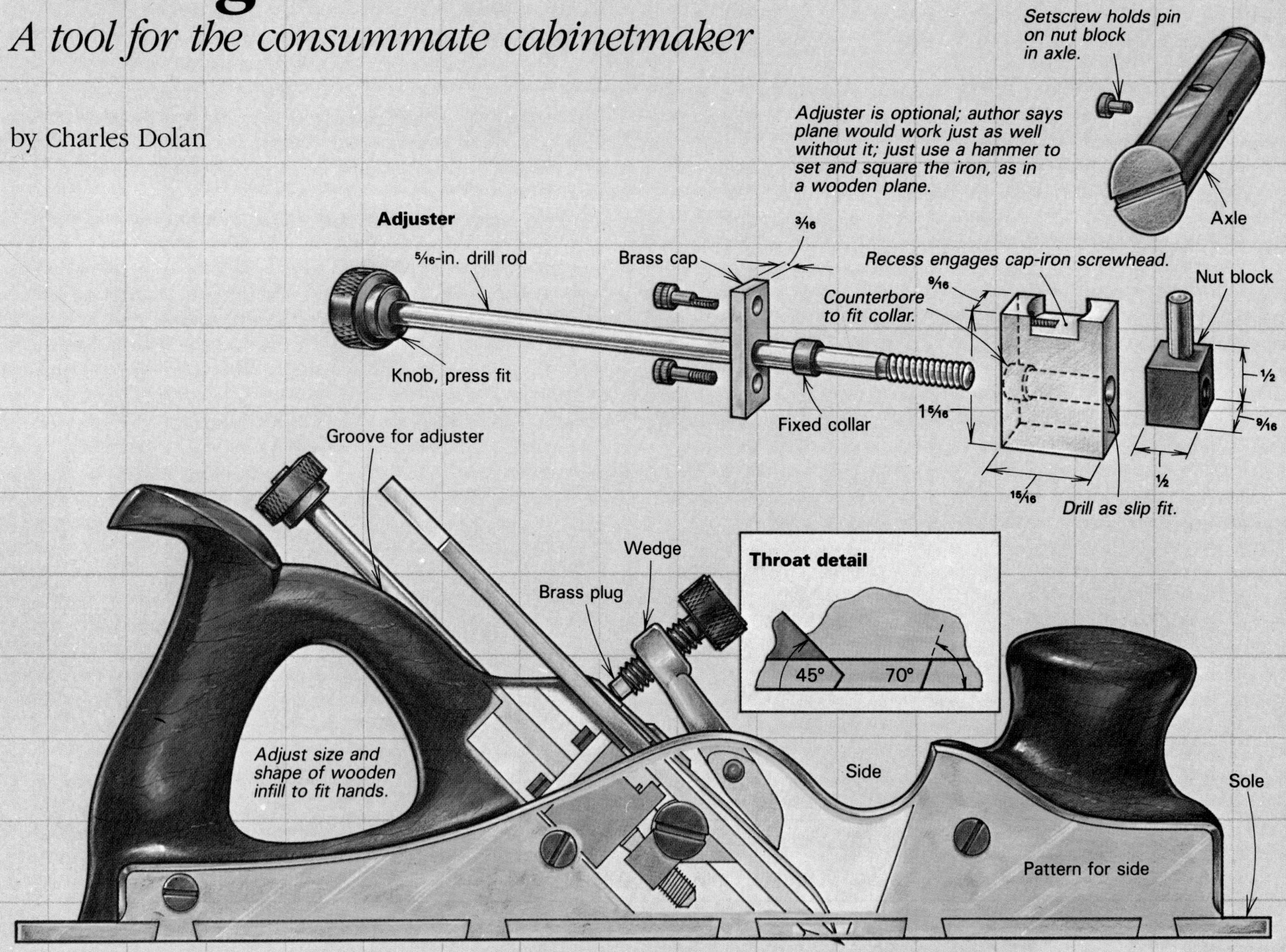

Setscrew holds pin on nut block in axle.

Adjuster is optional; author says plane would work just as well without it; just use a hammer to set and square the iron, as in a wooden plane.

Axle

Adjuster

⁵⁄₁₆-in. drill rod

Brass cap

³⁄₁₆

Recess engages cap-iron screwhead.

Nut block

Knob, press fit

⁹⁄₁₆

Counterbore to fit collar.

Fixed collar

1⁵⁄₁₆

½

⁹⁄₁₆

½

Groove for adjuster

¹⁵⁄₁₆

Drill as slip fit.

Wedge

Brass plug

Throat detail

45°   70°

Adjust size and shape of wooden infill to fit hands.

Side

Sole

Pattern for side

Some years ago I was fortunate enough to acquire an old cast gun-metal smoothing plane made by J. Rodgers of Minshull Street, Manchester, England and bearing the date 1886. The plane, however, lacked its original iron, and after much searching in vain, I finally decided to try making one for it myself. The resurrected plane performed so well that I thought I'd attempt to make a companion for it—a 16-in. panel plane of similar design—from scratch. A panel plane is the cabinetmakers' refined equivalent of the jack plane used by carpenters and joiners.

At first glance, making a tool such as this might seem too daunting, yet I found the task pleasant on the whole, and ultimately very rewarding. I use the plane almost daily in my work as a specialty contractor and restorer, and I continue to be amazed at the way this hefty tool seems to sit down on the wood, leaving me free to push and control it rather than having to force the iron into the work.

It is very unlikely that a tool such as this could ever be made commercially today and few of the old ones ever find their way to the marketplace. When new, this grade of plane cost several times the price of the Stanley/Bailey tools, which were, in turn, much more expensive than the wooden planes in general use. Planes like this were the prerogative of the most conscientious craftsmen executing consummate work to the highest standards.

The first step is to make the iron, a process described on p. 49. Those who have already made steel tools will be quite familiar with how it is done. This article, however, is more concerned with cutting and soldering the body and flattening the plane's sole. Even if you never make a plane, flattening is a process that you can use to bring any plane sole to very close tolerances, something the factories can no longer afford to do.

Cutting the body—My first inclination was to have a casting made, as the idea of making a wooden pattern and having someone else translate it into shiny gun-metal was particularly appealing. However, none of the foundries that I approached would cast fewer than five pieces (at substantial cost). Plane makers at the turn of the century often made plane bodies by joining the sides to the sole with through dovetails in the metal. I decided to do the same, soldering the joints together. This proved to be a first-class way to fabricate a body in brass and I am sure that it will do just as well in steel for those who prefer it.

I bought one bar of rolled brass 3 in. by ¼ in. by 16 in. and two of 2⅝ in. by ³⁄₁₆ in. by 14 in. The two smaller pieces had been cut from sheet and accordingly required some flattening with a ham-

From *Fine Woodworking* magazine (November 1985) 55:60-63

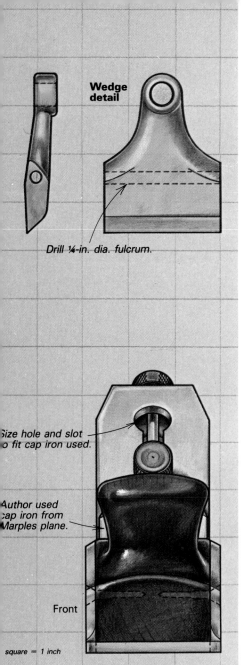

Wedge detail

Drill ¼-in. dia. fulcrum.

Size hole and slot to fit cap iron used.

Author used cap iron from Marples plane.

Front

square = 1 inch

A plane like this is comparable to the highest grade commercial tools at the turn of the century. Such tools are scarce, and rarely reach the marketplace, but you can make one from dovetailed brass plate. The author spent many hours working on the screw-type adjuster (right), but realized at the end that he seldom changed the set of the iron. He recommends that readers omit the adjuster and simply set the iron's depth and lateral adjustment by tapping with a hammer, as in a wooden plane, with the wedge screw snug but not fully tight.

mer. [Conklin Brass, 345 Hudson St., N.Y.C., N.Y. 10014 sells brass by mail order. The bars should cost about $70, postpaid.]

Using blue layout paint (a colored shellac that cuts down glare and allows you to see fine scribed lines), I marked out the sides very much as I would a drawer joint. I cut the narrow tails in the sides first and used these to mark out the broad pins in the sole.

A number of methods will work to remove the waste—jigsaw, hacksaw, jewelers' piercing saw, metal-cutting bandsaw, whatever is most convenient. Various files serve to work down to the layout lines. Files that have been used on steel don't work too well on nonferrous metals, and it is worthwhile having a set for each. The most difficult part of the job is to produce flat square lands between the tails on the side plates. I ground one edge of 10-in. second-cut file (a medium-cutting file) to an angle that allowed me to clean out right into the corners (photo, p. 48).

When the tails are finished, use them to mark the sole. Rough cut first, then clean up with a four-square file with one of its sides ground smooth to act as a safe bearing surface. When the joints are as near perfect as you can make them, you can drill a line of holes across the sole to begin the mouth slot. Clean up the edges by filing, but leave the throat undersize for the time being, because final shaping will be done after the iron is fitted.

Soldering—Ordinary 50/50 solder is not in any way difficult to work with provided three requirements are met: there must be adequate heat, a good flux, and surgically clean surfaces, as shiny and clean as a guardsman's buttons. Wire the parts securely together and use some pieces of hardwood to spread everything square and true. You can provide sufficient heat by placing the work on one of the rings of an electric cooking stove at medium heat for half an hour. Bring the work to a heat where the solder will just go pasty but not run freely and then heat locally with a propane torch, flowing the solder into the joints all around. Use plenty of solder or it may not completely fill the joints (I had to reheat some spots with the torch and refill them). It is safe to ignore any runs or drips—they won't stick to the stove rings, and the excess can be filed away from the plane when it has cooled.

When all is run in, stand back, turn off the stove and leave well enough alone until cold. Moving the work too soon will cause frosted joints that will have to be heated all over again. Then remove all the excess solder and file the work flat.

Making the infill—I chose walnut for the infill as it is both strong and easy to work. I recommend a bed angle of 45° for the general work to be expected of this plane. This can be cut on the

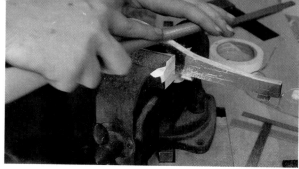

Brass can be bandsawn with an 18-TPI blade (top left). The metal has been sprayed with layout dye, a colored shellac that cuts glare and shows fine scribe lines clearly. With both sides clamped in the vise (top center), bandsaw marks can be filed away. To reach into tight corners (top right), grind the edge of a file to an angle that will fit. For soldering, pre-heat the brass on a stove (left) until it reaches a temperature where the solder almost flows. Use a propane torch to bring each successive joint up to full heat.

To flatten the sole, test it on a reference plate of heavy glass spread with blue oil paint (left). The thin paint transfers only to high spots on the sole. File and scrape these areas down, then test again on the glass, repeating until the critical areas at toe, heel and throat are fully covered by blue (for the rest of the sole an even spread of about 70% is adequate). A metal scraper (above) is used something like a paring chisel, working in a crosshatched pattern. The tool takes a series of fine, powdery shavings about ⅛ in. wide.

tablesaw using the miter gauge. I next cut the grooves for the adjuster. I put a lot of time into making the adjuster, but have decided it was more trouble than it is worth. I'd advise you not to bother with one, but simply to adjust the iron by tapping it with a hammer when necessary. The set of the iron in this sort of plane is not changed very often anyway.

For the actual shaping of the handle and knob, I simply drilled through the block to define the important radii inside and out, then I gradually shaped the wood with rasps and files, checking the fit and feel often. There are much faster ways to shape a handle, of course, and anyone in a hurry will doubtless use his own methods. But the handle and knob, to me, are critical parts of the plane, and I wanted to get mine right.

Making the wedge—The wedge is cut from a solid slab of ½-in. brass by drilling adjacent holes around its perimeter (line drilling). I began the shaping with a big rat-tail file, then moved on to a half-round, a small flat file, and a smooth file for the finishing cuts. I then evened out the surface with 200-grit wet/dry paper.

It remains to tap the wedge for the screw, and drill a hole clear through it for its pivot pin, which is a length of ¼-in. drill rod with one end peened slightly so it is a friction fit in one side of the plane body.

The wedge screw is best made on a metalworkers' lathe but an alternative would be to epoxy a hardwood knob onto the head of a ½-in. socket-head screw.

Finishing up and flattening—Mount the iron in the plane and start to refine the size of the mouth slot. I feel that there has been a recent tendency to overstate the advantages of a very narrow mouth and would personally never have one thinner than ³⁄₆₄ in. for a plane such as this, which will occasionally be required to "shift some stuff." Make sure that the mouth is square across the body and have the top of the front edge sloping away from the iron by a few degrees, as shown in the drawing on p. 46.

The last job is to flatten the sole. The heating of the body during soldering will inevitably have left some distortion, which will now have to be removed. The most suitable low cost way to flatten the sole of a plane is by filing and scraping, using a surface plate as a reference.

Flattening to a plate is a technique well worth learning as it allows precision flats to be put on any machine pieces or tools with just hand work and patience. You will need some good files and also a scraper, which can be bought quite cheaply or can even be made from an old file for nothing. You will also need a tube of artists' thalo blue or Prussian blue oil paint, some light oil and of course a surface plate.

If you do not expect to be doing much of this work, buy an 18-in. by 12-in. rectangle of plate glass, ¾-in. thick. To avoid twist, house the glass in a strong plywood box supported by only three feet. Plate glass is ground and lapped to quite fine limits of flatness to achieve optical truth and if treated carefully is more than adequate for this purpose—you should be able to flatten to tolerances well under a thousandth. If you intend to do more serious fitting than that, I would advise you to buy a granite bench plate of the same size. Avoid all used cast-iron plates like the plague. These are very sensitive to abuse and there is no easy way of diagnosing or correcting faults. A piece of new glass is infinitely preferable to an old iron plate that may have been used as an anvil.

Fit the iron in the plane and tighten the wedge screw to stress the tool to working conditions. Apply a thin glaze of paint and oil over the surface of the plate and lightly rub the sole of the plane on it. The blue will adhere only to the high spots.

Carefully file these blue areas away. For control and precision, press the front of the file down with your left thumb, and file in short strokes right on the mark. When the first set of spots has been filed off, repeat the marking and remove the new ones. The high spots will increase in number and gradually spread all over the surface of the sole.

When the file begins to do as much harm as good, change to the scraper, which can remove fine, precise shavings. The scraper should be kept sharp and is used rather like a paring chisel being pushed into the work. By repeated marking and scraping, the spots will progressively become more numerous until they cover the whole of the surface. Work slowly and deliberately and crosshatch the cuts frequently. There is no denying that this is a tedious business, but it is, in fact, very reliable.

You can now strip everything down and finish file the metal parts. A good rub with 120-grit wet/dry paper will give a very smart finish to the brass. All the steel parts can be blued with cold gun-bluing solution if such meets your fancy.

You now have a tool that will last several lifetimes and which will constantly delight you with its performance. I hope that the use of the plane as well as the elementary fitter's skills that you have learned in making it will provide you with greater scope and more satisfaction in your trade. □

Charles Dolan lives in Montreal West, Quebec, Canada.

Making the iron

I feel that the principal reason old irons (and modern Japanese ones, for that matter) are held in such high regard is that they have great weight and thickness, and not that the steel is superior to modern alloy steel. For my iron I chose an alloy of carbon, manganese, chromium, tungsten and vanadium, a steel made in Sheffield by Sanderson Kayser Ltd., and sold as Precision Ground Flat Stock Oil Hardening Non-Distorting Pitho Alloy Tool Steel. Similar tool steels are available from any industrial hardware supplier and should work as well, as long as they contain tungsten and vanadium for toughness.

Blanks are available in a great size range—mine (18 in. by 2½ in. by ¼ in.) cost $18. There is still enough of it left for two more irons. The steel is sold in the annealed, soft state—22 on the Rockwell hardness scale. With a little patience, a good hacksaw, some sharp files and a drill press, an afternoon is all you need to make as good an iron as can be had at any price.

Much has already been said elsewhere about making tools in general, so at this point I will just concentrate on some fine points. I decided to hacksaw the iron to length at a 25° bevel angle, in order to save a lot of filing afterwards. Not much has been written about hacksawing. A rigid frame and a good high-speed blade make a lot of difference. Saw with long full strokes without forcing the blade. Some 3-in-1 oil in the kerf will ease friction. If the blade begins to lead off the line, lightly dress the teeth on that side with a whetstone to get the blade going

straight again. If it continues to run out, put in a new blade and saw from the other edge until the cuts meet.

To file the bevel, position the iron with the bevel uppermost and horizontal in a vise. I'd recommend a clean, sharp 14-in. mill-bastard file for this job. It helps a good deal to rub chalk over the faces of the file and use it only until it starts to slide. Then clean the file with a file card and remove any "pins" with the point of a soft iron nail. Then chalk the faces again and continue.

You will by now have seen how much effort is needed to work this stuff, but there should be some light at the end of the tunnel. You must next mark out the size and position of the hole and slot for the cap-iron screw. I used the cap iron from a Marples plane.

Drill a hole the width of the slot at the bottom and one big enough to clear the head of the screw at the top. Back the iron with a piece of mild steel to prevent the drill from grabbing when it breaks through. Then drill carefully with the drill running slowly, and use enough pressure on the quill to make the drill really cut. It is essential to clamp the work firmly. Trying to hold the work free-hand would be very dangerous. The swarf will be coming off the drill at a very high temperature and will certainly burn skin. Lastly, be sure to wear good eye protection.

The slot is cleared by drilling a row of adjacent ⅛-in. holes around the perimeter of the piece to be removed. When the row is complete the cutout will fall free, looking something like a metal centipede. If any of the holes don't quite touch each other the waste can be cleared by sawing or chiseling. The edges of the slot are cleaned up by "drawfiling" smooth, a technique in

which the file is used crossways along the work, using only enough pressure to feel the file cut. Next file the top corners of the iron at your chosen angle and finish-file all the edges smooth. Do all the filing now as the next step is to harden the steel, after which it can be shaped only by grinding.

I'd read about using a propane or acetylene torch for basic heat treating of tool steel, but this plane iron is heftier than many tools. I found I needed a charcoal barbecue force-drafted by a hair dryer to generate enough heat. Also, I tested the temperature of the steel by using a magnet, because it is very difficult to discern color changes in the midst of the fire. I attached the magnet to a longish wire, and gradually fanned the flame hotter, testing from time to time until the magnet was no longer attracted to the steel. Then I quenched the iron in 2½ gallons of old motor oil in a 3-gallon metal bucket. Quenching produces all sorts of spectacular fulminations—have the bucket's lid handy in case the oil catches fire, and on no account use a plastic bucket.

If you have used the magnet correctly and not overheated the steel, no scale will have formed—the iron will come out of the oil clean and smooth, apart from some minor surface staining. I cleaned the surface with 200-grit wet/dry paper and tempered the iron in a kitchen oven at 220°F for two hours. This brings it to a hardness of about 60 RC, tough enough to be driven through a nail without chipping and capable of taking an edge you could shave with. Despite the myths about laminated irons, Victorian blacksmiths, magic swords and hobbits and dragons, I am certain that properly heat-treated modern alloy steel is in every way superior to the old stuff. —C.D.

A shoulder plane's sides and sole are milled perfectly square so it can shoot along the face of a tenon to true up the shoulder. Its top edge is contoured to provide finger grips when used on large tenons. Made to refine rather than create joints, a shoulder plane is a precision tool.

Shoulder Plane
Unmatched for precise trimming in 90° corners

by Maurice Fraser

It's hard to imagine life without a trusty shoulder plane. When you need to trim a tenon's end-grain shoulder, fine-tune a rabbet joint or smooth flush up to an obstruction, you can rely on the control and finesse of a shoulder plane. While its cousin, the rabbet plane, efficiently cuts joints, the shoulder plane was born to refine or correct existing ones: The joint is its shooting board. If things always went perfectly, correctives wouldn't be needed. But erring, reportedly, is human, and that's when these tools can be "divine."

Shoulder planes probably didn't appear much before the mid-1800s. They are likely a product of the burgeoning of metal technology during the Industrial Revolution, when metal sheathing was applied to wooden objects, from handplanes to ships. Metal tools have several obvious advantages over wooden ones, including dimensional stability and the wear resistance of contact surfaces. A more subtle point is how metal elevated the plane body from a mere blade holder to a major contributor to the finesse of cut. The shoulder plane is a prime example—a classic wooden rabbet plane that was not simply ironclad but transformed into something quite new.

Before the Industrial Revolution, worn, wide-mouth wooden planes were a fact of life. Toolmakers could shrink mouth openings by flipping the blade, bevel upward, and thereby eliminate the gap between the mouth's rear lip and the blade's cutting edge. But this combined the blade's 30° bevel with the plane's 45° blade-seating angle, resulting in an unworkable 75° total cutting angle. A 15° blade-seating angle would compensate, but would result in a very thin sole behind the mouth. Such a thin sole, impossibly fragile in wood, *was* possible in metal. The new mouth, narrower by more than 300%, not only supports the cutting edge better, but makes the cutting action almost integral with the sole itself, as though a sharp rear lip of the mouth were cutting. These durable, hair-fine mouths (see the left photo on the facing page) promised a way to refine planing, parallel to that offered by the then new-fangled cap iron. Other finessing tools evolved this way as well: the miter plane, chariot, thumb and small miter block (today's block plane). But only the shoulder, from out of the rabbet plane's body, carried this genetic trait: It could work into corners.

Shoulder or rabbet?—Today, books and catalogs, as well as their readers, confuse shoulder planes with rabbet planes. That's understandable: Simple rabbet planes are near look-alikes of shoulder planes. Both are slim, unhandled and have blades, at full body width, coming through the plane's sides. Besides, manufacturers love to blur terminology to make the buyer think he is getting both in one.

The right photo on the facing page compares shoulder planes to rabbet and dado planes. Because they're designed to cut joints, "complete" rabbet planes have fences, depth gauges, cross-grain

From *Fine Woodworking* magazine (May 1989) 76:38-41

scoring spurs and handles. Shoulder planes, meant for trimming, don't need these accessories. Rabbet planes, for good chip clearance, are big mouthed; shoulder planes conversely are soft-spoken. Both cut at the same 45°-50° angle, but shoulder planes do so with their bevel up and a low 15°-20° seating angle (see the drawing detail on the next page). Add to this that the tops of shoulder planes have curves, to provide a grip when shooting along a large tenon, and they are always metal bodied (some with wooden cores). Rabbet-plane bodies are either all wood (old style) or all metal.

There's a third species, I'll call a trim-rabbet plane, that might be an intermediate stage from wooden rabbet to shoulder plane. It has a steel body with a wooden core and its blade bevel is up, but it has a steep 58° cutting angle. In effect, it's a high-angle shoulder plane, good for highly figured long grain and cross-grain in rabbets, but cranky on endgrain.

Uses of the shoulder plane – One of the principal uses of the shoulder plane is correcting tenon shoulders that have been cut high, round or canted. When doing so, clamp the work horizontally and rest the plane's side on the tenon's face, as shown in the photo on the facing page. Begin by pressing the nose of the plane onto the work surface, to avoid tilting the plane during the first inch of the cut. In addition, tenon faces can be planed cross-grain if minor corrections are necessary.

There's also a subspecies of shoulder planes, bullnose planes, that add considerable versatility. They are easy to grip in one hand, and their bobbed nose lets them work almost smack up to a wall. Other than their small size and nose, they are identical in design and performance to shoulder planes.

Shoulder and bullnose planes excel at fine-tuning frame rabbets, where panels or glass can't be trimmed; softening tongue or groove corners; and paring (or thinning) tongues to ease insertion, especially with breadboarded tabletops. Correcting lap or halved joints, or dadoes, with "petite" models is a snap. They're indispensable for cleanup in tight areas, like lap dovetails behind lipped drawer fronts, tablesawn raised-panel bevels or tool-torn quirks on moldings and rule joints. And, no other handtool forms knuckle-joint "necks" or secret dovetail miters as precisely.

Grinding and setting the blade – The cutting edge of a shoulder-plane blade must be kept perfectly square with the blade (and plane) sides when it's sharpened. Other plane blades correct easily, with lateral adjustment, but any corrective tilting here will make it impossible to set the blade so it protrudes equally from each side of the plane body. You have to grind the cutting edge perfectly. Even the smallest discrepancy in blade-corner depth can spoil joints.

After grinding a 25° bevel on the cutting edge, insert the blade into the plane body so it protrudes equally from both sides. Inspect the barely emerging cutting edge. If it's not square, scribe a pencil line behind the blade's edge, bearing against the rear lip for reference. Then, regrind to this line. Persistent small errors can be honed off on a medium-grit stone, using greater hand pressure at the appropriate corner.

Next, remove the burr and hone in a 5° second bevel, either a traditional full one, with a medium stone, or a microbevel, with a hard Arkansas or its equivalent. (Both styles total 30°.) I prefer the latter, because the microbevel can easily be removed by honing to the 25° bevel and started anew, as opposed to retaining and enlarging it with each honing. With this method, you can rehone easily for a long time and postpone the need for the perfect regrinding of the primary bevel. Some prefer honing a single 30° bevel.

Insert the sharpened blade diagonally into the oblong entry opening with care, to avoid nicking it on the plane's interior. When the blade appears in the mouth, guide it to rest with the left hand. For endgrain or difficult figured grain, the front lip of an adjustable mouth should be set between 1/100 in. and a full 1/64 in. from the cutting edge. On most hardwoods, between 1/64 in. and 1/32 in. will probably allow sweet, clog-free shearing. The depth of cut should be just enough to produce a continuous shaving. Sawdust means too light a cut; an opaque chip, too heavy. On some planes, the final tightening of the hold-down lever or wedge gives a microadjustment toward a fuller cut. If so, learn to compensate.

Choosing a shoulder plane – Let me share some hard-earned prejudices. First, large, heavy shoulder planes offer more delicate control and refinement of cut than the smaller versions – even on small work. Their length lends linear accuracy; their mass acts as a

A fine mouth opening is a sign of quality. The Norris (top) has a minute cutting aperture of .010 in.; the Mathieson (middle), an acceptable .025 in; and the Record #042 (bottom), a marginal .051 in.

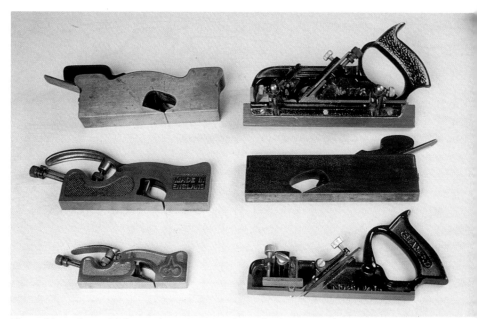

The rabbet plane (right, top) and dado plane (right, bottom) have fences and depth gauges for cutting joints. Shoulder planes (left), for trimming joints, never do. They have fine mouths, with their blade bevel up. The trim-rabbet plane (right, center) has a steeper cutting angle than shoulder planes and a straight top.

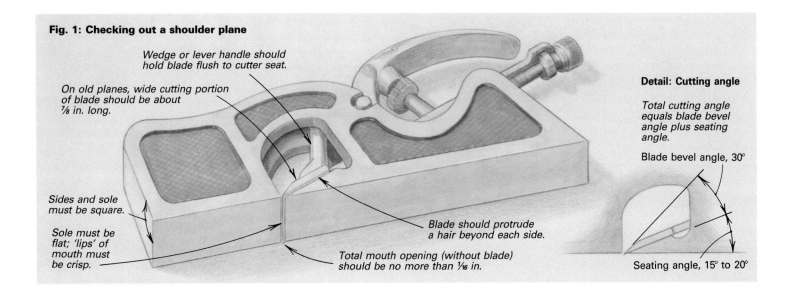

Fig. 1: Checking out a shoulder plane

Wedge or lever handle should hold blade flush to cutter seat.

On old planes, wide cutting portion of blade should be about ⅞ in. long.

Sides and sole must be square.

Sole must be flat; 'lips' of mouth must be crisp.

Blade should protrude a hair beyond each side.

Total mouth opening (without blade) should be no more than ⅟₁₆ in.

Detail: Cutting angle

Total cutting angle equals blade bevel angle plus seating angle.

Blade bevel angle, 30°

Seating angle, 15° to 20°

shock absorber for cut resistance; their weight seats you into the cut, adding momentum; and their high profile adds a welcome reference surface, especially when working the plane on its side. On narrow ledges, if most of a wide plane hangs over empty space, there's no harm, so long as your fingers feel in control.

Second, if the big tool perches on the workpiece like a horse on a high chair, then it's time to reach for the junior size. Although small planes sometimes chatter and deflect on hardwoods, they will compensate: They are pocketable, will follow slightly bowed surfaces, cut in confined places and work easily in one hand.

Third, two extreme sizes do more than one middling. In the mid-range are Stanley's #93 (6½ in. long) and Clifton's 3-in-1 plane (6 in. long). The latter has interchangeable noses to go from shoulder to bullnose plane, or it can drop its nose to become a chisel rabbet plane. These well-made planes work satisfactorily, but they lack the authority of larger planes and the maneuverability of smaller planes.

The chart on the facing page lists models currently being made and available through many large mail-order tool companies and local suppliers. Of these, the most versatile package consists of Record's massive but refined #073 (mouth and blade adjustment) partnered by the compact Stanley #92, plus Stanley's #90 bullnose for small or enclosed work (see photo below)—David and Goliath, plus a mascot, on the same team.

The chronology of shoulder and bullnose planes. Top to bottom: (19th- to mid-20th-century British), bronze and ebony Norrises; (20th-century British), Record #042, with depth adjustment, and Preston bullnose; and (20th-century American), Stanley #92, with adjustable blade and mouth, and Stanley #90 bullnose.

Shopping for a classic or a bargain—The tools mentioned earlier are currently made...and are good. But, a working antique *might* be better, especially cheaper. Antique tool dealers and auctions are worth a look, but you must be knowledgeable about the types and merits of the planes you'll find.

The photo below, left, shows three shoulder planes and their bullnose counterparts. Each represents one of three basic categories, based on when, where and how they were made. The best shoulder planes are the original British models: simple, solid and elegant. They were hand-assembled, from Victorian times until World War II, by firms like Slater, Spiers, Mathieson and Norris. The tool's dovetailed steel shell houses a rosewood core and wedge, which sandwich a stout Sheffield blade that is adjusted manually by sight and touch. It takes a little practice, but once set, requires little readjustment. These tools are still available, but you'll pay in the range of $150 for a workable tool to $600 for a fancy bronze and ebony model in mint condition. What you get in return is buttery planing—the legacy of a standard of workmanship now, sadly, historical.

A second category of shoulder plane, the all-metal, screw-adjusted, 20th-century British variant, was pioneered (circa 1900-1930s) by Preston. Originally semi-mass produced but hand-fitted, their hollow iron castings were heavy and well machined, though campy-ornate. In the 1930s, the line was continued by Record, who added an adjustable mouth to the large sizes. There was some post-war decline of quality, the only plus being the elimination of Preston's glitzy nickel plating, which wears badly. Record also deleted many models, a few of which have been reissued recently by the Clifton firm. These tools have proportions and profiles roughly similar to the historic type (Norris, et al.) and at best, can work...oh, nearly as well. And, with their blade-adjusting screw, they *are* user-friendlier. In price ($50 to $120), as in quality, they stand in the middle ground between the Norris type and the current U.S.-designed tools.

The third version of the shoulder plane, the 20th-century American all-metal one, is Stanley's. They've manufactured the #92 and #93 models since 1902, avoiding the term "shoulder plane" in their literature and calling them instead "cabinetmaker's rabbet planes." Lighter, shorter and lower slung than analogous English versions, they trade off some mellowness and alignability for compactness and versatility. They are wickedly adjustable—far exceeding Norris' and Preston's—by screw action. You can change mouth width or blade depth, or drop the nose for close-up (chisel-planing) cuts. The machining quality is as good as ever, despite their auto-bumper nickel plating.

Regardless of class, shoulder planes are finicky. Roughly made (new) or roughly used (old) planes are rarely fine-tunable and

Drawing: Bob La Pointe

Models currently made					
Tool model and type	**Dimensions W x L**	**Mouth adjustment**	**Convert to chisel plane**	**Approx. price**	**Comments**
Shoulder plane: Record #073	1¼ by 8⅛	Yes	No	$94 - $99	The last large classic shoulder plane still made.
Clifton #420	¾ by 8	No	No	$100	As above, but less massive. Specialized for shooting narrow ledges. Medium mouth. Remake of Record #042.
Clifton #410	⅝* by 5⅜ * some are 11⁄16 in. wide	No	No	$98 - $100	The smallest shoulder plane now made. Handy. Good partner to large plane. Proper mouth. Remake of a classic.
Stanley #93	1 by 6½	Yes	Yes	$57 - $60	Middle member of Stanley's original trio: #92, #93, #94. Useful. Well made and designed. Curious size.
Stanley #92	¾ by 5½	Yes	Yes	$49 - $52	Smaller version of #93. Size close to Clifton #410 with added versatility if needed. Good partner to a large plane.
Bullnose plane: Record #077	1⅛ by 4	Shims to 4 widths	Yes	$52 - $55	Fine appearance. Good Weight. Nose section a bit thick.
Stanley #90	1 by 4	Yes	Yes	$46 - $49	Despite glitzy look, a good tool. Better mouth adjustment than #077. Thin nose section cuts closer to obstructions.
Stanley #75	1³⁄32 by 4	Yes	Yes	$25	Remake of Stanley's 1879 "el cheapo." Poorly machined; still no bargain.
Clifton #400	⅜ by 3¼	No	No	$70	Remake of Preston. Wedged blade. Narrowest bullnose available.
Combination plane: Clifton "3 in 1"	Shoulder: 1⅛ by 6 Bullnose: 1⅛ by 4⅞	Shims to 4 widths	Yes	$110 - $115	Ingenious idea, but clumsy in hand. Pricier and less useful than set of Stanley #92 and #90, but more compact.

should be avoided. Features to watch for are shown in figure 1 on the facing page and listed below:

1. Fine mouth openings are essential for precise work. On fixed-mouth planes, total mouth width should be no more than 1⁄16 in. (3⁄64 in. or less is ideal) and equal all across. Any filing of "lips" to straightness will widen the mouth—a cure worse than the disease. Test adjustable mouths to see if they close parallel and all the way to the blade's edge (zero opening). A skewed front lip can be filed straight. A skewed rear lip, filed back, loses its thin support at/under the cutting edge and is worse off. Better leave it alone.

2. The sole must be machined flat in length and width and not reflect a wavery shine when turned slowly under a light. The mouth must be a crisp slot and not round inwards like lips sucked in. If the sole is slightly out of flat, rub it on wetted 150-, then 220-grit wet-or-dry abrasive paper supported by a thick glass plate. If flaws are great, don't buy it. Skilled machining is expensive, with the risk of mouth-widening or distortion.

3. Sides and sole must be perpendicular to each other. Check this with a good square. Some unscrupulous old-tool dealers grind out pitting and patina...and alignment! Never be suckered into buying these shiny but functionally dead tools.

4. The blade should protrude just a hair beyond each side. It must never be narrower than the body. A blade flush with or narrower than the sides will leave a series of steps with each pass, instead of a single, clean corner. Nowadays, shoulder-plane blades often come too wide for their bodies: Remove the blade and file its edges until they protrude between 1⁄100 in. to a scant 1⁄64 in. on each side. If you find a shiny old tool with an over-width blade, beware: Likely the plane body got narrowed (and distorted) by ruinous "cleaning." Original owners rarely left blades too "full."

5. On old tools, the wide, cutting portion of blades should be at least ⅞ in. long (after nick removal on edges and corners). On wedged models, the blade stem should protrude back beyond the wedge for easy malleting. Avoid pitted blade backs: Flattening is tedious and unremoved pits eventually become gaps in the edge. If a lightly pitted blade back is the worse flaw on an otherwise desirable tool, you might level it on a coarse-grit, polka-dot diamond stone. Out-of-true water stones are fatal here.

6. Blades should be held flush to the cutter seat by the clamp, lever handle or wedge. Be wary of replaced wedges. Fine, continuous wedge fit is essential for a solid blade hold-down. Realistically, a cobweb-thin glimmer of light under the blade, though undesirable, is less of a problem with thick-bladed, wedged, old models (with a generous contact area around a rigid blade) than with newer models with thin blades and scanty hold-down levers. So, look a gift shoulder plane in the mouth—a sound one is a boon to craftsman and woodbutcher alike. ☐

Maurice Fraser teaches woodworking at the Craft Students' League in the Y.W.C.A. at 53rd and Lexington Ave., New York City, N.Y.

Tuning a Japanese Plane
Taking the tool to its full potential

by Robert Meadow

Fig. 1: Plane anatomy

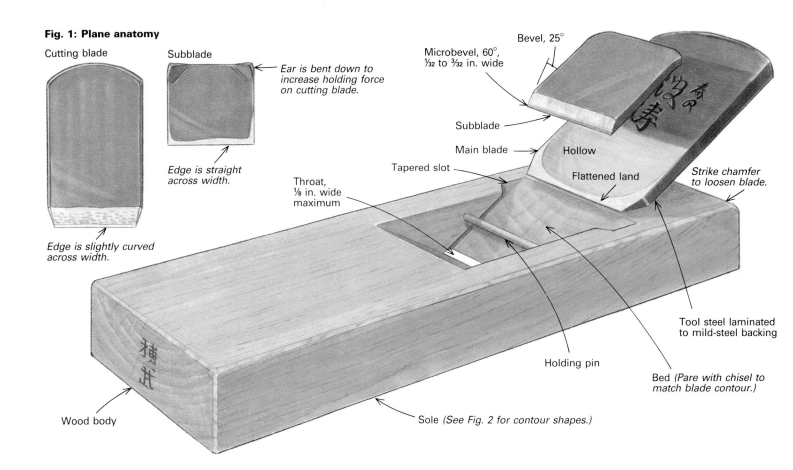

Cutting blade

Subblade

Ear is bent down to increase holding force on cutting blade.

Edge is straight across width.

Edge is slightly curved across width.

Bevel, 25°

Microbevel, 60°, ¹⁄₃₂ to ³⁄₃₂ in. wide

Subblade

Main blade

Hollow

Tapered slot

Flattened land

Strike chamfer to loosen blade.

Throat, ⅛ in. wide maximum

Tool steel laminated to mild-steel backing

Holding pin

Bed *(Pare with chisel to match blade contour.)*

Wood body

Sole *(See Fig. 2 for contour shapes.)*

H andplaning at its best is perhaps the most pleasurable of all woodworking surfacing techniques; at its worst, it's one of the most frustrating. The handplane can surface even the most figured woods, such as bird's-eye maple, to a mirror-like finish, producing far better surfaces than possible with a cabinet scraper or sander. As a musical instrumentmaker, I have conducted many tool demonstrations, and my students invariably are astonished at how my Japanese planes produce long ribbons of tissue-thin shavings with any wood. They sometimes think some magic or trickery is involved. There isn't. But to make these fine cuts, you need a well-designed, high-quality plane that has been meticulously fine-tuned. The planing itself requires a high degree of concentration and sensitivity. You must be aware of what is going on at the blade's edge as it moves through the wood, continually adjusting your plane and technique to achieve the best results.

A newly purchased Japanese plane possesses the potential for superior performance, but it won't work well right off the dealer's shelf: The wooden body may have dried out and shrunk since it

left the moist Japanese climate. The blade and subblade also must be shaped, sharpened and fitted to the body. But before you make these adjustments, you need to understand a bit about the planes themselves.

I was introduced to Japanese planes by my friend Makoto Imai, who apprenticed as a temple builder in Japan and now works in California. Although I had been getting good results from Western planes for years, it wasn't long before I abandoned them in favor of the Japanese planes. Their heavy irons can be sharpened to an incredible edge, and their wood bodies can be customized to make fine cuts in any wood.

The Japanese plane appears primitive alongside a metal Western-style plane. It has few parts: a wood body with tapered slots that hold the cutting blade, also tapered, and a subblade wedged tightly behind a pin that spans the width of the plane. Figure 1, above, shows the plane's anatomy. There are no built-in adjusting mechanisms. The Japanese plane, unlike its Western counterpart, is normally pulled rather than pushed. One hand grasps the long

Drawings: Bob La Pointe

part of the plane's body in front of the blade to provide downward pressure and to pull the plane over the workpiece. The other hand, positioned behind the blade, guides the plane. At all times, one must be sensitive to the balance between the pressure of the two hands.

The blades used in Japanese planes are thicker than those used in today's Western planes and are laminated from two pieces: a thin, high-carbon steel layer that forms the cutting edge and a thicker, wrought-iron back. This thicker blade rigidly supports the cutting edge, and because the bulk of the blade is a fairly soft metal, its cutting edge and bevel can be shaped more easily. The key to superior performance, however, is in the steel itself. The Japanese use unalloyed high-carbon tool steels, which they call "white steel." Western tool steels have alloys added. High-carbon tool steel without alloys warps when it is quenched in hardening. This warpage can be controlled by laminating the tool steel to a thicker backing. One great advantage of white steel is that it can be worked over a wide range of temperatures, so the size and shape of the metal grains can be manipulated. The edges of these flattened crystals are hard yet still flexible. The round crystals of alloyed tool steels used in Western planes (and the so-called "blue steel" in some Japanese planes) lose flexibility as you increase hardness. The process of "tapping out," which will be discussed later, aligns the flat crystals of white steel so their hard edges form the cutting edge of the blade. This gives you a blade that wears evenly, rather than one that dulls or chips.

Because the bodies of Japanese planes are made from solid wood, they can be affected by changes in temperature and humidity. Fortunately, these effects are small, and in any event, correctable. As mentioned earlier, the cutting blade is held in position by the tapered slots in the wood body. The blade is sprung when it is held in the body, which helps it to resist deflection as the tool cuts. The range of elasticity of the wood body affects its ability to spring the blade without requiring excessive force to get the blade in and out. Metal has too little elasticity to work well in this way, and a soft wood doesn't have the stiffness to support the blade sufficiently. Japanese white oak, the wood commonly used for the best planes, has the best balance of these characteristics. Additionally, as will be discussed later, the plane's wood sole can be reshaped for the particular task at hand, whether it be roughing, trueing or finish-planing.

Conditioning the plane—You must understand what happens when you plane a piece of wood before you can grasp the rationale involved in conditioning a plane. As you pull the plane, the forces on the blade deflect the cutting edge down into the wood. When working with softwoods, such as pine, these forces are not great, so the blade easily resists deflection. The forces on the blade increase, however, when taking heavy cuts or when working with hardwoods. Eventually, these downward forces can exceed the stiffness of the blade, causing it to pull down into the wood abruptly. As the blade snaps back to its original, nondeflected position, the wood will tear out. We think of steel as being a hard, rigid substance, yet in reality, it is flexible and whippy. Students are amazed at how the blade's edge is easily deflected simply from fingernail pressure applied along the back of the blade near its cutting edge. No small wonder then that even a slight change in edge angle has a great effect on how the blade flexes and how it feels as it moves through the wood. The trick in getting a plane to work well is to adjust the body to provide maximum support for the blade as it's carried across the wood surface, and to shape and sharpen the blade to resist deflection. A well-conditioned plane shaves cleanly, is easy to use and control, and doesn't vibrate.

Shaping and sharpening the cutting blade—Begin by disassembling the plane. Remove the blade and subblade by sharply hitting the chamfered surface on the back end of the body with a hammer. Keep your thumb on the blade to keep it from popping out. Note how the hard, high-carbon steel side of the blade has a flat at the cutting edge, then a dish-shaped area. The hollow is formed as the blade cools when it is being hardened; the thin, high-carbon steel layer contracts more than the plane's thicker, mild-steel back. The flat area is an essential part of the cutting edge and must be maintained at all times.

The process for maintaining the flat, or land as it's often termed, is called tapping out, and it's the first step in the blade tune-up. In addition to aligning the metal crystals as previously discussed, this process gently curves the edge of the blade to provide metal for shaping the flat. Over time, the flat wears away, so it's a good idea to tap the blade out a little each time you resharpen it. Using a cross-peen hammer, I gently tap on the mild-steel portion of the bevel, as shown in the photo on the next page. The blade has to be supported directly under the hammer blows; I use the rounded spot on the corner of an anvil. Begin tapping at the heel of the bevel, moving the blade back and forth like a typewriter carriage, and progress down the bevel toward the weld line between the mild steel and the tool steel. Don't tap on the hard, tool-steel laminate, because you're liable to chip it.

Once you've finished tapping out, you can flatten the land along the edge and alongside the hollow. The land along the edge should be perfectly flat, but the blade is slightly concave along its length. To preserve this slight curvature, don't place the whole blade down flat on the sharpening stones. Instead, begin at the edge, supporting the weight of the rest of the blade, and move farther into the stone in a controlled manner. Coarse and medium stones are used to form the flat area; it'll be polished later. Check for flatness using white light (the reflection of your light source) to highlight any uneven areas. The photo below shows an example of a well-prepared flat, along with some examples of problems to be avoided.

The next step is to prepare the bevel on the other side of the blade. Steep bevels support the edge best, making it more resistant to deflection, but this configuration, because of its bluntness, also decreases the blade's slicing effectiveness. A shallower bevel cuts more effectively but is weaker and more prone to chipping. Optimally, hardwoods require a larger bevel angle than softwoods, but for Japanese planes, a 25° bevel is a practical compromise for most planing applications. The bevel itself should be perfectly flat, but as you shape the bevel, you want to form a slight convex curve

Photo: Michele Russell Slavinsky

The left blade has been tapped out correctly, and the flat land is well defined. The other blades need to be tapped out. The flat area on the middle blade extends too far back, forming a groove. The flat on the right blade has almost disappeared from repeated sharpenings.

From *Fine Woodworking* magazine (March 1989) 75:82-85

The author uses a small cross-peen hammer to gently tap out the blade, which is supported on the rounded corner of an anvil. Only the mild-steel portion of the bevel is struck. In this way, the hard tool steel, which is laminated to the mild steel, can be gently curved.

across the width of the edge by applying more pressure when stoning the outside edges than in the center of the bevel. The deviation from straight should be about five times the thickness of the shaving you want to take. This allows for the angle and deflection of the blade by the body and prevents the corners of the blade from nicking the planed surface. I carefully remove the burr formed during sharpening with a slower-cutting medium stone (3,000 to 4,000 grit), working alternately on the back side of the blade and the bevel. The objective here is to cut the burr off cleanly without work-hardening the edge. If you bend the burr back and forth to remove it by causing the metal to fatigue, the edge will work-harden, dull more quickly and be more prone to chipping.

Finally, finish the edge by polishing it on fine stones. As before, work alternately on the back side and the bevel. Again, as you proceed, use reflected white light to make sure that these surfaces are smooth, flat and free of imperfections. When the white light reflects uniformly off the bevel and no longer reflects off the edge of the blade itself, the job is done.

The subblade – The subblade directs shavings up and over the cutting blade and out of the plane, but its major function is to deflect the cutting blade so it resists being pulled down into the wood. As the cutting edge dulls, the planing forces will increase and the subblade's role becomes more important. For finish-planing, where the goal is to produce a smooth and shiny surface and not to remove a lot of wood, the planing forces are minimal, because extremely fine shavings are made. Here it's possible to use the plane without its subblade and produce gleaming, mirror-like surfaces, because the subblade is not changing the shaving's angle as it leaves the plane.

The subblade, like the cutting blade, is made by laminating tool steel to mild steel. It is conditioned in the same way as the cutter, with a couple of important differences. Because the subblade isn't used for cutting, the keenness of its edge is not critical. Its bevel should be formed accurately, but it doesn't need to be polished. To provide additional support at the subblade's edge, I blunt the end of the bevel by forming a 60° micro-bevel. The micro-bevel should be polished. For hardwoods, where the most support is required, I make the width of the micro-bevel about ³⁄₃₂ in.; for softwoods, about ¹⁄₃₂ in. If you are working with a wide variety of hardwoods and softwoods, the hardwood width will do for all the work. This eliminates the need to keep two sets of planes with different blade angles for use with hardwood and softwood. The

edge is made straight so that when the subblade is aligned with the cutting blade, this edge will sit back just far enough from the cutting blade's curved edge to prevent shavings from getting jammed.

Fitting the blades to the body – Changing the plane's white-oak body to compensate for climatic effects and to fit the blade and subblade is not very difficult. The purpose here is to adjust the body so the cutting blade and subblade conform to their mating wood surfaces. Once these initial adjustments are made, you shouldn't have to make any major adjustments, as long as you use and store the plane in a reasonably constant environment.

The width of the tapered slots and the cheeks, which support the subblade, need to be adjusted first. The blades should be centered in the body and fit snugly, not tightly, at the bottom. At the top, leave about ¹⁄₃₂ in. of play on each side of the blades to allow for lateral adjustment. Use a chisel to carefully pare the sides of the tapered slots and cheeks. Keep the shoulders of the tapered slots square and clean. If you have any question about the fit, you should err on the side of tightness; you can always loosen the fit later, if necessary.

The back of the cutting blade must lie firmly on the bed. Adjusting this area is a matter of "cut and try." Cover the back of the blade with lead from a soft pencil and gently tap the iron into the body. When you remove the blade, the lead marks left on the wood will highlight areas where the blade interferes with the bed. Because the blade and the bed have small curvatures, some of the marks can be misleading, thus not all the marked areas should be pared away. Instead, look for how the blade skews to one side or the other as you tap it in. First pare the high spots, where the blade hangs up, repeat the marking procedure and check the fit again. Repeat this process until the blade can be positioned smoothly, with the tightest fit near the throat in the center of the plane.

Once the blades fit the body properly, adjust the subblade to apply the desired amount of pressure on the underlying cutting blade. The subblade is tightly wedged between the holding pin and the cutting blade. Contact between the two blades is made by the beveled edge of the subblade and the "ears," the bent-over top corners of the subblade. The ears are formed by hammering over the top corners of the blade, using the tapping-out process described earlier. As before, the blade has to be supported on the rounded corner of the anvil when being struck. If the ears are unevenly bent, the subblade will rock, so check for this before trying out the plane. If the cutting blade digs in or tears the sur-

The author uses winding sticks to check the sole of this plane for twist in the plane's body. Using a single stick, Meadow will later check the sole for flatness.

Meadow is shown here adjusting the sole of a plane, flattening its surface and removing any twist with a scraper plane. The wooden sole should be checked frequently so any necessary adjustments to compensate for wear or changes in environmental conditions can be made.

face, the blade is too loose and you'll need to bend the ears a bit more to increase the pressure on the blade. When working with hardwoods or when taking thick shavings, you may find it necessary to increase the pressure to resist the increased planing forces on the blade. The pressure is about right when you get shavings of the same thickness whether you plane with or against the grain.

Checking out the sole—Before using a wooden plane, you should carefully check the plane's sole. When a plane is not cutting smoothly, it almost always involves a problem with the bottom of the plane. Either the shape of the sole is not right for the job at hand, the body is twisted or the sole is not flat across the plane's width.

The first step is to check the body for twist with a pair of winding sticks, a matched pair of wooden parallel straightedges. Place one stick on the sole just in front of the plane's throat and the other at the front end, as shown in the photo above, left. Sight across the top edges of the sticks. If the end of one stick is higher than the other, the body is in winding—twisted. Use a scraper plane, working across the grain, to eliminate the high spots, as shown in the photo above, right. The scraper plane, because of its near-vertical blade, takes fine, dust-like shavings, so the adjustments can be made gradually.

When you're sure the sole is flat with no twist, you can modify its shape along its length. The shape of the sole depends on how you intend to use the plane. For trueing, the idea is to remove local high spots from the wood's surface and make it flat. To do this, the plane has to bridge the high spots, so the sole is supported at the far ends of the plane and near the blade. For rough-surfacing or finish-planing, the idea is to remove the wood uniformly. For finish-planing, the sole must conform to the trued, flat surface of the workpiece, so the plane is supported only at its front end and at the blade. For rough-planing, more relief is needed between the support points to allow the sole to conform to the more irregular surface of the wood. Figure 2 at right illustrates the ideal sole configurations for trueing and for roughing or finishing. Use the scraper plane again to contour the sole. Finally, you want to clean up the throat of the plane without enlargening it any more than necessary. The opening should be small, not larger than ⅛ in. Your aim is to make the plane as immune as possible to subtle changes in grain and wood hardness. The most critical point of support for the plane is at the throat opening: The closer this point is to the edge of the blade, the easier it will be to control the plane.

Now that you've worked your way through the tune-up proce-

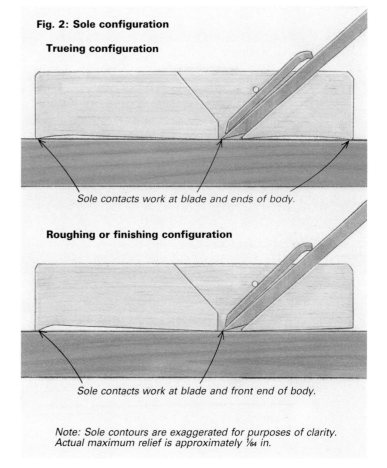

Fig. 2: Sole configuration

Trueing configuration

Sole contacts work at blade and ends of body.

Roughing or finishing configuration

Sole contacts work at blade and front end of body.

Note: Sole contours are exaggerated for purposes of clarity. Actual maximum relief is approximately ¹⁄₆₄ in.

dures, it's time to see how well you've done. Try your plane out on a wood that's hard to surface, such as bird's-eye maple or quarter-sawn cherry. If you've tuned everything right, the plane should produce wide, uniform shavings. The plane should also feel good, be easy to handle and be free of vibration or chatter. And, it should be quiet: The only sound should be that of the blade slicing into the wood. If things are not quite right, you probably need to increase the pressure on the cutting blade or check the plane's sole configuration. □

Robert Meadow is an instrumentmaker. He and his wife, Bonnie Robiczek, who helped prepare this article, operate The Luthierie in Saugerties, N.Y.

Hollows and Rounds

Making the most of a common pair of planes

by Graham Blackburn

A few of the author's hollows and rounds, a mixed bag bought over the years—some so recently that they have yet to be reconditioned. At far left is a pair of English planes with skewed irons; at far right is a pair of side-cutting rounds. Unlike most molding planes, which are named for the shapes they cut, hollows and rounds are named just the opposite, for their profiles.

Of all the wooden molding planes that are still to be found in antique shops, at flea markets and at the back of many workshops, the hollow plane, and its mate the round plane, are among the commonest. They hardly appear at first glance to be among the most useful of tools, but their relative abundance is an indication of the important position they once held in many woodworkers' tool kits. I well remember, as a boy in England, seeing rows of them in my school workshop and watching with fascination as they were used for all manner of work. Today, more than 30 of them have a place in my own workshop and find frequent employment in my custom-furniture business. The photo above shows a good range of sizes, from a variety of makers here and abroad. While these are by no means a complete set of graduations, these are typical of what you might easily find for sale, and a selection such as this is sufficient

to accomplish most of the purposes I will discuss in this article.

Hollows and rounds are often represented as being the poor relations in the family of molding planes. While other molding planes—the ogees, the cavettos, the astragals and the beading planes, for example—all cut a distinct molding, the hollows and rounds are said to be used only in lieu of a more particular plane, in a makeshift effort to reproduce the desired molding. While it is true that hollows and rounds can duplicate moldings made by specialized molding planes, this is by no means their only job. They are also invaluable for completing and trimming moldings begun by more specific planes, for sculptural shaping, and for working hollow and round shapes in their own right—of which perhaps the crowning example is the imitation of draped cloth in wood known as linenfold paneling.

Old books written at the time when machines were increasingly

From *Fine Woodworking* magazine (March 1988) 69:81-83

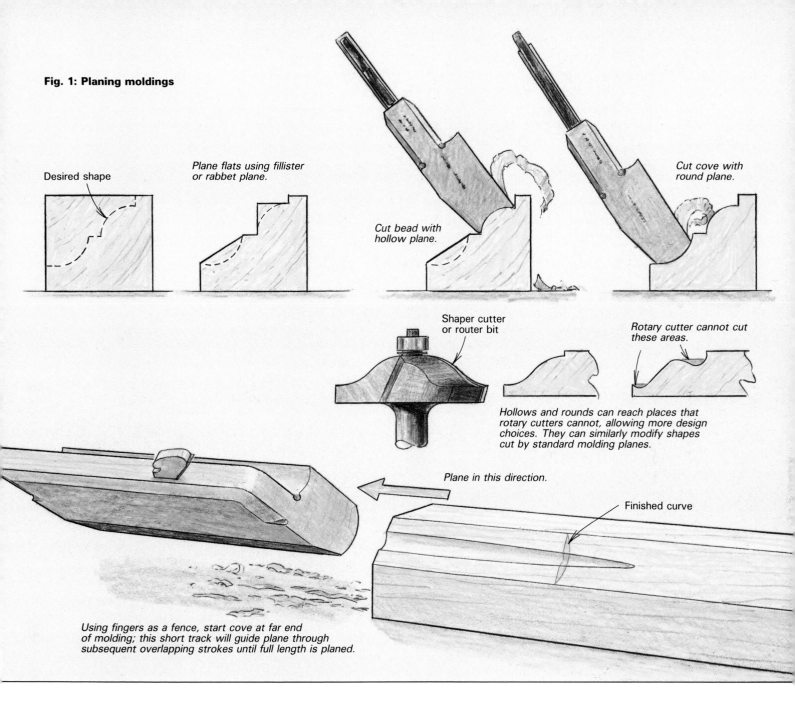

Fig. 1: Planing moldings

Desired shape

Plane flats using fillister or rabbet plane.

Cut bead with hollow plane.

Cut cove with round plane.

Shaper cutter or router bit

Rotary cutter cannot cut these areas.

Hollows and rounds can reach places that rotary cutters cannot, allowing more design choices. They can similarly modify shapes cut by standard molding planes.

Plane in this direction.

Finished curve

Using fingers as a fence, start cove at far end of molding; this short track will guide plane through subsequent overlapping strokes until full length is planed.

replacing planes in the production of commercial molding, and when the fashion for moldings was decreasing anyway, often advise the beginner that hollows can be dispensed with by substituting flat-soled planes and sandpaper. This is roughly the equivalent, in today's terms, of suggesting that you don't really need to learn joinery, because everything ought to be put together with dowels or metal fasteners. In fact, a hollow plane could be your most useful tool when, for example, you need to round over edges. Rather than setting up a router, or being limited by the size of available roundover bits, reach for the nearest-size hollow plane. Draw the exact profile you desire on the stock and plane to the lines. You will find the hollow plane does not have to match the required profile exactly, as does the router bit; neither is it limited to a perfect quarter round.

Of course, if you have any kind of footage to prepare, a router is the method of choice. Yet even in this case, hollows and rounds can lend a hand, refining machine-made moldings and allowing the benefits of quick production without unduly limiting design choices.

Before we examine exactly what these planes can do, and how they do it, let's take a closer look at the variety of hollow and round planes you might find.

Varieties—The planes were originally sold in pairs of matching hollows and rounds, and numbered according to the width of the iron. Markings are not always consistent, but one of the most common systems in America was to number planes using even numbers only, from 2 through 30, for planes starting at ¼ in. and increasing by increments of about ⅛ in. up to 2 in. In Britain, a frequent method was to sell sets of 18 pairs, ranging from ⅛ in. to 1½ in., rising by 1⁄16ths, and using both odd and even numbers—which also made possible the selling of so-called half-sets of nine pairs consisting of only the odd or the even numbers. You might also find the size stated as a fractional number, such as 4/8, denoting a width of four-eighths, or ½ in. Other numbers may refer to the manufacturer's catalog listing or a store code. Most planes are stamped with the manufacturer's name and address, and many are stamped with the owner's name, an obvious effort to keep the tools from wandering.

The most common arc for hollows and rounds is about one-sixth of a circle (60° of arc), but this will vary somewhat from one manufacturer to another. Therefore, you can't assume that by collecting a group of planes, made by different firms, stamped from 1 through 15, for example, you will have a graduated, fully matched set. Various manufacturers indicated the exact shapes by charts of measurements, diagrams and printed tables. One manufacturer, the Ohio Tool Co., found it necessary, after having merged with another plane manufacturer, to publish two tables: one for their own planes and another for those of the company they had absorbed.

To complicate matters further, there are different kinds of hollows and rounds. The commonest sort by far have straight irons bedded at various pitches between 45° and 50°. (In general, the 45° planes are designed for softwoods and hence are carpenters' tools, while the 50° planes are for cabinetmakers working in hardwoods.) Then, less common, are planes with skewed irons, which are usually set at a higher pitch, around 55°. In addition, the overall family of hollows and rounds includes a number of specialty planes. I'll describe some of these briefly.

Planes with arcs comprising virtually one-quarter of a circle (90° of arc) are called table hollows and rounds, and are used specifically for cutting the two halves of a rule joint—by means of which drop leaves are joined to drop-leaf tables. The better quality table hollows and rounds were made with fences—unlike regular hollows and rounds—and this kind is the easiest to use when cutting rule joints. The lower grade, unfenced, table hollows are less easy to recognize—the clue is that both sides of the plane body, or stock, are beveled instead of just one. If you chance upon a pair (or even one) of table hollows and rounds, seize them, for they can be very useful in conjunction with regular hollows and rounds.

Yet another variety is the side round. This type can have a profile consisting of a quarter round or a half round and was made in mirror-image pairs, as shown in the photo on p. 58.

Lastly, there is a group of planes that, while not strictly hollows and rounds, nevertheless cut these shapes and so deserve mention. These planes, which often have wide bodies like bench planes, include such exotics as ship hollows and ship rounds, gutter planes, forkstaffs and nosing planes. For those interested, all these tools are shown in R. A. Salaman's *Dictionary of Tools* (Charles Scribner's Sons, Front & Brown Sts., Riverside, N.J. 08075; 800-257-5755).

Plane shopping—Now that you know what to look for, what are you likely to find? There is a good chance of coming across matched pairs of planes, especially if you buy from knowledgeable dealers, who are unlikely to split pairs up. Occasionally a set of hollows and rounds will turn up, often in some purpose-made box or chest, and such a find would be a great pleasure. But do not think that a single plane is useless without the "rest of the set" or even its mate. It is up to you how many you collect, and use, just as it was to the original purchasers. Cabinetmakers, and those joiners who worked in shops rather than on-site, kept many more sizes and types than a carpenter would have carried around with him, and indeed manufacturers themselves were by no means in agreement as to how many planes properly constituted a "complete set."

I keep a list in my wallet of the particular sizes and arcs that are missing from my collection. But my main strategy is simply to pick up all that appear on the horizon and trade any duplicates with other woodworkers or interested dealers or collectors. I find it astounding that these tools can be bought for as little as $7 to $10 in the open marketplace, for surely they represent much more intrinsic value. For the price of a router bit, I can buy a tool whose working life is longer than my own.

When you look for a plane to use, I'd suggest that something from the middle of the size range will be best to start with; leave the extremes until later. How to judge the serviceability, and if necessary how to effect some basic restoration, was dealt with in my article "Old Wooden Planes" (see pp. 40-45), so I shall mention here just a few correctible, yet critical, points.

The profile of the edge *must* match the profile of the plane's sole, otherwise one of two things will happen: Either the high area of the iron will take a coarse shaving, leading to tearout in the cut, or, if the iron is lowered to take a finer shaving, the plane will bottom out after a few strokes and be unable to cut the full profile. In the days when hand tools were the mainstay, planes were properly maintained by their owners; but in the days since, inept sharpening by bunglers is likely to have changed the profile of the iron. When examining a plane, you should assess how much work it will take to grind and hone the iron to match the sole, until the iron can be made to project through the mouth of the stock the same amount across its entire profile.

If the wedge is warped, bent or split, you may have to refit or remake it so it supports the iron evenly against its bed. If the wedge is blunted, it may be necessary to angle and repoint the tip so shavings exit cleanly.

Secret weapons—It should be obvious that hollows and rounds can cut independent rounded-over profiles and coves of various sections. It follows that they can finish up and trim similar sections of other profiles. This use is extremely valuable because of the main inherent weakness of most molding planes—they can work in only one direction. Thus, they cannot be reversed if grain direction changes in the middle of the workpiece.

To minimize tearout due to changes of grain direction, molding planes are tuned to take extremely thin shavings, which requires many passes of the plane to finish the job. When possible, the bulk of the material is removed with other planes, such as a rabbet plane or a fillister. Aside from speeding the work, this has the added advantage of doing most of the job with a plane whose iron is easily resharpened. Yet despite paying the best attention to stock selection, some tearout may occur. The hollows and rounds are the secret weapons that can step in and clean up the work by going in the opposite direction. Without these, no set of molding planes is truly complete.

The side hollows and rounds have tight arcs and the fact that they are made in pairs makes them reversible. They will be found to be of great use, as will certain auxiliary planes designed for cleaning up quirks and fillets, such as side snipes and snipesbills, and various shaped side- and V-rabbet planes—but these planes take us beyond the present discussion. A little experimentation will amaze you with the possibilities that hollows and rounds offer in the realm of molding adaptation and duplication—try skewing them to alter the cut, for example.

As to which sizes work best for any given profile, preferences will vary with experience. To start with, the planes you own will dictate the shapes you can attempt, but improved skill will seem to make each plane capable of an increased range. At this stage, hollows and rounds can become an extension of your eye and your intent. They will then compete with the Surform and rasp for rough shaping of sculptural forms as well as being always to hand for delicate trimming of a variety of shapes. Last, but not least, the sound they make when properly tuned and used is infinitely preferable to the threatening whine of any machine. □

Graham Blackburn is a contributing editor to FWW *and has written numerous books on woodworking and tools. His shop is in Santa Cruz, Calif.*

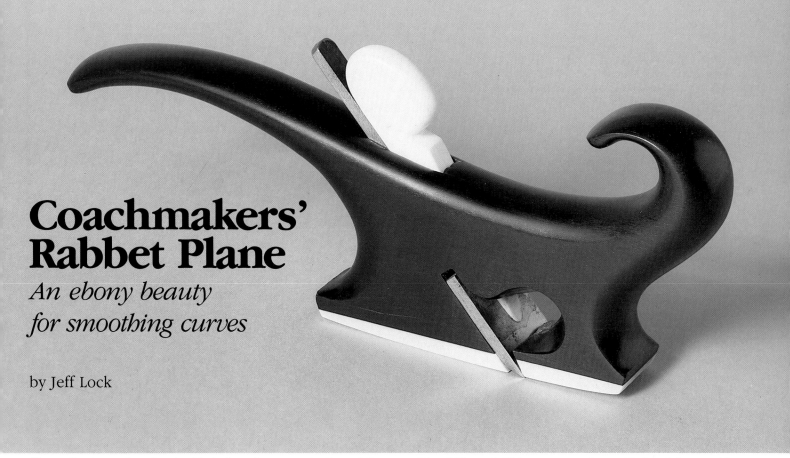

Coachmakers' Rabbet Plane

An ebony beauty for smoothing curves

by Jeff Lock

The author's coachmakers' rabbet plane is a reproduction of those used by 18th- and 19th-century artisans. Made of ebony with a bone sole and wedge, it's used as a finishing tool to clean up the marks left by gouges and chisels on curved surfaces.

Custom planemaking is ideal for those who find pride and beauty in handworkmanship. It's for the person who understands that patience and concentration are necessary to produce the best work—the person who puts cost effectiveness in its proper place. Those who appreciate the subtle distinctions between a hand-carved pediment and the cold perfection the shaper yields will grasp the essence of this craft.

Our ancestors fully appreciated the spirit of producing things of beauty—including the tools they used to make those products. Coachmakers, violinmakers, cabinetmakers and coopers all had their own specialty planes. Of these, I find the planes used by violinmakers and coachmakers to be the most beautiful.

I started making my own planes because I feel my woodworking and violin restoration warrant the most effective tools possible. Also, many of the planes I need are now available only as high-priced antiques.

The coachmakers' plane shown above is typical of those used by 18th- and 19th-century artisans. Its gently rounded sole allows it to be used to smooth curved surfaces—even the curved rabbets often found in carriages and musical instruments. It can also be made with a sole flat along its length for working straight rabbets. To provide enough clearance for the cutter to clean up the sides of a rabbet, the cutter is 0.005 in. wider than the plane body at the cutting edge, then tapers from the edge to the tang—the long, narrow part of the cutter.

The plane's body is ebony, its sole and wedge are beef bone and its blade is made from a discarded file. (For more finely crafted planes, see pp. 22-23.) A cutter from the Stanley No. 75 bullnose plane (available from Highland Hardware, 1034 N. Highland Ave. N.E., Atlanta, Ga. 30306) is thinner and will need some re-grinding, but works well. The plane may look awkward to those accustomed to standard bench planes, but rest assured that its design is efficient, having been refined and streamlined over the centuries. I never use this tool for rough work, but instead reserve it for finish-planing. I find it invaluable for smoothing the ridges left by chisels and gouges in shaping a violin's top plate, for instance, but there's no reason why the plane couldn't be used to clean up the ogee in a chest's bracket feet, too.

Begin the plane by selecting materials. If exotic woods aren't available, beech, cherry and apple are all traditional plane-body woods. You can make the plane with a wood, bone or ivory sole. You may find it difficult to locate ivory, but if you decide to use it, a good source is antique piano keys for thin soles or billiard balls for thick ones. If you're using an applied sole, dimension the plane accordingly. I usually make an applied sole about $\frac{3}{16}$ in. thick at its center.

If you plan to use bone, visit your local butcher and get a fresh piece of shinbone from the front leg of a steer. These bones have a thick wall and are ideal for soles and wedges. Saw off the knuckles to expose the marrow on both ends of the bone, and boil it in a large pot for two to four hours. Adding an onion to the water will speed the process, and also helps bleach the bone. After all of the marrow has been cooked away, hang the bone in the sun to dry or place it in a pan on a south-facing roof for a few weeks (bring the bone inside if it starts to rain). The bone is ready when sawing it produces fine, dry powder.

Bone can be worked like dense hardwood. It dulls chisels quickly, so sharpen your tools to a less acute angle than normal—about 30° to 35°. I use resorcinol glue to attach the bone to the plane's sole. Mix the glue to the consistency of a paste; if you mix it to the directions given on the package, it'll be too thin. Also, score both the bone and the mating surface of the wood with the corner of a file or with 40-grit sandpaper. This helps the glue adhere to both surfaces. Be careful to keep all score marks about $\frac{1}{16}$ in. away from the edges of the sole, lest the marks show on the glue joint after the plane is finished. If you use an exotic

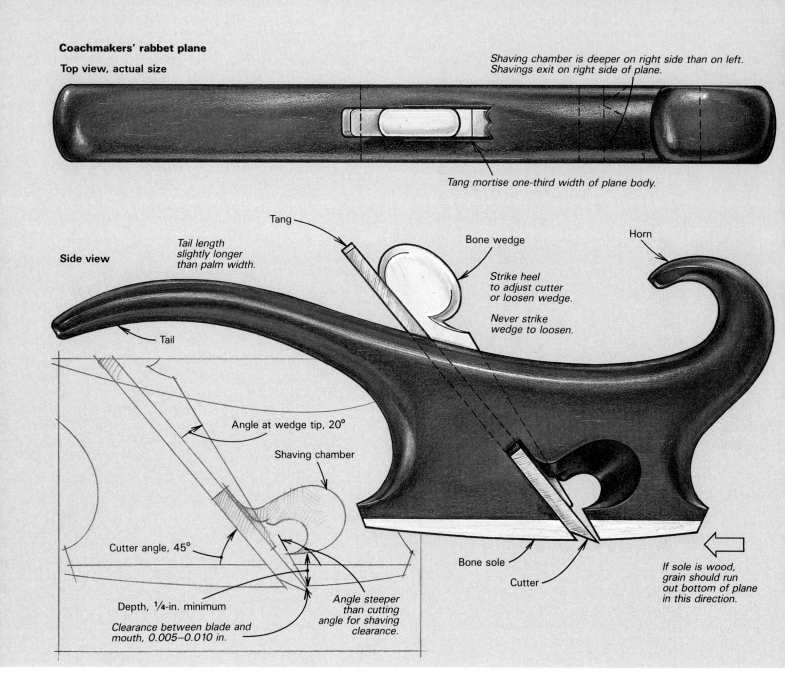

Coachmakers' rabbet plane

Top view, actual size

Shaving chamber is deeper on right side than on left.
Shavings exit on right side of plane.

Tang mortise one-third width of plane body.

Side view

Tail length slightly longer than palm width.

Tang

Bone wedge

Horn

Tail

Strike heel to adjust cutter or loosen wedge.

Never strike wedge to loosen.

Angle at wedge tip, 20°

Shaving chamber

Cutter angle, 45°

Bone sole

Cutter

If sole is wood, grain should run out bottom of plane in this direction.

Depth, ¼-in. minimum

Clearance between blade and mouth, 0.005–0.010 in.

Angle steeper than cutting angle for shaving clearance.

---

wood, remove traces of resin by wiping the wood's mating surface with lacquer thinner after the scoring is completed.

Now, draw the profile of the plane body on the blank you've selected and cut it out on a bandsaw. If you're making a wooden plane that's self-soling, be sure the grain runs out the bottom of the sole *opposite to* the direction in which the plane will be pushed. (Think of the grain as cat's fur: If you move with the grain, you lay it down; move against the grain, and you raise it up.) Save the outline cutoffs, too—they're ideal for protecting the plane when it's clamped in a vise during shaping (see top left photo, facing page). Now, shape the plane body with chisels, rasps and files.

Next, lay out the 45° angle that beds the blade and the wedge. (Don't mortise for the blade or make the throat cutout until the plane's profile is completely roughed out—the body may crack from the clamping force needed to hold it in the vise during rough-shaping.) Make the tail slightly longer than the width of your palm. Also, your thumb should fit comfortably inside the horn.

Make the first cut for the 45° mouth slot with a fine backsaw, dovetail saw or bandsaw. Don't use a tablesaw—its kerf is too wide. Next, measure the thickness of the blade and make a second cut

that distance from the first. For now, you want the blade tightly seated in the opening. Later, you can pare or file away enough wood to shape the throat opening—the most critical dimension in making the plane. Cut out the shaving chamber with a scroll or coping saw, and bevel the chamber's edge using carving chisels and gouges. The bevel allows shavings to curl out after they enter the chamber. Otherwise, they jam up like an accordian's bellows.

Carefully bore down from the top of the blank to start the mortise for the tang. The wedge bears down mostly on the tang, so the bottom of this mortise must be flat and smooth. Otherwise, the cutter will have a tendency to slip under cutting force. I clamp the plane in a vise and bore the tang mortise hole by eye, judging the angle by the layout lines drawn on the side of the plane. Stay clear of the layout lines to avoid chewing up the final bed surface. I use an extra-long drill bit (also available from Highland Hardware) in an "eggbeater" hand drill for boring this hole. You could make a jig and use an electric drill instead, but I prefer doing this by hand since it allows me to proceed slowly and carefully. The top of the mortise is pared to the wedge angle, and the bottom of the mortise is finished by paring as described later. Make the mortise ⅛ in. wider than the tang's width to allow the cutter lateral adjustment.

Cutter

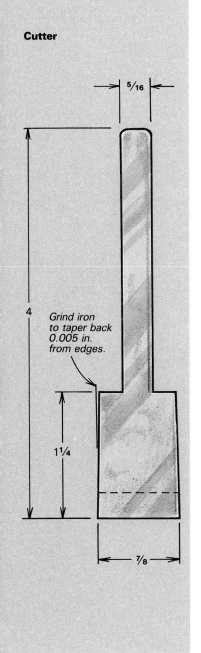

5/16

4

Grind iron
to taper back
0.005 in.
from edges.

1¼

⅞

Save the outline scraps from the plane's body to help clamp it in place during shaping (above, left). Flatten the cutter bed after the mouth is cut out by clamping the plane in the vise and filing the bed in line with the top of the vise jaw (above, right). Test fit the cutter after its mortise is completed (below), and hold the plane up to the light to reveal any gap between cutter and bed.

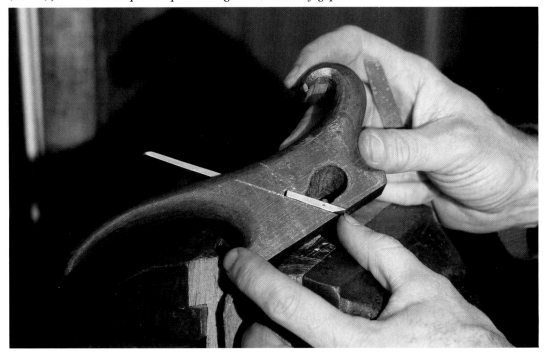

Clamp the plane in a vise with its bed parallel to the vise jaws and extending about ¹⁄₃₂ in. above them (see top right photo). Then, flatten the bed with a fine, thin file, using the top of the vise jaw as a guide. Use a mortise chisel to bring the tang mortise in line with the bed. Slip the cutter in place, and hold the plane up to a strong light to check that it fits precisely to the bed. It's critical that the blade bed down accurately. If not, the plane will chatter during use. After making minor adjustments, make a final light check to ensure that the blade beds precisely. Chalk or graphite rubbed on the blade's back will mark any remaining high spots. Be careful not too remove too much material when bedding the iron or you'll risk making the mouth too wide.

Now, bandsaw the wedge and test-fit it. Trim it as needed—with a file if it's made out of bone, with a block plane if it's made out of wood. The wedge should slip easily into place and bear against the top of the tang mortise, not the sides. If it rubs against the sides of the mortise, the wedge won't snug up properly, and you could crack the plane along the mortise trying to tighten the wedge by driving it in place. The wedge should require only a light tap with a small mallet to seat properly.

Now, check the throat opening for chip clearance with the blade wedged in place. Remove the blade and file or pare the mouth so there's a 0.005-in. to 0.010-in. space ahead of the blade—to allow for chip clearance. Automotive feeler gauges are great for checking this dimension.

Dry-sand the plane, beginning with 120-grit paper and following it with 220, 320, 400 and 600 grit. I also wet-sand the body and the sole, and final-polish with polishing compound, such as jewelers' rouge. I finished my plane with ten coats of Minwax Antique Oil Finish.

Cutter adjustment with these planes is simple, requiring only a light touch. Deepen the cut by gently tapping the back of the tang. Back the cutter out by tipping the plane forward and lightly tapping the plane at the heel. Loosen the wedge by tipping the plane forward and firmly striking the plane's heel (*never* loosen the wedge by striking it directly or working it back and forth).

The plane is demanding to build in that it requires concentration and careful workmanship. But I didn't pay attention to how long it took to build—I was enjoying myself too much to care. For me, one's enjoyment while working is the real bottom line. □

Jeff Lock is a woodcarver and violin restorer in Tallmadge, Ohio.

Photos this page: David Sloan; drawing: David Dann

The results obtained from a well-tuned scraper are evident here. The wide, fine shavings are indicative of the blade's sharpness. When the blade no longer produces these fine shavings, it's time to rehone its edge and form a new cutting hook.

Souped-Up Scraper
Old-time hand tool challenges belt sander

by Kelly Mehler

Whenever I run into my former apprentices, I'm always curious about whether any of the things I taught them have turned out to be valuable tools for making a living. Invariably, I'm told that one of the best tricks is how to tune-up a cabinet scraper—not the steel hand scrapers most woodworkers are familiar with, but the old metal-body ones with spokeshave-like handles and a reputation for not working. But I've found that once you learn how to handle this scraper, you can take wide, fine shavings off any hardwood with ease; it's especially effective on highly figured woods where you have cross-grain. With a well-tuned blade, you can smooth a tabletop faster than you can with a belt sander.

My scraper is a Stanley No. 80, pictured at the top of the facing page. You can order it or a similar version from most woodworking-supply houses. As with a plane though, you want to make sure your tool has a flat, smooth bottom. The scraper, as it comes from the manufacturer, is usually not flat or smooth enough to do a good job. My scraper has a sole that's 3¼ in. by 2⅝ in., so it's not much of a job to flatten and polish the sole with a piece of fine

silicone carbide paper supported by a glass plate or other flat surface. The scraper blade itself is 2¾ in. wide and 2⅜ in. long. It's held in position by a flat metal clamp and two screws. The only other part is a thumbscrew that bears against the blade to keep it from chattering and to flex it. The more the screw flexes the blade, the heavier the cut.

I started using this scraper years ago when it seemed I was sanding all the time and getting sick of the dust and noise. I also don't think a sanded surface finishes as well as a scraped one. I did a lot of reading to see how other craftsmen handle the problem and decided these old cabinet scrapers, which traditionally were used for smoothing after planing, offered a lot of possibilities. Many craftsmen are reluctant to use them, perhaps because of the perceived difficulty in tuning the tool: It's more complex than sharpening a plane blade or chisel, because it requires forming a hook, which does the scraping, on the blade edge after the blade has been sharpened. At first, I couldn't get the tool to work well. It took awhile to master the technique of getting the correct combination of bevel angle, straight edge and hook angle.

The cabinet scraper used by the author is a Stanley No. 80. For a newly purchased tool, it's necessary to flatten and polish the sole and modify the scraping blade to produce the best smoothing results. A carefully tuned tool will produce a surface ready for finish-sanding.

My procedure for preparing the blade is much like the one used with the more familiar hand scraper, except the blade for the Stanley No. 80 requires a beveled edge. The blade is square when it arrives from the factory, so I shape a 45° bevel using a bastard mill file. This angle permits a fine cut with hardwoods and is critical, because unlike a hand scraper, the angle formed by the clamped blade and the work surface is not adjustable. I've never used the scraper on soft woods, but I suspect that a lower angle and a blunter bevel might work best.

My vise is located near a wall. To gauge the bevel, I've penciled in a 45° line on the wall at a height where I can sight along the blade's edge as I file. The system is surprisingly accurate. You can also double-check your work with a combination square. The important thing when filing the bevel is to keep the bevel flat and straight. Always check for flatness with a straightedge, or put the edge on a flat surface, such as a bandsaw table, and check where light comes through between the blade and table. This flattening operation should create just a slight burr, barely large enough to feel with your finger.

I remove the burr by polishing the back side of the blade on a 1,000-grit waterstone, but a medium or fine Carborundum stone will work as well. It will probably take eight or nine strokes to remove the burr. I also polish the bevel itself on the stone using the angle on my combination square to check my progress. A really smooth edge is necessary to make the finest cuts. Polishing the bevel again raises a small wire burr, so I finish up with a few strokes on the back side to remove it.

The next step is to turn over a hook on the cutting edge; the hook does the actual cutting. As with a conventional scraper, I form the hook with an oval steel burnisher. With the blade lying on a flat surface, bevel side down, I first burnish the back side of the blade, keeping the burnisher flat but with a little additional pressure on the edge to "draw" the metal toward the edge. Next, I clamp the blade vertically in my vise. I start burnishing at a 45° angle, pulling the burnisher toward me using light pressure while keeping it in contact with the full surface of the bevel. I continue to burnish while gradually decreasing the angle and increasing the pressure. I stop when I reach a 15° angle, which I again gauge by referring to a line marked on the wall, as shown in the photo at right. By this point, I have shaped a sharp hook evenly along the length of the blade's edge.

I always put the blade into the scraper from the bottom, with the bevel side facing toward the thumbscrew. I set the body on a flat surface, such as a workbench, and push the blade down so it is even with the bottom of the scraper body. Then, I tighten the screws (but not the thumbscrew) to secure the blade. I hold the blade down as I tighten the screws, offsetting the blade's tendency to be forced up.

The thumbscrew is turned so it just touches the blade, exerting

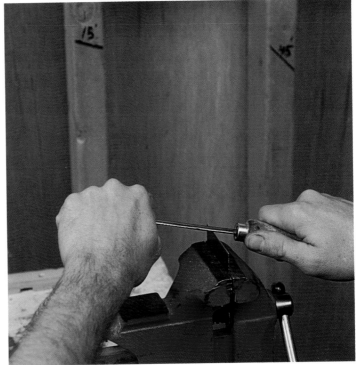

The final step in tuning the scraper is to form the cutting hook on the edge of the blade. The author is shown here burnishing the scraper's edge using a 15° line marked on the wall as a guide. Earlier, in preparation for forming the hook, the blade is flattened and its edge is made straight and filed to form a 45° bevel.

almost no pressure. I take a few practice strokes to be sure the blade is scraping evenly across its entire width and make any necessary adjustments by tapping the blade's top edge. As scraping proceeds, the hook gets worn. You can compensate for this by tightening the thumbscrew, which causes the blade to flex and increases the hook's "bite."

Using the scraper is much like using a plane. Grab the scraper handles firmly, keep the sole flat on the surface and push. Take long strokes with even pressure. Lift the scraper on the return stroke to prevent dragging the blade and consequently dulling it. It's also a good idea to take skewed cuts with the scraper held at a slight angle to the cutting direction, as shown in the photo on the facing page, because this produces a smoother cut and prolongs the life of the hook. From then on, it just takes practice until you can produce a shaving as wide as the scraper body. When the shavings become crumbly, producing more dust than shavings, it's time to go back to the stone, rehone the blade's edge and burnish a new hook. □

Kelly Mehler builds custom furniture and operates the TreeFinery Gallery in Berea, Ky.

The Hand Scraper

A *sharp burr makes shavings, not dust*

by Stephen Proctor

The term scraper brings to mind a tool for cleaning blistered paint from the sides of a house, or for chipping rust from the deck of a ship. It seems a poor term for such a fine tool, a tool capable of the finest of cuts and the heights of accuracy, an almost indispensable tool around a furniture shop. The term is something of a misnomer, for when sharpened to a burr edge, a scraper cuts rather than scrapes, much like a very low angle plane blade or chisel, slicing off paper-thin shavings of wood. As useful as the scraper is, it's surprising how few people understand how to sharpen and how to use it.

Scrapers come in various sizes and thicknesses and the methods I will describe for sharpening and use are the same for all. A standard scraper, good for most work, is a 2½-in. by 5-in. piece of steel, about ⅟₃₂ in. thick. Scraper hardness varies; I have had little luck using my methods on scrapers advertised as having hardened edges. For curved surfaces, a thin flexible steel that will conform to the curve is better. A gooseneck scraper (the whale-shaped one in the photo at right) contains a variety of curves that can be used on tight curves or moldings. I have four or five scrapers around so I don't have to stop and sharpen so frequently.

A rectangular scraper consists of four narrow edges and two broad faces. The cutting is done by a small burr formed at the juncture of a face and an edge (such a juncture is called an arris, as indicated in the drawing on the facing page). The quality of the burr, and of the cut it makes, is entirely dependent on the quality of the intersecting surfaces. Two smooth, blemish-free surfaces produce a stronger burr with fewer of the microscopic serrations that produce a rough surface on the wood.

To sharpen the scraper, first dress the two long edges with a single-cut mill file. Clamp the scraper vertically in a vise and draw the file along the edge, trying to achieve a straight edge, perfectly square in cross section. All four arrises should feel sharp to the touch, if not, refile until they do.

Next, polish the faces of the scraper with a medium India stone followed by a fine, hard finishing stone—I use a hard black Arkansas stone. Be careful to keep the scraper flat on the stones, or you'll round the arris. Then, holding the scraper vertically between both hands, polish each long edge, rubbing the scraper to and fro along each stone in turn. Hold it diagonally across the stone to prevent uneven wear to the stone. Don't be tempted to polish on the edge of the stone, using the box holding the stone as a 90° guide—repeated polishings will wear a groove in the stone and round the edge of the scraper. After this operation, all four edges should again feel sharp to the touch.

A burnisher is required for the next step. It must be smooth

A scraper, most often nothing more than a piece of thin steel, can be any of a variety of shapes. Common commercial scrapers are rectangular and gooseneck, shown in the center above.

After filing, work the faces and edges of the scraper on a medium and a hard stone. Hold the scraper diagonally across the stone's width to prevent wearing the stone unevenly.

From *Fine Woodworking* magazine (May 1986) 58:59-61

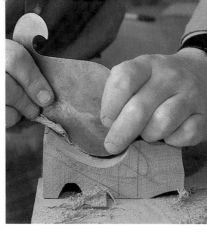

Scraper sharpening

Arris — Face

Edge

Step 1

Burr

Burnish almost parallel to the faces to begin the burr. (Size of burr exaggerated.)

Step 2

Burnish almost perpendicular to the faces to turn the burr.

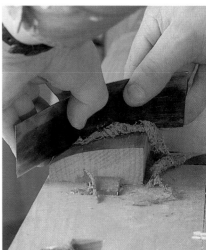

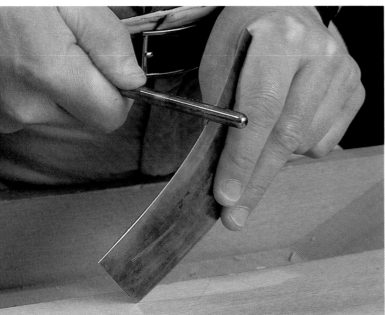

To raise the burr, hold the burnisher at a slight angle to the face and stroke it firmly back and forth along the arris. To turn the burr, make a single firm pass along the arris, the burnisher held slightly less than perpendicular to the face.

To scrape a flat surface (right), hold the scraper as nearly perpendicular to the work as possible and push or pull it to take wide shavings. A gooseneck scraper is ideal for tight curves (top). A flexed rectangular scraper can scrape shallow concave and convex surfaces (bottom).

and of a harder steel than the scraper. If it isn't smooth, it will abrade the scraper and damage the burr. You can buy burnishers, but many things will work as well. My preference used to be the back of an old gouge. Currently I use a buffed-up pushrod from an automobile engine. Whatever you use, it may help to apply a little lubricant between burnisher and scraper. Oil is fine, or just rub the burnisher across your nose—it really does work.

Two steps are required to make a burr: raising the burr and turning it. To raise the burr, lay the scraper flat on the edge of a firm surface, hold the burnisher almost in the same plane (a few degrees off horizontal) and stroke it firmly back and forth along each arris. You should hear a loud tick as the burnisher goes off the end of the scraper at the end of each stroke. Hence the term ticketer, as the burnisher was once known. The resulting cross section is shown in the drawing and can easily be seen on the scraper with the aid of a magnifying glass.

There are many methods of turning the burr—the following one works well for me and is quicker than others I have tried. Holding the scraper vertically in the left hand, stick one of its corners into the bench, push it firmly into the surface to create a slight curve in the steel. Then, starting the burnisher near the top corner of the scraper and holding it at a fraction less than 90° to the face of the scraper, take one firm stroke down the arris, as shown above. Finish the small unburnished section at the top with a short upward stroke. Repeat this process on the other three arrises, making sure to turn the burr on the concave arris

each time. It isn't necessary to curve the scraper to turn a burr, but I think that it puts a little tension in the burr once the curve is released, and this makes the burr a little stronger.

Taking several passes will turn a large burr, which will take a large shaving. However, a large burr takes longer to turn than a small one, and I've found them to be more brittle, possibly because of metal fatigue caused by the repeated passes made when turning the burr. In addition, a large burr has relatively little substance behind it to dissipate the heat generated during a cut, and this also tends to make it degrade rapidly. I prefer a small burr because it's less work in the long run. Gooseneck scrapers are sharpened by the same method, though the curves make the job a little more difficult.

Scrapers are most commonly used to remove a fair amount of wood from a flat surface. Why scrape, rather than plane or sand? A plane may tear interlocking or curly grain, but the scraper can manage nearly any awkward grain. The scraper face immediately behind the burr acts like a very finely set chip breaker, fracturing the severed wood fibers before they can tear out. A scraper also removes material quickly and leaves a finished surface, unlike coarse- or medium-grit abrasive paper, which removes the same amount of material, but leaves scratches.

To maintain the flatness of a large surface, like a tabletop, it is essential to cover as large an area as possible with one stroke of the scraper and to introduce as little curvature to the cutting

edge as possible. A curved scraper will make a concave cut—the greater the curvature, the greater the concavity. To avoid curvature, hold the scraper with your fingers behind the cutting edge and thumbs in front. Maintain a constant angle to the wood, as close to perpendicular as possible, and draw the scraper toward you, attempting to produce a shaving almost the full width of the scraper. Proceed across the surface with a series of long and slightly overlapping strokes. I prefer to pull the scraper, but you can push it, too, as shown above. It's easier to curve the tool when pushing, so be careful.

Unlike a plane, the scraper has no sole and may, therefore, ride up and down over hard and soft areas and create ridges on the surface. To avoid this, the scraper should be slightly diagonal to the direction of the wood grain. Alternate the diagonal orientation every other stroke, so that the edge will only take material from the high spots, leaving a flat surface.

For a fine, finishing cut, a small, sharp burr is needed; if the scraped surface isn't good enough, re-stone the scraper and turn another burr. Hold and move the scraper as described previously, keeping it as perpendicular to the surface as possible. Obstinate grain may require that the angles diagonal to the grain be increased to produce a skewed cut.

The third basic scraper technique is for shaping or truing concave or convex surfaces. Depending on the curves, use a flexible rectangular scraper or a gooseneck scraper, as shown on the previous page. By springing the scraper between fingers and thumb, the cutting edge can be made to conform to a variety of curves. As the curve of the scraper tightens, the cutting angle of the scraper is inevitably lowered. As the scraper is lowered, the burnishing angle of the burr must also become more acute to maintain the proper cutting angle of the burr to the wood. You may need to experiment with various angles at first, but you'll get the feel of it with experience.

The most common fault when using a scraper is to concentrate all your energy on one small flaw—a slight tear or, most frequently, an edge joint in a veneered surface. The resulting surface looks as though it has been bombarded by billiard balls or has had a drainage ditch cut down it. To avoid this natural attraction to flaws, a good rule of thumb is to take two strokes either side of the flaw for every stroke on it. Also, try to cover as much ground as possible with each stroke.

As soon as the scraper no longer takes a shaving, it's time to resharpen. It is possible to re-turn a burr with the burnisher several times before having to go back to the file and the stones. Burnish the face first, then turn the burr at the desired angle. When the burr is ragged and leaves striations in the wood's surface, it's time to go back to the beginning of the process. Putting off sharpening because of laziness costs time and energy. The joy of using a sharp scraper is well worth the effort that it takes. □

Stephen Proctor, a woodworker for 34 years, is Dean of Instruction for the Wendell Castle School.

9-in. steel square from Garrett Wade

Getting Squared Away
Finding the perfect perpendicular

by Paul Bertorelli

Whether you actually have need for it or not, a well-made tool has an attraction that's hard to resist. Polished brass milled into some interesting-looking geegaw practically begs to be picked up and examined, if not bought. Owning a trunk full of perfectly serviceable tools doesn't make you immune from this peculiar urge either, as I found out at a woodworking show last year when I bumped into John Economaki. He's an Oregon furnituremaker who has met rousing success selling precious, pricey measuring and marking tools. Barely a minute after I approached his booth, I'd coughed up $34 for a 5-in. trysquare to add to the three I already own. A year later, even with a few scratches and dents, the square shimmers with a satisfying gleam.

Of course, a good trysquare is more than just a trinket. Much woodworking begins and ends with this humble tool. For stock preparation, a trysquare tells when a board's edge is square to its face. A trysquare is indispensable for marking out joints, setting the tablesaw's miter gauge or the jointer's fence and then checking how precisely they've done their work. It's worth having a good one and taking care of it. Practically every mail-order catalog offers trysquares in several sizes and styles. The better-known tool houses are giving splashy play to Economaki's Bridge City Tool Works line alongside the popular brands made in Europe. Not knowing much about how squares are made, I decided last fall to investigate by visiting three square manufacturers. During the course of my travels, I learned that despite big variations in price ($8 to $100 and beyond) there's really not much practical difference between one square and the next. Given reasonable standards of accuracy, they will do the same job. But, some are clearly better buys than others.

Bridge City Tool Works is housed in a cavernous defunct furniture factory near the center of downtown Portland, Ore. As is the fashion in old industrial buildings, the open bays have been walled off into spacious, high-ceilinged rooms. When I arrived on a chilly November morning, sunlight streamed through the south-facing windows, illuminating a pall of dust suspended in the air, an unappetizing mix of brass and rosewood: squaremaking here, and elsewhere, is mostly an abrasive process. "It's pretty awful in here right now," Economaki explained. "We've designed a dust-collection system. I want to get it in by next month." With Christmas just six weeks away, Bridge City was filling last-minute orders at near-frantic pace while Economaki hurriedly prepared for a weekend sales trip to North Carolina.

What with the dust and hubbub, the scene was almost surrealistic. It must seem especially so to Economaki. Three years ago he was working alone in the same shop, building furniture commissions and small production items. "I was doing well with my furniture. I had plenty of work but I couldn't see myself working those kinds of hours when I'm 40 or 50," Economaki recalls. Wanting the regular hours of production work, Economaki turned to toolmaking. For some ten years he had made short runs of fine little brass and rosewood trysquares that had sold well in galleries. It was logical to pitch them to a broader market. To say the tools have caught on is an understatement. The day I visited, Bridge City's three toolmakers were cranking out one hundred fifty 5-in. trysquares, and had orders for that many more standing by. By the end of last year, Economaki's sales were well into six figures.

Bridge City makes two sizes of trysquare, the 5-in. Jointmakers' square I had bought, and an 8-in. model that sells for $47, plus a scratch awl, a T-square, a miter square and some specialty items. The square designs are based on Stanley's 8-in. trysquare and evolved from Economaki's days as an industrial arts teacher when he had his students make them as a ninth-grade shop project. Where Stanley has a beech handle and steel blade, Economaki has substituted a sweet combination of rosewood and brass. Brass wear strips protect both edges of the handle and the blade rivets are set into brass strips inlaid into the handle. Brass, rivets and wood are all sanded perfectly flush.

Apart from an automatic screw-setting machine and a dial-indicator jig for checking accuracy, Economaki makes squares with essentially the same tools he used for furniture work. Brass is sawn on the tablesaw, just like wood. "We use the Forrest Manufacturing blade. I could do a great testimonial...it cuts brass like it was walnut." Like virtually all wooden-handled squares,

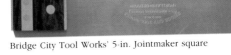

Bridge City Tool Works' 5-in. Jointmaker square

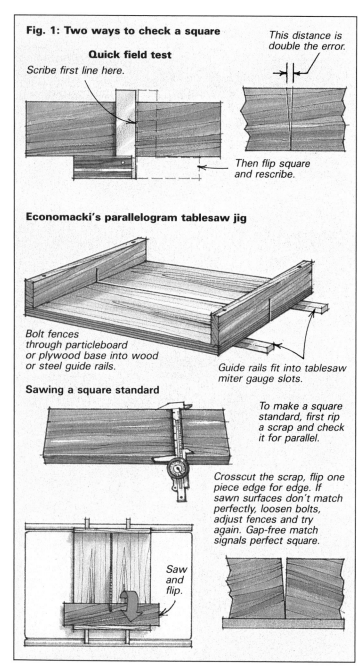

Fig. 1: Two ways to check a square

Quick field test

Scribe first line here.

This distance is double the error.

Then flip square and rescribe.

Economacki's parallelogram tablesaw jig

Bolt fences through particleboard or plywood base into wood or steel guide rails.

Guide rails fit into tablesaw miter gauge slots.

Sawing a square standard

To make a square standard, first rip a scrap and check it for parallel.

Crosscut the scrap, flip one piece edge for edge. If sawn surfaces don't match perfectly, loosen bolts, adjust fences and try again. Gap-free match signals perfect square.

Saw and flip.

To ensure the accuracy of each of his squares to 0.002 in. over the length of the blade, Economaki devised the dial-indicator jig shown here. Referenced against the steel pins, the square's angular error is converted to a directly readable linear run out.

Economaki's are made by inserting the metal blade into a slot milled in the handle. Before the blade is mounted, it's carefully sanded parallel in width and to reasonably uniform thickness.

Economaki is methodical about accuracy. He achieves it in one of two ways. Each blade is set into its handle with a dab of fast-setting cyanoacrylate cement. Moving smartly before the cement hardens, the square is either clamped against a National Bureau of Standards certified angle block or, more usually, checked on a dial-indicator jig, which measures how close the blade is to perpendicular. It's adjusted, if necessary, then riveted once the cement sets. Although no Federal inspectors come poking around square factories, the government does publish accuracy standards for woodworking squares. A General Services Administration regulation says that squares bought for government use must not run out more than 0.001 in. per inch of blade length, a standard also observed by European manufacturers. Economaki promises a finicky plus or minus 0.002 in. over the entire length of blade, inside and out. That last distinction is an important bit of square lore. The vast majority of woodworking trysquares are meant to be square only on the *inside* edges. "That's why nesting two squares together, outside edge to inside edge, to test one against the other is a dumb thing to do," Economaki explained.

How, then, do you check accuracy without a sophisticated instrument? The usual way is to joint a straight edge on a scrap then, guided by the suspect square, scribe a line perpendicular to the edge. Flip the square then align it with your mark. If it matches up, the square is okay. If not, the runout represents double the error. Economaki argues that it's better to check a square against a known standard, such as an accurate machinists' square or a gauge block. In this way, you will find the actual error.

Lacking a known accurate standard, you can make your own standard square block out of wood by empirically deriving a perfect 90°. Economaki's method involves the shop-built tablesaw sled shown in the drawing. He uses the sled for all kinds of accurate cutoff chores and the fences can be adjusted to shallow angles for joinery work. Square blocks cut on this jig are accurate enough to test squares or to set miter gauge and jointer fences.

With a reliable standard available, correcting a faulty square is quite straightforward. I learned one way of doing it at the L.S. Starrett Co., the second stop on my tour. During its 106 years of existence, Starrett has established itself as the best-known maker of precision measuring and marking instruments, mostly for the machinist trade. In a sprawling brick complex in Athol, Mass., Starrett manufac-

Ulmia 350mm rosewood-handled trysquare

At Starrett, blades are soldered not riveted to the beams. Scott Songer, above, heats both sides of the beam with a dual-tip burner then feeds solder in as the joint warms. Once soldered and quenched, he tests the soundness of the joint by gently tapping the flat of the blade on his vise. A bright, tuning-fork ring indicates a good joint and the square is ready for testing.

tures a staggering assortment of 3,000 tools, including a line of precision machinists' trysquares popular with woodworkers. Scott Robinson, a Starrett toolmaker, was assigned to show me around the place.

Following Robinson onto the factory floor reminded me of In-dustry on Parade, a Commerce Department gee-whizzer I watched on television as a kid during the 1950s. Amid the perva-sive odor of warm machine oil, there's a constant clatter of ma-chine tools, some attended by operators, others spitting out parts at the command of tape- or computer-driven controllers. At every turn, we encountered dollies stacked high with minutely ma-chined parts, each of which Robinson seemed able to identify.

Intriguing as the machines were, the real fascination for me was the amount of handwork that goes into making a precision measuring tool. Scattered throughout the factory are rows of workbenches where toolmakers deburr and clean parts prior to assembly. Each finished part is calibrated and tested before it's carted off to another department for final inspection. Nowhere is this fussy work more demanding than in Department 9, a warren-like room off the main factory floor where Starrett machinists' squares are assembled. The squaremaker's benchroom is kept dark, about like a movie theater. Better to see the bare sliver of light that squeaks between a pair of square blades being checked against a light source. It's hot, too. Open gas burners furnish the heat for silver soldering each square blade to its handle.

Starrett makes eight standard sizes of hardened-steel machin-ists' squares, from a tiny 1½-in. model to one with a 36-in. blade. You can special order a giant square with a six-foot blade but

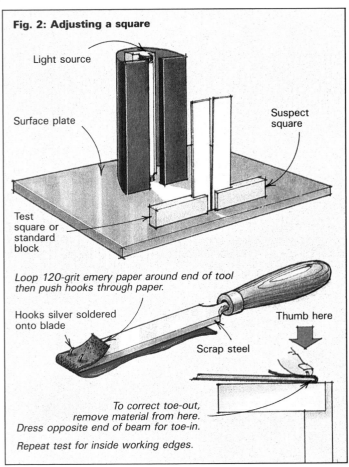

Fig. 2: Adjusting a square

Light source

Surface plate

Suspect square

Test square or standard block

Loop 120-grit emery paper around end of tool then push hooks through paper.

Hooks silver soldered onto blade

Thumb here

Scrap steel

To correct toe-out, remove material from here. Dress opposite end of beam for toe-in.

Repeat test for inside working edges.

Drawings: Joel Katzowitz

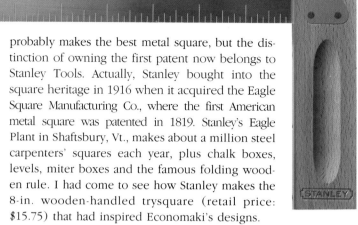

better plan on having a muscular friend help you move it. He can also help shovel money out of your wallet. Starrett squares are expensive. The 6-in. model 20-6, shown in the photo below, retails for $91.50, a 12-in. sells for $187.25. Even at these prices, a Starrett square is no more than an ordinary right angle, but one that is manufactured to a high standard and designed to hold the tight tolerances necessary in machine work. For thermal stability, the square's beam (handle) consists of three precision-ground steel blanks riveted together and then ground again to final size. Soldering instead of riveting the blade keeps the beam from being distorted during assembly.

Once my eyes had adjusted to the darkness, I settled into a corner to watch squaremaker Scott Songer assemble a 6-in. square. First, he slid the blade into the beam slot then clamped both into an angle-block fixture that holds the parts square. With everything aligned, a dual-tip gas burner mounted on a single pivoting arm is swung into position to heat both sides of the beam evenly. Fifteen seconds later, an even bead of silver solder melts into the joint, followed by a water quench to finish the job. The acid test of a good joint is a bright, tuning-fork ring when the flat of the blade is tapped lightly against a metal surface. A dull thunk signals trouble. Songer says any metal machinists' square with a soldered blade should be ring-tested occasionally.

Songer's work brings a square close to the final tolerances. Richard Dill, another Starrett squaremaker, does the fine tuning. Dill works in front of a precision-ground cast iron surface plate on which is positioned a fluorescent tube shaded to form a bright vertical slit as long as the blade of the square being tested. To check a square, he positions it upright on the plate in front of the light slit, blade-to-blade against a square of known accuracy. As the blades converge, there's the sensation of a door being closed against a brightly lit room. An accurate square shuts out the light completely the instant it touches the test square, then breaks or shows an even hairline of light when the two are moved gently apart. This method is extraordinarily accurate. A gap as small as 50 millionths of an inch is detectable by the human eye, a tolerance far finer than woodworkers or even machinists need. Starrett aims for light-blocking perfection but will allow a run out of no more than 0.0002 in. per foot of blade length.

Adjusting a square is a simple matter of removing minute amounts of metal, usually from the beam, to correct toe-in or toe-out. Dill uses 120-grit emery paper wrapped around a burnishing tool he made from a piece of scrap steel, as shown in the drawing on the previous page. The tool is capable of abrading quite a bit of metal so Dill sands sparingly, dressing a 1-in. or 2-in. spot at the butt end of the beam to close a gap at the bottom of the blade and at the opposite end of the beam for a gap at the top. A few passes over the length of the beam feathers-in the spot. An indentical procedure trues the inside of the square. Dill's method will work with any metal or metal-bound wooden square. For a surface plate, you can use a flat jointer or tablesaw top or, best of all, a piece of ½-in. plate glass. If the square's blade hasn't been badly bent or the joint loosened by a careless drop on the floor, it can be trued as often as necessary. Starrett

Starrett 6-in. hardened steel machinists' square

probably makes the best metal square, but the distinction of owning the first patent now belongs to Stanley Tools. Actually, Stanley bought into the square heritage in 1916 when it acquired the Eagle Square Manufacturing Co., where the first American metal square was patented in 1819. Stanley's Eagle Plant in Shaftsbury, Vt., makes about a million steel carpenters' squares each year, plus chalk boxes, levels, miter boxes and the famous folding wooden rule. I had come to see how Stanley makes the 8-in. wooden-handled trysquare (retail price: $15.75) that had inspired Economaki's designs.

In principle, Stanley squares are made just like Economaki's are, but in a more automated way. Twenty years ago they used rosewood handles, but rising costs and declining sales forced a switch to beech, which is harvested from a 4,000-acre woodlot Stanley owns in northern Vermont. The steel blade (inscribed with rules graduated to ⅛ in.) is attached to the handle via three steel rivets set in a triangular brass seat, and the handle's inside edge is protected by a brass wear strip. As at Starrett, an angle-block jig holds the parts square during assembly, but instead of soldering, an operator inserts the parts into a pneumatic hammer that flattens the rivets in about a second. Stanley isn't nearly as fussy about accuracy as are Starrett and Bridge City. Paul Harris, the plant's chief engineer, showed me a simple go, no-go tester that employs a microswitch to flash a warning light if a trysquare is more than 0.001-in. out of square per inch of blade length, the U.S. and European standard. When I asked how an errant square is brought into line, Harris picked one up from a nearby bin and unceremoniously whacked the corner of the blade against the worktable. I couldn't hide a flinch. "We don't try to move them much," Harris later told me, "If they're too much out, we scrap them."

In another part of the plant, we watched carpenters' steel squares being die-stamped out of giant sheets of cold-rolled steel, like so many cookies. I was surprised to learn that Stanley makes two grades of steel squares in two sizes, plus a top-of-the-line aluminum square. The high-grade square is accurate to 0.005 in. in 15 in. of tongue length (in a large square, the blade is called a tongue) and 0.015 in. in the lower grade. Each square is hand-flattened and hand-hammered to tolerance.

Lew Levine, an Eagle toolmaker, demonstrated. First he flattened the square's tongue and body by hammering the faces atop an anvil made of end-grain maple. Using a dial-indicator jig like Economaki's, Levine tested the square. To open the angle, he gently hammered the tongue close to its edge at the inside angle. Hammer blows near the edge of the outside tongue closed the angle. Levine is fast and seems to hardly need the dial indicator to check his work. Although he is allowed 0.005 runout, the indicators hardly budged off zero during the entire time I watched him. Stanley's aluminum squares, by the way are considered the most durable. Besides resisting rust, aluminum has a better "memory" than steel, so, if a square is dropped, it returns more closely to the orginal shape than does steel.

At the end of my Eagle Square tour, I had formed some definite opinions about what makes a good square. First and foremost, a square ought to be accurate. How accurate is as much a

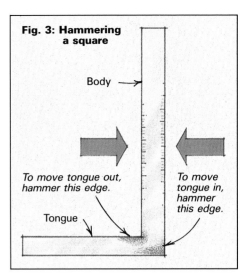

Fig. 3: Hammering a square

Body →

To move tongue out, hammer this edge.

To move tongue in, hammer this edge.

Tongue

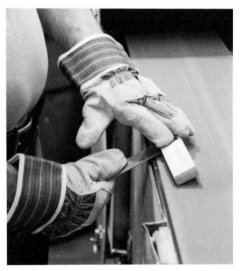

Stanley's best carpenter's squares are hand-hammered to tolerences of 0.005 in. in 15 in. of tongue length. Lew Levine first flattens the tongue on an anvil of end-grain maple, above. Then he trues the square by hammering it as shown in the drawing. A dial-indicator setup similar to Economaki's measures run out. Abrasives (right) play an important role in squaremaking. After the blades are riveted at Stanley, they're sanded flush and sharp metal edges are eased on a large beltsander.

function of pocketbook as it is of skill. I liked Economaki's squares best of all. They are very accurate, beautiful and priced just far enough shy of outrageous to be affordable. A far-from-exhaustive survey I did while researching my article turned up two other wooden-handled trysquares that tested accurately against the Starrett, but are cheaper than Bridge City's tools. Garrett Wade sells an Ulmia 350mm trysquare (catalog 90N01.03) of brass-bound rosewood for $30.25. The finish is not quite as nice as Economaki's, but it's precisely square inside and out. Woodcraft sells a bargain 6-in. trysquare (catalog 14C11-CL) for $8.95. The one that I bought showed barely a peep of light next to the Starrett. Given the finish quality and prices of these squares, the Stanley seemed like less of a good buy at nearly $16.

If you decide to lay out a lot of money for a square, you are buying two things: good materials and guaranteed precision. In that regard, Starrett leads the pack. You won't find a better quality tool. But if Starrett's prices are too rich for your budget, there are better buys for woodworking purposes. The very best value I found is a 9-in. steel engineers' square sold for $32.40 by Garrett Wade, catalog 39N04.02. The one I purchased is well-made and has a pleasing heft that suggests it will retain its accuracy. The manufacturer, an English firm called O. Fisher and Co., promises accuracy of 0.004 in. over the entire length of the riveted blade.

One tool merchant I talked with told me it doesn't make sense for a woodworker to buy expensive precision squares given the sloppy tolerances of woodworking machines and the cantankerous, changeable nature of wood itself. He's right; you don't absolutely need Class-A toolroom precision in a woodworking square. But how much inaccuracy can you tolerate before everything comes out just a little off? To do the very best work on a tablesaw whose blade wobbles like a top or a jointer with 0.015 in. runout in the cutterhead, you need *something* to rely on. A good, well-maintained square can help. □

Paul Bertorelli is editor of Fine Woodworking. *Starrett, whose address is given below, operates a small musuem with exhibits illustrating its toolmaking history. Write the company for more information.*

Sources of supply

Woodworkers' trysquares, engineers' squares
Garrett Wade, 161 Avenue of the Americas, New York, N.Y. 10013

Woodworkers' trysquares, combination squares
Woodcraft Supply, 41 Atlantic Avenue, P.O. Box 4000, Woburn, Mass. 01888

Machinists' squares, combinaton squares
L.S. Starrett Co., Athol, Mass. 01331

Inexpensive machinists' squares
Penn Tool Co., 1776 Springfield Avenue, Maplewood, N.J. 07040

Wood and brass measuring and marking tools
Bridge City Tool Works, 2834 N.E. 39th Ave., Portland, Ore. 97212

Inexpensive measuring and marking tools
U.S. General, 100 Commercial Street, Plainview, N.Y. 11803

Shopmade Sash Clamps
Two bars are better than one

by Antoine Capet

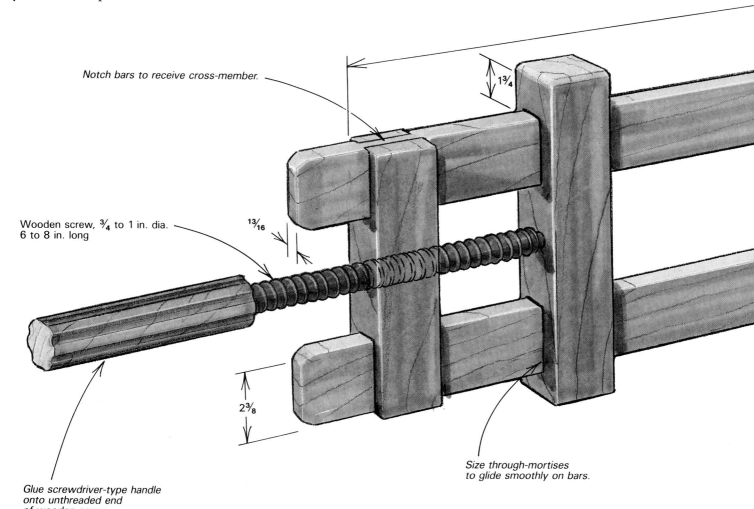

Notch bars to receive cross-member.

1¾

Wooden screw, ¾ to 1 in. dia.
6 to 8 in. long

¹³/₁₆

2⅜

Glue screwdriver-type handle
onto unthreaded end
of wooden screw.

Size through-mortises
to glide smoothly on bars.

C lamping—an essential step in most woodworking jobs—
just doesn't seem to get the same attention given to other
major operations, such as sawing or planing. Yet the experienced woodworker will agree that faultless clamping equipment is a precondition for a businesslike approach to gluing,
with no fiddling about and no frayed nerves.

Today, it seems that wooden sash clamps have been superseded
by metal equipment. Steel-bar or pipe clamps, however, don't
provide a complete answer. They are cumbersome, heavy and
require a number of precautions to avoid denting the work being
clamped. Moreover, they are quite expensive and cannot be
made in the average woodworker's shop.

I've made several pairs of these wooden sash clamps and have
found them to be extremely useful. There's no bending stress on
the wooden bars whatsoever, since they're positioned on both
sides of the press screw. And the bars won't break easily when
clamping pressure is applied because they stretch slightly.

Wooden sash clamps can be made by even the inexperienced
woodworker, and I strongly encourage readers new to the
hobby to make at least one pair. Besides equipping themselves

for a lifetime of good clamping, the construction techniques
required will give them good practice in performing basic,
fundamental woodworking operations.

Before getting into the actual construction of the clamps, we
must first decide on the species of wood to be used and the
desired capacity of the clamp. In Europe, hornbeam has long
established itself as the superlative species for clamps and
presses, as it possesses the right combination of strength,
elasticity and resistance to abrasion and splintering. Although
hornbeam is sometimes available in America, ash, maple or
beech would certainly be acceptable substitutes. The ideal
wood for the screw would be a rather uncommon species
called service wood *(Sorbus domestica)*. However, any strong,
dense hardwood will do.

I decided that my clamps should have a useful capacity of 50 in.
in length and 4 in. in depth, although you may make them any size
you wish. This size will accommodate the widest tabletop and
the thickest benchtop I'm ever likely to make, not to mention
doors, windows and other frame-type constructions. I made the
bars from 60-in.-long 4/4 stock, and the fixed and sliding cross

From *Fine Woodworking* magazine (May 1987) 64:46-47

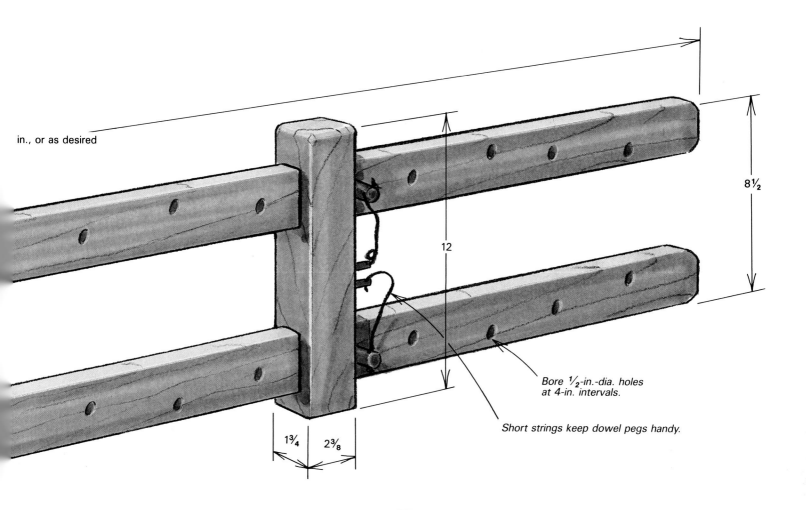

in., or as desired

8½

12

1¾ 2⅜

Bore ½-in.-dia. holes
at 4-in. intervals.

Short strings keep dowel pegs handy.

members from 8/4 stock, with everything cut 2⅜ in. wide.

After all the parts are planed to dimension, the ends of the fixed cross member are slot-mortised to receive the bars, which have been notched on both sides. The resulting bridle joint will later be held in place by glue alone, so a reasonably true fit between these parts is desirable.

Each of the sliding cross members is provided with two easy-fitting through mortises, cut approximately ¹⁄₁₆ in. oversize so they can slide smoothly over the bars. Don't overdo it though—if the mortises are too big, the sliding cross members will not remain perpendicular to the bars and will tend to wedge themselves and bind.

The bars can now be drilled at 4-in. intervals with ½-in. holes (for the adjustable stop pegs), starting about 2 in. from the bottom end. The holes should not be aligned dead-on center, as any incipient split would be encouraged to travel the length of the bar. Instead, arrange them in a zig-zag pattern so that no two subsequent holes are in line. I didn't bore the bars all the way up, as it's unlikely that my clamps will ever be used for very small jobs.

It's now time to drill and thread a hole for the press screw in the fixed cross member, and to bore a shallow, flat-bottomed hole in the upper sliding cross member to receive the end of the screw. It's also prudent to cut the male part of the screw now, so that it can be tested in its "nut" before everything is glued up. You can use a ¾-in. or 1-in. thread box and tap set to make a wooden screw as I did, or substitute a metal veneer-press screw. (Both the thread set and press screw are available from Garrett Wade, 161 Ave. of the Americas, New York, N.Y. 10013.) A screwdriver-type grooved handle is then fitted on the end of the shaft. It's very comfortable to use and easy to make on the

lathe—the grooves are cut with a small gouge or router jig.

The fixed cross member may now be glued to the two bars, with the sliding pieces left in position at the other end to ensure parallelism. While the glue is setting, cut two short stop pins from dowel scraps and tether them with short strings to the bottom sliding piece so that they will not be mislaid.

When completed, rub linseed oil or your favorite finish over the entire surface of the clamp, except the wooden screw. The screw can be finished by soaking it in hot tallow or a mixture of paraffin diluted in mineral spirits. A nice final touch is to permanently glue a thick layer of felt (off-cuts of carpet would do in a pinch) on the surfaces of the cross members that will contact the clamped work.

The finished clamps are extremely easy to use. The screw is first fully retracted so that the upper sliding cross member can rest against the fixed one. The pegs are then inserted in the appropriate holes, depending on the length of the workpiece. The bottom slider is positioned against these pegs and the clamp is ready to be tightened. You can also remove the end crossbar and thread the clamp through the work before reassembling and tightening the clamp.

The greatest advantage of this double-beam clamp becomes obvious when it's tightened. The more pressure you apply, the straighter the bars become. Plus, the clamping faces stay square—the complete opposite of conventional one-bar clamps.

Storage is always a problem for long clamps, but the flat nature of these clamps, combined with their relatively light weight, makes hanging them a breeze—two long nails driven in the shop wall will do nicely. □

Antoine Capet teaches at the University of Rouen in France.

Using a brace and bit is a quiet and efficient, if somewhat antiquated, way of boring holes in wood. Here the author sights the bit against a square as he bores a perpendicular hole. The orange paper tells him when the bit is through the workpiece.

The Brace and Bit

This old standby can do more than just bore holes

by Richard Starr

A joist brace, with it's ratchet action, can work in spots too tight for even an electric drill. The brace's relatively short height allows it to bore even inside a box, and the long drive handle provides exceptional power to drive the bit.

Despite all the motorized drills available to woodworkers, the old-fashion bit brace is still a useful tool in today's shop. I use mine for boring holes when I don't want to mess with a power cord, and it's fun to use, too. I also use it for driving screws, tenoning, chamfering dowels and doing other jobs you might expect to do on a lathe or with a drill press.

Before the brace was invented, early craftsmen drove large boring bits with a simple cross handle, something that looks like a giant corkscrew. Although the cross handle may still be the most powerful tool to use for boring a big hole, it is hard to steer and the hand-over-hand motion is slow. It's also difficult to apply pressure on the cross handle to advance the bit through a hole. The brace is a surprisingly recent improvement, appearing in Europe only 600 years ago. Its design overcomes the problems of the cross handle by providing a top handle to push down on and another handle to drive the bit around in a circle. A simple crank that multiplies the rotating force of your arm, the brace's sweep (sometimes called swing) is the diameter of the circle your powering hand travels around the tool. To determine the sweep, measure the horizontal distance from the chuck to the handle and double it. The wider the sweep of the brace, the more your efforts are multiplied and the more torque (or rotary force) the brace puts out. Although a wide-sweep brace is more powerful, there is a trade-off: Your hand must travel in a larger diameter circle, so a wide-sweep brace bores slower than a brace with a narrower sweep. Thus, wide-sweep braces bore big holes better, while narrow ones bore smaller holes more quickly.

Unlike cross handles, which have one bit permanently attached to the end of a shaft, braces have an adjustable chuck that allows them to hold and drive different bits of varying shank styles and diameters. Bits used in braces may have round or square shanks, but most have a threaded leadscrew in the center that pulls the bit through the wood during boring. Some braces even feature a ratchet that powers the brace with a short reciprocal stroke instead of a full-sweep cranking motion. This feature is helpful for boring in a cramped location.

Choosing the right brace—In the days when they occupied a more prominent spot in the woodworker's tool chest, braces came in many sizes, and you could find one exactly suited for the job. Braces are still readily available in two sweep sizes: 6 in. and 12 in. A 6-in.-sweep brace is just the ticket when you don't need much torque, such as when boring holes up to ½ in. in diameter or when driving screws. The brace most commonly found in shops today, however, has a 12-in. sweep, which works fine for boring holes up to about ⅞ in. dia. in hardwoods or for forming up to ½-in.-dia. tenons. But you'll get frustrated if you try to use it for driving a large expansion bit. For that job, you'll do better with an old 14-in.-sweep brace. This brace will easily bore a 2-in.-dia. hole in hardwood, or with a hollow auger, will gnaw a 1-in.-dia. tenon on a chair leg. Unfortunately, as far as I know, 14-in. braces are no longer made. You might get a welder to modify a smaller one for you. Just make sure he keeps the alignment of the head and chuck perfectly straight, or the brace won't turn true. Otherwise, you'll have to scour the flea markets for an old 14-in. brace. With luck and for not much money, you may find a tool better made than any today.

Many braces feature a built-in ratchet that's handy in tight spaces where you can't make a full turn with the brace's handle. Located just above the chuck, it works like a mechanic's socket wrench, driving the bit only in one direction, then allowing the handle to return freely in the opposite direction. You can set the ratchet to work in either direction, for instance, to drive or remove screws. The ratchet allows you to use the your arm muscles in their most powerful direction, pulling toward your chest to drive the brace. There's also a tool that's built especially for ratcheting bits called a joist brace, so named because it is designed for drilling holes between joists. Joist braces are available from Woodcraft Supply Corp., 41 Atlantic Ave., Woburn, Mass. 01888; (800) 225-1153, or (617) 935-9278 in Massachusetts; part #01G11. Instead of having a crooked drive handle like a regular brace, the joist brace has a 10½-in.-long nearly straight handle you drive with a back-and-forth ratchet action (see the photo above). Besides allowing you to bore in a tight corner, the joist brace's long drive handle gives you tremendous torque—equivalent to a 21-in.-sweep brace.

The most important thing to consider when buying a brace is the chuck. A good chuck is one that opens and closes easily and holds a bit securely. Most chucks will easily grasp a square-tang bit, because the bit's tapered, square shank is designed to center and drive without needing a super-tight grip from the chuck. Round-shank bits, however, are harder to grasp and slip more easily than square-tang bits in most brace chucks, and some of the older split chucks can't accept them at all. The chuck used on most modern braces has alligator jaws that are held together at the base by a spring, which spreads them at the open end of the chuck—like a hungry reptile's mouth. V-shape channels on the jaws' inner surfaces taper down at the tip to allow the chuck to engage square-tang or round bits.

If you decide to buy an older brace, you'll be confronted with an astounding variety of chuck designs. In my collection, I have at least eight very different styles ranging from split chucks that tighten with wing nuts to chucks that use ball bearings to reduce friction between the jaws and the collar, making tightening easier. Before you buy an older brace, examine the chuck to make sure its jaws and the collar surrounding them aren't cracked and that the spring that retains and spreads the jaws is in good shape—it can be difficult to replace. The threads between the collar and threaded core (at the end of the brace's shaft) of most chucks are meant to fit loosely to make the chuck easier to tighten, but check to see if they've been damaged from overtightening or worn so they don't tighten at all. But don't necessarily reject a brace just because it has a bad chuck: I once resurrected a hard-to-come-by 14-in. brace by welding on a good chuck from an old junker. My woodworking students now use it every day at school.

The most-abused parts of old braces are usually the wooden handles. Drive handles often split and fall off. Screws that hold

From *Fine Woodworking* magazine (July 1988) 71:46-49

These old braces from the author's collection illustrate the variety of chucks found on older or antique tools you may encounter at flea markets. The split chuck, at far left, will hold only square-shank bits, and it locks them in place with a thumbscrew. The chuck next to it and the one at far right are both more modern designs, with alligator-type jaws with grooved inner surfaces that can hold square- or round-shank bits. Both have rotating locking collars that tighten against the threaded end of the brace, but the chuck at right has ball bearings inside the collar to make tightening the chuck easier. The chuck that's second from the right is a peculiar design in that its jaws project forward of the locking collar and are tightened by rotating the collar outwards—exactly opposite of an alligator-jaw chuck.

the top handle to its collar sometimes wear their way loose, the handle can then fall off and often ends up "missing." Fortunately, new wood parts can usually be turned and fitted. If the brace's handles are in reasonable shape but won't turn freely, a drop of oil may get them moving again. A bent brace can usually be wrestled back into alignment by clamping it in a vise and levering the braces with a monkey wrench with its jaws padded.

A brace should be properly lubricated. There's usually an oil hole in the collar below the top handle, but on better braces, including premium Stanleys, these handles turn on ball bearings, which need lubrication less often. A couple of drops of oil should also be applied to the ratchet mechanism where it meets the chuck shaft and on the pawl pivots. A touch of white grease on the threads of the chuck and on the jaws is also a good idea. The drive handle doesn't usually need lubrication.

Boring a hole—Using a brace and auger bit to bore a hole is smooth, quiet and safe. Regardless of how awkward cranking a brace seems at first, with a little practice, you'll be able to bore as straight and true with a brace as with a drill press. First, chuck up a bit by holding the bit between the chuck's jaws, keeping the locking collar from turning with one hand and rotating the brace to close the jaws with the other hand. Make sure the chuck's jaws are grabbing the bit concentrically as you tighten, because tightening the chuck on a misaligned bit can stress and fracture a jaw or damage the spring. Tighten the collar until it's hard to turn, but never use more than hand pressure.

When boring a perpendicular hole, the bit must be kept aligned in two planes. I set up a square next to the bit and sight along the axis of the bit to the square's edge. I also peek from the side to see that the bit lines up in that direction, and I check both views frequently as I bore. I use the same method for boring angled holes, except I use a bevel gauge instead of a square to align the bit.

Once you've engaged the bit in the wood by the first few turns of the brace, the auger's threaded leadscrew should drag the bit through the wood with very little down pressure as you crank. Hold the brace's head steady while you crank the handle: If you allow it to wobble, the leadscrew may lose its grip in the wood. Some craftsmen prefer to rest their forehead on the hand grasping the brace's top handle, but I like to bend my elbow far enough to let my shoulder bear on that hand (see the photo on p. 76). If you want to bore horizontally, rest the head of the brace on your belly or thigh. If you find it very hard to turn the brace, try one

with a wider sweep. Switching to a larger brace for boring a big hole is like shifting your bicycle to a lower gear for climbing a hill—it gives you more mechanical advantage. If you only have one brace, use your pull stroke with the ratchet on to ease the work.

Any bit will leave a ragged exit hole as it bursts through the far side of a board. To avoid this, clamp your stock to a scrap backing board to support the wood fibers as the bit cuts through. A quick way to determine when the bit has gone through the workpiece is by using a backing board of a different color wood or by clamping some brightly colored paper between the boards. Watch for the signal shavings to show you are through. If you're boring at an angle, crank the brace a few extra turns to be sure you are completely through. Another way to ensure a clean exit hole is to bore until the point of the leadscrew protrudes from the other side of the board, then bore back in from that side. You can tell that the screw is through by pulling gently up on the brace when you are nearing the bottom of the hole. If the screw is out, the auger will simply stop boring. When you bore in from the other side, extra pressure is needed on the brace to drive the bit through, because the screw is chewing air, not wood. To bore a stopped hole to a specific depth, stick a tape flag or a piece of a dowel to the bit's shaft. When the tape flag sweeps away the shavings or when the end of the dowel touches, the depth has been reached.

Auger bits—For general hole boring, auger bits are the most commonly used and come in lots of lengths and diameters. An auger bit's main cutters slice away wood at the bottom of the hole. The spiral body of the bit removes chips from the hole with a screw-like action as the boring progresses. The spur cutters, located on the outside edge of the main cutters, shear the wood fibers at the circumference of the hole. For the smoothest holes and easiest boring, all the cutting edges should be kept as sharp as possible. You'll know the bit is dull if it produces crumbly looking dust rather than clean, spiral-shape shavings or if it takes excess pressure to advance the bit. A light touch-up with a file is usually all that is needed to sharpen a bit, filing on the beveled edge of the cutters and the inside edges of the spurs. You can modify an auger bit for boring endgrain by simply filing off the spurs, just don't use the bit for cross-grain boring, because it will leave a very ragged hole. If it takes a lot of down pressure to keep a sharp bit advancing into the cut, the leadscrew probably needs some filing. The screw's tip must be sharp-pointed, and the threads should be clean and unbent. If the threads are damaged, you may be able to restore them with a needle file. Bent threads can sometimes be straightened with the point of a knife.

If you accidentally bore an undersize hole, don't just plunge in with an auger bit to enlarge it: The bit won't center properly and will cut eccentrically. Instead, bore the larger hole in a hardwood scrap and clamp it concentrically over the smaller hole. The scrap will keep the larger bit from wandering as you bore, but you'll have to use more down pressure to advance the bit, because the leadscrew won't engage the wood. You can also chuck a regular twist drill—the kind used for drilling metal—in your brace. It has a conical end that will center in the auger hole and bore an enlarged hole that's clean and concentric with the original. The brace's low speed and high torque are helpful here.

Expansion bits—If you want to bore a hole that's larger than any of your standard auger bits or a hole of precise size that falls between standard bit sizes, an expansion bit is the answer. Unlike a regular auger bit, which has fixed cutters and spurs, an expansion bit has a moveable cutter that adjusts in or out to change the diameters of the hole. Setting the bit to an accurate size, especially with a cheap bit, is a trial-and-error effort. Use the scale on the cutter to get into the ballpark, and check each setting by boring a trial hole in scrapwood before doing critical work. Be sure to lock the setting securely so it won't slip.

While boring with an expansion bit, try to keep the brace true and smooth-running. Since the bit has only one cutter rotating around the leadscrew, even a little wobbling at the head of the brace can cause the cutter to dig in and jam. If you're boring a deep hole, stop periodically and clear the shavings from the hole. The expansion bit has no spiral body to lift shavings out of the hole, and if you let them accumulate, you'll have a dreadful time yanking the bit out when you're done. If you bore through the workpiece, you *must* use a backing board. Without one, the leadscrew quits guiding the cutter in a circle before the hole is through, and you're left with half a hole to whittle clean.

Cutting tenons—One job you might not think of doing with a brace is cutting tenons. An adjustable jig called a hollow auger can cut round tenons on the end of sticks for chair legs or rungs. The hollow auger, with its plane-like blade that's adjustable for tenon diameter, cuts tenons quickly and with far less skill than it takes to cut them on a lathe. Unfortunately, hollow augers are becoming increasingly hard to find—even at old tool sales. I wish someone would manufacture them again.

A tool used in the brace that's more commonly available is the dowel pointer. A scaled-down version of the old-time spoke pointer (often used for chamfering the end of a stick before tenoning with the hollow auger), the dowel pointer is a hollow cone-shape tool that works like a kid's school-bag pencil sharpener. You can use it to neatly chamfer the end of a dowel or round tenon—up to about ¾ in. in diameter—to make it easier to insert into its hole or mortise. I usually set the stock in the vise so the axis of the dowel or stick is vertical. Then, I do my best to keep the brace plumb as I shave down the chamfer. (For more information on using hollow augers, see *Woodworking with Kids*, Taunton Press, 1982.)

Driving screws—Although high-tech cordless screwdrivers are rapidly becoming the standard tool for driving screws in the woodshop, many craftsmen prefer using a brace fitted with a screwdriver bit. Unlike a motorized driver, a brace lets you sense just how tight the screw is, and with a little practice, you'll never again snap the head off a screw or have its threads tear out of the wood.

A brace with a 6-in. sweep is ideal for driving screws, because

Driving dozens of screws is a breeze with a small-sweep brace, like the 6-in. model shown here. The brace provides more than enough torque for the job, yet provides a sensitive feeling, so screws can be driven to precise depth.

After chamfering the end of a chair rung with a spoke pointer, fitted in the brace in the foreground, the author uses an adjustable hollow auger to form a tenon on the rung. A plane-like blade on the bottom of the auger cuts the tenon by paring a shoulder around the tenon.

you can turn it quickly and its driving torque is limited. A larger brace will work, but is less sensitive, so use some extra care during those last few turns. A 6-in. brace is also great for boring small pilot holes or for countersinking with a rose-head countersink.

It's best to use Phillips head screws and the appropriate-size screwdriver bit when using a brace, because the bit stays centered in the screw head. If you must drive slotted screws, try to keep the top of the brace aligned with the screw's axis as you crank. You'll also need to put extra down pressure on the brace to keep the screwdriver's blade from sliding sideways out of the slot and gouging the work. □

*Richard Starr is an author (*Woodworking with Kids, *Taunton Press, 1982), teacher and woodworker in Thetford Center, Vt.*

Testing Wood Chisels
Lab finds no secrets in the steel

by Bill Stankus

A wood chisel is a very simple tool, but there are so many brands to choose from, and such a wide range of prices, that deciding which one to buy is anything but simple. It helps if you can examine a chisel, try the edge with your thumb, and heft the tool to feel how well the handle fits your hand. It's important that a chisel *feel* right. But what about the most important part—the steel? Are the more expensive chisels made of better steel? Just by looking, there's no way to tell how a chisel will sharpen or hold an edge. Advertising copy isn't any help either. Some tool-sellers' claims notwithstanding, there hasn't been a magic blade forged since Excalibur.

As a tool consultant and woodworker I've used many chisels over the years, and I've noticed that they don't all perform in the same way. Determined to find out why, I enlisted the help of Paul Horgan, a metals quality-control manager and amateur woodworker. We decided to run a series of metallurgical tests on chisel blades to see if steel quality differs between brands and, if so, what effect this has on sharpening and edge-holding properties. *Fine Woodworking* agreed to pay for the tests, which were conducted by Anderson Laboratories, Inc. in Greendale, Wisconsin, and confirmed by another Wisconsin lab. We don't claim our tests to be the last scientific word on tool-steel metallurgy, but the results do shed some light on a confusing subject.

We couldn't test every chisel on the market, so we chose 11 popular brands: Craftsman and Stanley (United States); Footprint, Marples and Sorby (England); Hirsch and Spannsage (West Germany); Iyoroi, Oiichi and Sentora (Japan); and Mifer (Spain). So we wouldn't base our findings on a chance bad chisel, we tested two of each brand bought from mail-order and retail outlets around the country. To correlate the lab analysis with performance, I sharpened the chisels on waterstones (800-, 1200-, 4,000- and 8,000-grits) and worked with them at the bench.

Interestingly, despite the wide range in price ($7.60 for the Footprint to $31.95 for the Oiichi), the tests showed that 8 of the 11 chisels tested are made of very similar water-hardening tool steels. The lab tests did show some variations in carbon content and alloys, but no significant differences except for the Sorby, which was a different type of tool steel, and the Sears Craftsman, which was a plain carbon steel with a low carbon content. The other U.S.-made chisel, the Stanley, was made of a plain high-carbon steel. Differences that directly affect how the tool sharpens and holds an edge—hardness and grain size—were more pronounced and quite noticeable during sharpening and use, suggesting that the type of steel probably has less to do with how well a chisel works than does how carefully the factory forges, grinds, and, most importantly, hardens and tempers the tool.

To make sense of the lab tests, it's helpful to understand a little about tool metallurgy. To cut well, a wood chisel needs steel hard enough to hold an edge for a reasonable time but soft enough to be sharpened on benchstones. It also has to be tough enough to resist chipping when hammered through dense wood such as maple. Mild steel, the stuff found in angle iron and I-beams, won't do the job because there's no practical way to make it hard enough.

Adding carbon to steel—anywhere from 0.45% to 1.40%—makes steel hardenable. Plunged red-hot into water, brine or oil, carbon steel's crystalline structure changes to a brittle, harder form. A cutting edge made from this brittle steel would fracture, so the hardness is reduced slightly by reheating the steel to a lower temperature. This is called tempering and makes the steel much tougher. Tool steels, which were actually developed not for hand tools but for industrial applications such as stamping dies and metal cutters, are a type of high-carbon steel that has been alloyed with metals such as chromium, manganese and vanadium to improve hardenability and wear resistance. The main difference between plain high-carbon steels and the tool steels commonly used for chisels is in the quality control. Tool steel is manufactured to a more rigorous set of quality standards than is ordinary high-carbon steel. Its chemical makeup is constantly tested, and each batch is routinely inspected for microstructure, cleanness, hardenability, and surface and internal flaws. This consistency means that the consumer is less likely to get a bum tool, but it also makes things easier for the manufacturer since, theoretically, each batch of steel will react about the same way when it's forged and hardened, thus producing tools of identical quality.

We had the labs perform three basic kinds of tests on the chisels: chemical analysis, hardness testing and inspection of the steel's microstructure. First, they mounted the $300 worth of new chisels on an abrasive cut-off wheel and sawed them up into small chunks in order to get at the steel inside. A spectrographic analyis of the pieces revealed their chemical makeup to be very similar. It's worth noting that steel standards vary from country to country, but all of the foreign-made chisels closely matched the U.S. definition of a family of tool steels called W-type water-hardening, except for the Sorby, which is a shock-resistant S-type tool steel. Both U.S. chisels were non-tool-steel grades of carbon steel. Carbon content of the 11 tools varied widely, from a barely hardenable 0.50% in the Sears to 1.24% in the Footprint.

Hardness, the quality most discernible at the bench and that which most governs a tool's edge-taking and edge-holding properties, was measured with a tool called a Tukon tester. Here's

From *Fine Woodworking* magazine (March 1985) 51:44-48

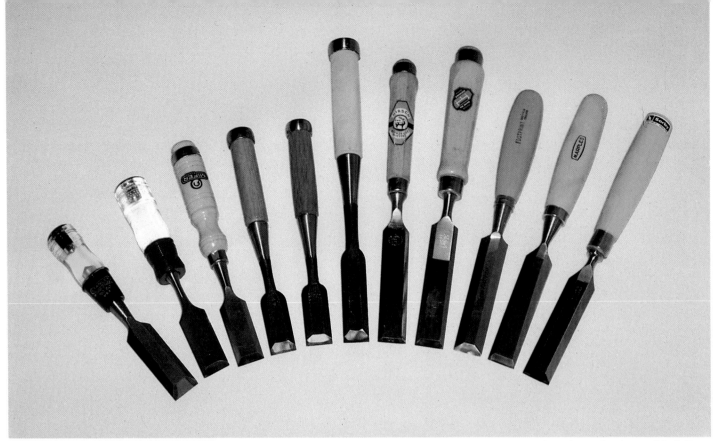

The test chisels had a wide range of handle styles and blade lengths—both important factors to consider when selecting a chisel. From left: Stanley, Craftsman, Mifer, Sentora, Oiichi, Iyoroi, Hirsch, Spannsage, Footprint, Marples and Sorby.

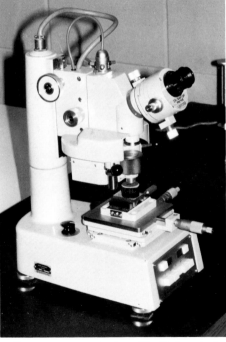

To measure hardness, two slices from each chisel were cast in plastic and polished, then they were mounted on the Tukon tester (above right), which calculates hardness by measuring the penetration of a diamond stylus.

how the test works: One longitudinal and one transverse slice of each chisel's blade are cast into a small disc of thermosetting plastic. The sample is polished and mounted under the tester's microscope. A tool with a tiny, diamond-tipped stylus called a Knoop indenter is next placed on the steel. Weighed down by a 500-gram weight, the indenter penetrates minutely into the steel; the deeper it goes, the softer the steel. The depth of the nick is measured and converted to a hardness number on the Rockwell C scale. The microscope allows the technician to place the indenter away from soft spots or contaminants that might give a false reading. For our tests, three separate readings were taken near the cutting edge on each sample and the results averaged.

As the chart on p. 82 shows, the chisels varied in hardness by as much as 7.5 points on the Rockwell C scale (RC), which ranges from 20 to 70. At 56 RC, the Sears Craftsman was the softest of the test chisels—too soft to hold an edge. The three Japanese chisels were the hardest at more than 60 RC.

Hardness tells only part of a tool's metallurgical story. Peering through a microscope, a metallurgist can learn a lot about a steel's properties just by looking at it, reading its texture just as a wood technologist might study pores to identify a wood sam-

Chisel Characteristics

	Brand name	Price (1-in. chisel)	Steel	Average hardness at cutting edge*	Carbon content	Grain size	Blade thickness at top of bevel	Handle	Edge-retention rating
United States	Stanley	$10.25	High-carbon (AISI 1095), trace of carbides	59.5 RC	0.94%	#11	9/64 in.	Plastic, round	Very good
	Sears Craftsman	$ 7.99	Plain-carbon (AISI 1050), no carbides	56.0 RC	0.50%	# 9	5/32 in.	Plastic, round	Poor
England	Footprint	$ 7.60	W-type tool steel	59.0 RC	1.24%	**	9/64 in.	Beech, oval	Very good
	Marples	$13.15	W-type tool steel	60.0 RC	1.18%	# 6	1/8 in.	Boxwood, round	Fair (edge breaks down when dull)
	Sorby	$11.75	S-type tool steel, no carbides	57.5 RC	0.57%	#10	11/64 in.	Boxwood, round	Very good
West Germany	Hirsch	$14.95	W-type tool steel, no carbides	58.5 RC	0.80%	#11	3/32 in.	Ash, octagonal	Very good
	Spannsage	$ 9.25	W-type tool steel, no carbides	59.5 RC 62.0 RC	0.81%	#11	9/64 in.	Ash, round-flats	Very good
Japan	Iyoroi	$27.95	W-type tool steel, mild steel back	61.5 RC	1.04%	# 8	7/32 in.	Boxwood, round	Excellent
	Oiichi	$31.95	W-type tool steel, mild steel back	63.5 RC	1.09%	# 9	11/64 in.	Red oak, round	Excellent
	Sentora	$ 9.95	W-type tool steel, mild steel back	60.5 RC	0.81%	#10	3/16 in.	Red oak, round	Excellent
Spain	Mifer	$ 8.10	W-type tool steel	59.5 RC	1.10%	# 8	9/64 in.	Boxwood, round	Fair (edge breaks down when dull)

* *Knoop indenter, 500-gram load. Average of three readings.*
** *Not determined.*

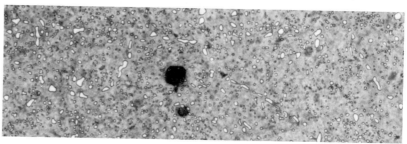

The chart above lists significant chisel characteristics. The prices given are the retail prices paid for the test chisels; current prices may vary. The edge-retention rating is based on the results of the bench test. The micrograph at right (magnified 100X) of a section of the Marples chisel shows the steel's microstructure. The small white particles are primary carbides, a hard-wearing combination of carbon and iron that improves edge retention. The large dark island is an oxide inclusion.

Anderson Labs

ple. The lab tests sought two important microstructures in our chisels: carbides and grain. Carbides are a compound of carbon and iron present in the steel as it comes from the mill. Ideally, when the chisel is heated and quenched, some of these very hard carbide particles will disperse throughout the crystalline structure of the steel. The higher the initial carbon content of the steel, the more likely it is that the heat-treated chisel will contain carbides. Carbides are desirable because they greatly increase the wear resistance of the steel. In theory, a blade with fine and evenly distributed carbides will hold an edge longer than will a blade of the same hardness with no carbides.

Grain refers to the crystalline particles that make up the steel. The size of the grain is a measure of the "fineness" of the steel. A fine grain is important for edge retention and, in combination with evenly distributed carbides, will give the longest edge life. Grain is measured on a numerical scale: #1 is extremely coarse, #10 or above is extremely fine. Any steel with a grain size of 8 or higher can be considered a fine-grain steel.

Again, the results of the laboratory tests more or less agreed with my findings at the bench. But the really interesting thing that the microstructure analysis showed is that hardness alone doesn't necessarily mean the best edge retention. After sharpening each chisel, I pared away at a variety of hardwoods and pine

until the edge dulled, then I resharpened. I noticed a considerable difference in edge retention between brands. The six chisels that contained carbides (Footprint, Marples, Mifer, Oiichi, Iyoroi and Sentora) seemed to take an excellent edge from the waterstones. With their hard edge and evenly distributed carbides, the Japanese chisels held keen edges longer than any of the Western chisels. The Hirsch, Spannsage, Sorby and Stanley—all fine-grained but slightly softer than the Japanese chisels—took and held very good edges. The Mifer and Marples are almost as hard as the Japanese chisels, yet when dull their edges seemed to fragment and become ragged. It took longer to get them sharp again because more steel had to be removed during the sharpening process. This is due, I suspect, to their relatively coarse grain. The Sears Craftsman chisel fragmented badly as it dulled.

A common complaint about Japanese chisels is that they're brittle, and tend to chip. I experienced this once when I cut a mortise with a new Japanese chisel without first sharpening it. Perhaps because I removed a fair amount of steel at the initial sharpening, however, chipping wasn't a problem with any of the Japanese chisels in the test.

The lab examined each steel sample for impurities such as slag. These are called inclusions (photo, above). From a metal-

A visit to a chisel factory

by David Sloan

Buck Bros. has been making woodworking tools in Millbury, Mass., since 1853, when Charles and Richard Buck picked out a spot with good water power. Water and steam turned the wheels at Buck Bros. until the 1940s, but today wood chisels are produced on modern machines. The factory also makes carving and turning tools, screwdrivers, scrapers, crowbars, spade bits, hatchets, and pitching horseshoes.

Last summer I visited the firm to see how wood chisels are made. According to the company manager, J.C. Cort, Buck Bros. manufactures all their chisels from plain high-carbon steel (AISI 1095) with manganese added to improve hardenability. They specify carbon and manganese content (each about 1%), and rely on their steel supplier for quality control. Buck Bros. does not test the steel.

Chisels are rough-formed by forging, but any romantic notions I might have had about wheezing bellows and ringing anvils were soon put to rest by what I saw. Hand-forging—at least for production tools made in the United States—is a thing of the past. Today, chisels are drop-forged in two-part dies.

The blacksmith's modern counterpart is the hammerman. He works in semidarkness as his predecessor did, but instead of a hammer and anvil, he presides over a hulking drop hammer that packs a 1600-lb. punch. Judging the temperature of the steel by the color, the hammerman seizes one of the long steel rods from the gas furnace at his side. With the timing and speed of a juggler, he brushes off scale on a wire wheel, then places the glowing end of the rod in the bottom half of a two-part die. Quick as thought, the hammer slams down, rises and slams down again, bringing the die halves together. The first blow rough-forms the blank, the second finishes it. A good hammerman handles two rods at once and can forge as many as 2400 chisels in an eight-hour shift.

Turning to a press, the hammerman separates the chisel from the rod and flash, the excess steel that squeezed out of the die. The still-glowing chisel travels down a conveyor and drops into a wheelbarrow.

When cool, the chisel is ready for heat-treating. First, the front, back and edges are ground by machine to remove surface imperfections. The chisels are heated in a device called a high-frequency induction heater coil. Twelve chisels are placed on end in a fixture. In a few seconds they're heated to a temperature of 1800°F. After 24 seconds at this temperature, the chisels automatically drop into a tank of quenching oil. A circular conveyor lifts out the hardened chisels and drops them into a soda wash to remove the oil. At this point, the steel has a hardness of about 64 to 65 RC. The clean, hardened chisels are then loaded into gas-fired air draw furnaces for tempering at 440°F. When the chisels come out, they have a hardness of 59 to 60 RC throughout.

Before 1950, one highly skilled man ground the entire chisel by hand. Today, it's done by machine in five separate steps: edges, front and back, side bevels, barrel, and cutting bevel. There's a separate automatic watercooled grinding machine for each operation. The loading and unloading of the machines was the only handwork I saw.

The machine that grinds the front and back holds forty-five 1-in. chisels in a circular fixture called a spider. The spider spins horizontally under an abrasive wheel. When one chisel face is finished, the chisels are manually turned over and ground on the other face.

After grinding, each finished blade is inspected by eye, and any rejects are cast aside. The ones that pass inspection are hand-wiped with oil to prevent rust. Then the blades are ready for handles.

Most of the chisels get plastic handles. These plastic-handled tools are intended for mass-market sales, so the blades get dipped in lacquer to prevent rust. Many of these chisels are packaged on cardboard cards, others go as sets in plastic pouches. A small percentage of the blades get wooden handles, but none were being fitted the day I visited.

I was surprised to learn that only about 15% of the total chisel production carries the Buck Bros. trademark. Some of the remaining 85% might carry the Great Neck brand (Buck Bros.' parent company). Others will carry the brand of the hardware or discount-store chain that ordered them (not Sears, however—Craftsman-brand chisels are made by Western Forge in Colorado Springs, Colo.). There's no difference in steel, manufacturing process or quality control—just a different name on the plastic handle and, most likely, a different price, too. Funny, before my visit I equated the name Buck Bros. with high quality, but who ever heard of Great Neck? I would have turned up my nose at the discount-store chisel, thinking that it was inferior.

I've never owned a Buck Bros. chisel, so I don't know how the blade stacks up to the German and Japanese chisels I use for fine work, or the 15-year-old Sears chisels

At Buck Bros., chisels are drop-forged in two-part dies. The monstrous drop hammer above slams the die halves together with a force of 1600 lb., squeezing the hot plastic steel between them. Two quick blows forge a chisel.

I carry in my carpenters' toolbox. From what I saw, Buck Bros. makes a chisel carefully and efficiently. The manager is well versed in metallurgy and knows what a woodworker expects from a tool. His dilemma is to try to satisfy the skilled user and at the same time avoid injuring the chap who grabs a chisel to pry open a paint can. This dichotomy dictates the tool he makes. When asked how his chisels would be different if serious woodworkers were his only customers, Cort replied, "We'd increase the hardness. The edge would be brittler, but much keener." □

David Sloan is an assistant editor at Fine Woodworking.

lurgical viewpoint, inclusions are a red flag because they often indicate sloppy quality control in the steel-making. The Sears Craftsman was the only chisel we tested that had a metallurgically unacceptable level of inclusions. The tests turned up some slag in the Iyoroi and Sentora chisels, but in the welds, not in the steel itself. Adhering to tradition, the Japanese make their chisels by forge-welding (often by hand, with a power hammer substituting for a sledge-wielding apprentice) a hardenable tool-steel blank to a mild-steel billet that forms the tool's front face. Chemical segregation was another steelmaking quality-control problem that turned up in the Mifer, Spannsage, Sentora and Iyoroi chisels. This means that elements in the steel that should be thoroughly mixed weren't.

Apart from the metal quality and hardness, we noticed some other things about the chisels that shed some light on how carefully they are manufactured. The Japanese chisels were carefully prepared at the factory. They came accurately ground to the 30° bevel recommended by the manufacturers. Setting the steel ring on the handle was the only "tune-up" that these chisels required. The Western chisels, however, were less carefully prepared. Some were ground to a bevel that was way off the 25° most woodworkers aim for, and this required quite a few minutes at the benchstone to correct. The Stanley had a double-bevel knife-edge grind, so the back had to be ground down to remove the extra bevel. I found the Hirsch to be buffed so heavily that the edges were rounded, making it difficult to see if the cutting edge was square to the body or shank.

I always hand-sharpen chisels, and to me it's important for a chisel to have a perfectly flat back, especially in the area immediately behind the cutting edge. Stoning the bevel leaves a wire edge that must be removed by lapping the back of the chisel. If the back isn't flat, part of the wire edge won't contact the stone and may not be completely removed. A flat back rests solidly on the benchstone and eliminates the possibility that you might unintentionally lift the handle and stone a slight second bevel on the back of the chisel. A flat back also provides a bearing surface when you're using a chisel for paring. Except for the Sorby and

the Japanese chisels, which came from the factory with flat backs, all of the chisels failed the flatness test—some miserably. The backs of the Craftsman and Stanley chisels were so wavy that it was very difficult to remove enough steel by hand to get them flat. In contrast, the Japanese chisels all have hollow-ground backs, which makes deburring easy.

Having read the lab reports after actually using the tools, I came away with some very definite ideas about chisel buying. The main thing to consider, I think, is your attitude toward sharpening. With one exception, the Sears Craftsman, any of these chisels properly tuned and sharpened will work adequately. If you're satisfied with your sharpening skills but aren't really fussy about getting the best possible edge, any of the Western chisels, except the Craftsman, should do fine. The steel is so similar in five of the eight Western chisels that only a very skilled sharpener could consistently tell the difference between them. That said, you might just as well let tactile factors such as the tool's weight and balance, blade length and handle shape govern your decision. Or the price.

If you're adept at sharpening and strive for the keenest edge, the Japanese chisels may be for you. As the tests showed, they are harder and made of fine-grained steel with evenly distributed carbides. But as with all Japanese blades, they require careful hand-sharpening and they won't tolerate being bashed around loose inside a toolbox.

So which would I buy? My favorite Western chisels were the Footprint and the Hirsch. Both had very comfortable handles and good edge retention, and at $7.60, the Footprint is an excellent value. For the very sharpest edge and the best retention, my favorite was the Oiichi, although at $31.95 it was the most expensive of our test chisels. □

Bill Stankus is a tool consultant, lecturer and woodworker in Bayside, Wis. John Boyzych of Kelsey Hayes Labs and Ralph Mayer of Anderson Labs assisted in the preparation of this article. For more on tool steels, see Tool Steel Simplified *by Palmer, Luerssen and Pendleton, Chilton Company; and* Tool Steels, *from the American Iron and Steel Institute, Washington, D.C.*

A second opinion

by Paul Horgan

My initial interest in this article was as a technician. My background is in metals quality control, so I was suspicious of the high-flown claims in some tool catalogs. My intent in researching this article was to determine if the large differences in chisel prices were due to some measurable, physical difference in the tools. In my view, there is no measurable difference. The materials are all similar and the methods of manufacture aren't different enough to justify any substantial difference in price.

The lab rejected all tools softer than 59 RC, but I feel that this judgment is excessively harsh in the case of the Hirsch and Sorby chisels. The softer steel may require frequent sharpening,

but in my view this is a minor consideration. Besides, differences of up to four points on the Rockwell C scale are not necessarily significant because of variables in hardness testing.

The laminated Japanese chisels we tested were made in a style once found in Virginia in the 18th century. Steel was scarce then, so only a small piece was used for the cutting edge of the chisel. Iron was used for the body because it was less expensive. The Japanese continue their traditional practice of laminating blades for what I see as two reasons. First, the Japanese respect and revere tradition. Second, they understand the interest we in the United States have for the Orient, and for very

good business reasons they are exploiting the differences between our tool-making traditions. In selling laminated tools they are selling something different. These chisels are very well made, but their initial expense and the time required to maintain them makes them inappropriate for the beginner or the production professional, in my opinion.

My advice? Don't let the steel determine which chisel to buy. Pick any chisel that's reasonably priced and feels nice. Sharpen it as well as you know how. Any differences in the steel are so subtle that most woodworkers won't notice the difference. □

Paul Horgan lives in Torrance, Calif.

Paring Chisel Basics

Warm-up exercises
teach an essential skill

by Michael Podmaniczky

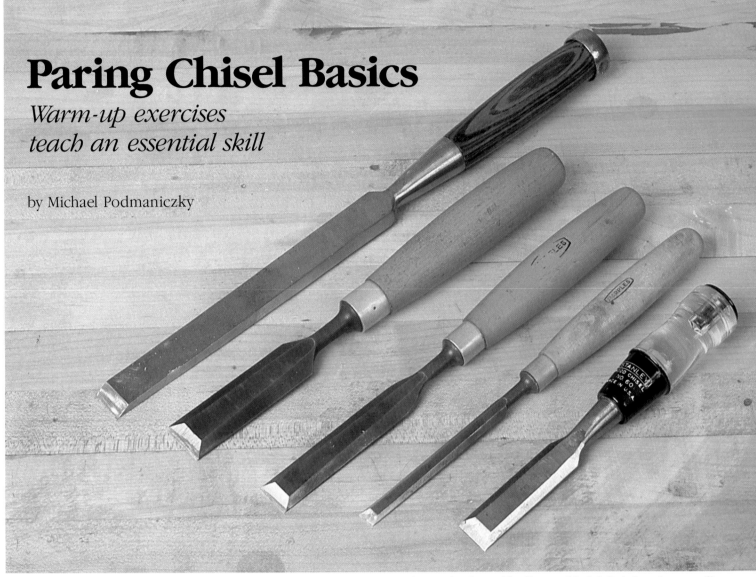

The three paring chisels, center, are lightweight tools shaped for precise work in tight places. The firmer chisel, left, is heavier overall, without side bevels, to resist the shock of hammering. The Stanley chisel, right, is an intermediate design for general work.

One of my favorite, and often enjoyed, times is the first slice I take with a paring chisel after a good sharpening. This most basic and useful tool is also the most versatile, doubling as a plane, a drawknife, even a cabinet scraper. But like any tool, it only performs for the hands that understand its basic personality—quirks and all.

There are many types of chisels, from the brutal timber framers' mortiser down to the tiniest carver, each one requiring a different technique. Here, I'll limit myself to an examination of the parer and how it's used for fine cuts. You *can* pare with any chisel, so much of the advice here will apply to all chisels. But the parer is a special case in that it is a lightweight, specially shaped tool that can get into places other chisels can't. Paring chisels are thin and light, with beveled edges to reduce weight and increase maneuverability. They are not expected to take hammering or prying. The nature of this tool is to remove light shavings of wood, usually with a finished surface as the intended result: sides of dovetails, tenon shoulders, etc.

The plane finishes large surfaces, the paring chisel finishes small ones. Incorrect use of a tool that's not necessarily intended for finish cuts—a drawknife for example—results in temporary frustration and extra work. Incorrect use of a paring chisel results in poor joints and ten years of irritation from having to look at them across the living room.

Any discussion has got to begin with the usual enjoinder: buy the best. There's no point in trying to master a second-rate tool.

But don't fret, I'm not suggesting that you buy a drawerful of expensive chisels. You can get by with two or three good parers, say, ⅜ in., ¾ in., and 1 in. or 1¼ in. You have many years to fill up that drawer. For rough-cut pounding, also pick up a couple of solid, inexpensive hooped socket or reinforced plastic-handled butt chisels. I like Stanley. There's no need to break the bank.

As I'll discuss further along, the action of paring—whatever sort of chisel you may be using—requires that the flat chisel back be used to "jig" the cutting edge in a straight line. It follows that the longer the blade, the longer the controlled cut. While this is true, it's also true that sometimes smaller areas need to be pared, and a long tool gets in the way...hmmm...what to do? Long-bladed patternmakers' chisels are really great for big work, and I go one step further and use cranked-handled ones—tools in which the shank of the chisel is bent so that the line of the handle is parallel with, but above, the line of the blade. With these, you can pare down a bung in the center of a sheet of plywood, if you really care to. But since these tools are extraordinarily expensive (not to mention hard to find), go for an average-length bench chisel, and it will take care of 90% of your needs.

It would be simple to describe some ideal working grip and, thence, the perfect handle for a paring chisel. You would then take it in hand, step up to the bench and find that the job you're doing is not ideal, and you'd end up with an entirely different grip and the shape of the handle would then be irrelevant, if it wasn't actually inconvenient. Better a plain handle that will give

From *Fine Woodworking* magazine (May 1987) 64:41-45

A mortising chisel, top, cannot get into tight corners because of its square sides; the paring chisel, above, has no problem because of its side bevels, which can be ground to almost a knife edge. Taking this thought one step further, the author modified a small parer's cutting edge to form a double-skew chisel, right, for slicing into dovetail corners. In all these cases, the right hand powers the cut, while the left rests against the work and grips the tool for control.

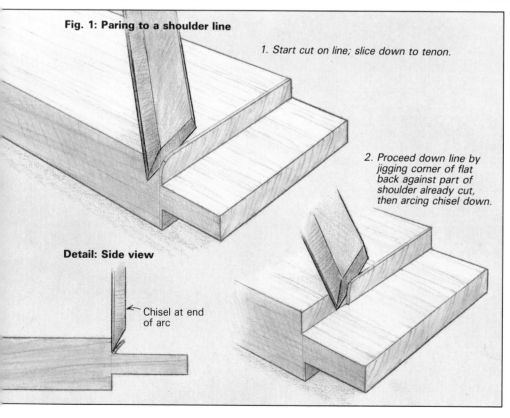

Fig. 1: Paring to a shoulder line

1. Start cut on line; slice down to tenon.

2. Proceed down line by jigging corner of flat back against part of shoulder already cut, then arcing chisel down.

Detail: Side view

← Chisel at end of arc

When paring a straight line, such as this tenon shoulder, the left hand backs up the tool for control, while the right hand pivots the cutting edge down. With a series of cuts (see drawing), the flat back of the chisel can jig itself along the length of the shoulder that has already been cut, as well as along the scribed shoulder line.

the versatility of grip so necessary to a proper job. The simple oval handles on Marples or Sorby tools are great, even though the smaller sizes may need a flat spot planed on one side of the handle to keep them from rolling off a not-so-level tabletop.

A very important detail is the finishing of the surfaces of the tool. It is imperative that the back of the chisel be ground flat, not belt sanded! This is easy to check if you're buying off the rack: just grab a steel ruler and hold it against the surface. You don't want to see light between the two. If you're catalog-buying and they send you a dud, send it back. It's the only way that manufacturers and distributors will ever get the picture.

As mentioned earlier, paring chisels have beveled side edges, and the care with which this is done is an indication of the overall concern the manufacturer has for the product. The maneuverability that side beveling gives you is apparent when working into an acute angle, such as next to a dovetail, as shown in the top photos on the facing page. You can re-grind this bevel almost to a knife-edge. To carry this idea a little further, I modified a ¼-in. bench chisel (shown in the large photo, p. 86) and made, in effect, a two-edged skew. Thus, I get a slicing cut (on either side), even when I push the blade in a straight line.

Now, I'm sure that you've already muttered something about my remarks that paring chisels are not for hammering on. I know, I know. . .I hammer on them, too, occasionally. But only with a wooden mallet, and then only lightly. Besides, paring is, by definition, done just with the hands. Blasting away with a mallet on a heavy mortising chisel doesn't permit the intimacy that develops between your hands and a paring chisel during a long day of cutting joints. Like a tiny stone in your shoe, a sharp edge or protruding piece of hardware can become a real irritant to your hand in a short time—which is another reason for choosing smooth handles (i.e. no butt hoops).

Manufacturers usually leave sharp corners where the body of the blade tapers back to form the shank. I grind these trailing corners off the blade to avoid opening up a finger if my sweaty palm slips, and I file any proudness off the edge of the ferrule, which ideally should be flush with the wood of the handle. This wants to be as comfy as an old loafer.

Now, before you can really understand the proper use of a paring chisel, you have to appreciate a key concept.

Ask yourself what would happen if you stuck a coil spring on the handle and held *it* while trying to take a shaving off an important piece of work. Why, as soon as you got near the end of the cut, the spring would unload, the chisel would jump and make a mess of everything in its way. You would have no control. Unfortunately, this can happen any time you go to work. The muscles and tendons in your hands and arms will act just like the spring unless you develop proper paring technique. There are

Bahco's ergonomic chisel

by Sandor Nagyszalanczy

I always thought that chisels were all about the same: a little fancier handle here, a little harder tool steel there. But my nonchalance was put to the test recently when I tried a chisel created by design methods usually reserved for jet cockpits and auto interiors. Made by one of the world's leading tool manufacturers, Bahco of Sweden, the Ergo line of hand tools is inspired by modern methods of ergonomics, or "human factors engineering." Bahco's aim was a chisel that would reduce hand and wrist fatigue while minimizing the risk of injury, common in hand-labor-intensive work.

Conny Jansson, director of R&D at Bahco, and a team of consultants began by videotaping woodworkers on the job and analyzing their individual physical movements. They also used computerized measuring devices attached to both people and mannequin-type figures to study worker functions and measure stress.

The collected data provided design criteria for the improvements incorporated in the Ergo chisel: a longer, textured handle large enough to accommodate two hands; a gently rounded, knob-like end to reduce palm pressure and protect the fingers when struck by a mallet; a smooth blade-to-handle transition to allow a closer grip for delicate work; and a shorter, stiff blade—angled in relation to the handle—for a higher angle of relief when working in close on flat surfaces.

I was impressed by the scientific treatment, but wondered if all the high-tech was worth it. To find out if the Bahco performed like a European sports car, I gave it a road

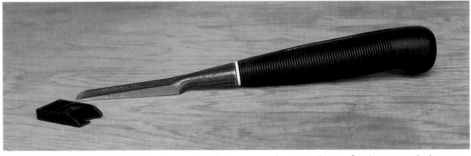

Sleek as a Swedish Saab, the Ergo chisel is as much a product of science as it is art.

test around the shop. The overall heft and feel of the chisel was gratifying. There was no feeling of cheapness, and the oval shape of the molded polypropylene handle gave a good sense of blade position relative to grasp. Since I have large hands, I appreciated its generous size, although I could only use the palm of my other hand on the chisel's butt end. I used it with a mallet and the handle felt very positive when struck; evidently, it won't mushroom over time. The socket-style attachment and angle of the blade gave the tool a feel similar to Japanese chisels I've worked with. At a claimed Rockwell hardness of 58 to 60, the blade sharpened and honed well and held an edge even after being pounded into dense rosewood.

I didn't much like the surface of the Ergo's handle. Despite the groove-textured surface, the black plastic was just a little too slick for my taste. Also, an indented area on the chisel's handle where Bahco molds in its trademark was uncomfortable to grasp, nearly negating, for the sake of product identity, all the

effort that went into making the tool's hand fit revolutionary.

So, is ergonomics a gimmick or a giant step in the evolution of hand tools? Although I usually choose a tool for the way it performs, I'd be drawn to Ergo's high-tech modern appearance, even if I knew nothing about all the computer-aided effort that went into its design. Bahco has created a high-quality tool that's got more going for it than a trendy design, but I can't say I'm ready to throw out all my antiquated chisels just yet; I still prefer the feel of a wood handle over plastic. If you're comfortable with the tool, you may not be with the price— $15 for the 1-in. model. But all that intelligent Swedish design—whether it's for hand tools or Saabs—doesn't come cheap. □

Sandor Nagyszalanczy is an assistant editor for Fine Woodworking. *Bahco's Ergo chisels are available from Woodcraft Supply, Woodworker's Supply of New Mexico and Garrett Wade.*

Successful paring demands forward pressure to make the cut and firm control to keep it in line. At top left, the controlling hand, the left, also acts as a brake so the chisel will not spring forward uncontrollably and chip out the wood at the far end of the workpiece. Below that is a practical one-handed grip—the heel of the hand acts as a fulcrum; the right thumb arcs the chis-el like a lever through the wood, slicing through the wood fibers. Control in paring comes easily when large muscles of the body are used to drive the tool. Shown above is one of the most common techniques: Podmaniczky uses his chin against his fist and the end of the handle, with the left hand helping to keep the tool on line. Other strategies include pushing with hip or chest.

two ways to overcome this problem: dampen the spring action, or substitute inertia of body mass for muscle power.

In most cases where I use my right hand to power the cut, I use my left hand to help guide the cut and restrain the cutting action. By squeezing the blade and resting part of my left hand against the work—sometimes the forefinger, other times the heel of my hand or whatever is convenient—I have real control and can stop the cut whenever I want, right on a dime. As I mentioned earlier, the back/side edge of any chisel has to be kept in good condition—actually sharp—so that there is a slight danger with this grip that you'll begin taking little slices off your finger. Try to apply the gripping pressure in the middle of the blade and you can avoid irritation.

As shown above, when I'm at the bench cutting straight down, I use my head. Despite what my wife occasionally thinks my head is full of, it is quite heavy, and my chin can really move that chisel. The idea is to keep the butt inside the fist so that the chin

pushes against soft meat. In practice, the handle creeps out, but you put up with it because it gives a bit more control.

A variation on this theme is to grab the chisel anywhere along its length and use the chin to push against the side of the handle and forefinger. Both these strategies eliminate the problematic springiness of arm muscles. You can use your hip, chest or other parts of your body in this manner, depending on the circumstances. Once in a great while, you'll look a bit foolish with one leg up on the bench in order to get the right angle, but you gotta do what you gotta do.

A plane is a jig that holds a "chisel" and forces it to cut in a straight line by virtue of a long flat sole. Without this jig, keeping the cutting edge going in a straight line is a bit harder, but as I mentioned earlier, you still have a way to partially jig the action. With the chisel flipped over on its back, start a paring cut. At first, the direction of cut is determined entirely by where you point the tool. As the cutting edge slices into the wood, it

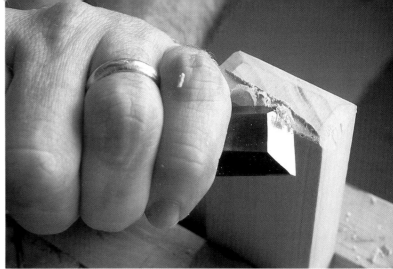

Chamfering is the first step in paring a flat end (see drawing). Then bring the surface down in steps, working toward the center.

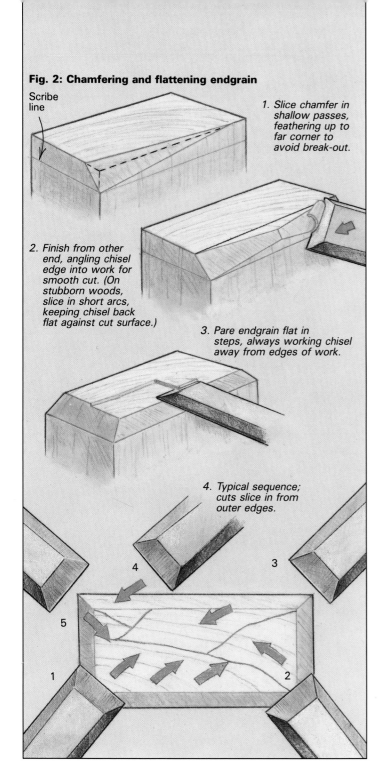

Fig. 2: Chamfering and flattening endgrain

Scribe line

1. Slice chamfer in shallow passes, feathering up to far corner to avoid break-out.

2. Finish from other end, angling chisel edge into work for smooth cut. (On stubborn woods, slice in short arcs, keeping chisel back flat against cut surface.)

3. Pare endgrain flat in steps, always working chisel away from edges of work.

4. Typical sequence; cuts slice in from outer edges.

develops a flat surface behind the cut. The back of the chisel can begin to rest on this surface, which it has itself created, and use the purchase as a guide for ever-increasing accuracy of direction. The longer the cut, the more controllable it becomes. If you use this help, you can all but eliminate digging in.

To practice the various techniques we've been discussing, I would recommend a short piece of a 1-in. by 2-in. poplar or mahogany. Using your combination square and a sharp layout knife, scribe a line around the stick about ¼ in. from one end. Your task is to pare to this line so that you have a nice flat end-grain surface. Figure 2 shows the basic approach, but every piece of wood is different—I won't go so far as to say contrary—so apply the principles in whatever way necessary to suit the job.

Clamp the wood vertically in the vise, sticking up three or four inches above the benchtop. Chamfer the long right-hand edge at roughly 45°. Trying to do this all at once will just get you broken-out wood on the other end of the cut—so don't do it. With easy

semi-circular slices, take ¹⁄₁₆-in. slices off the corner, aiming slightly up so that the cutting edge emerges from the wood before it gets to the other side. When you're down to your knife line at the corner, do the same on the other long edge, then finish the chamfers as shown in the drawing.

If you're right-handed, the first edge will be the easy one since you'll be able to rest your whole forefinger on the work. Moving to the left side will require a grip alteration, but a couple of tries will help you find a comfortable position. I half-heartedly try to do all operations with either hand. (I say half-heartedly because I'm not very good at it—but at least I try.) If you're paring or planing and run into reverse grain, you can flip the tool into the other direction a lot easier if you're a switch-hitter.

Now turn the work 90° and cut the two short edges. This will be easier since the following corners are cut down for this step, too. You now have a chamfer all around the end of the 1x2, right to your knife line. These can now be cut down flatter with the same grip and hand action. Slowly work two opposite chamfers down until you're almost on the flat. Turn the work 90° in the vise, and shoot across, square to the cuts you've just made, to finish off the flattening. If you're having trouble with break-out, rotate the work as many times as you need to, to be able to work "into" the surface. Finish off with a very light cleanup shave.

As you're working along an edge, keep in mind that the angle between the edge of the stock and the cutting edge of the chisel must be less than 90°, as shown in the drawing. Otherwise, the outside wood fibers will have a tendency to break away, being pushed by the chisel without anything backing them up. It can help if you imagine the cutting edge and the body of the stock as two scissor blades, shearing the fibers along the edge.

When you're satisfied with the flat end you've produced, scribe a new line, clamp the wood down horizontally on the bench and chamfer it again. You can either lay the work on a piece of plywood or directly on the surface of the bench, which will back up your cuts and prevent break-out, or you can hang the end out over the end of the bench, a position that more closely imitates situations you'll encounter in real life. This will be trickier, but better practice.

Try the other grips (including chin drive) that we've discussed, and cut the same way you did when the piece was vertical. The more you practice and the harder you make it for yourself (say, cut the end of the stock on a 120° bevel instead of square), the quicker and more accurate you'll be when it really counts. □

Michael Podmaniczky is a contributing editor to FWW.

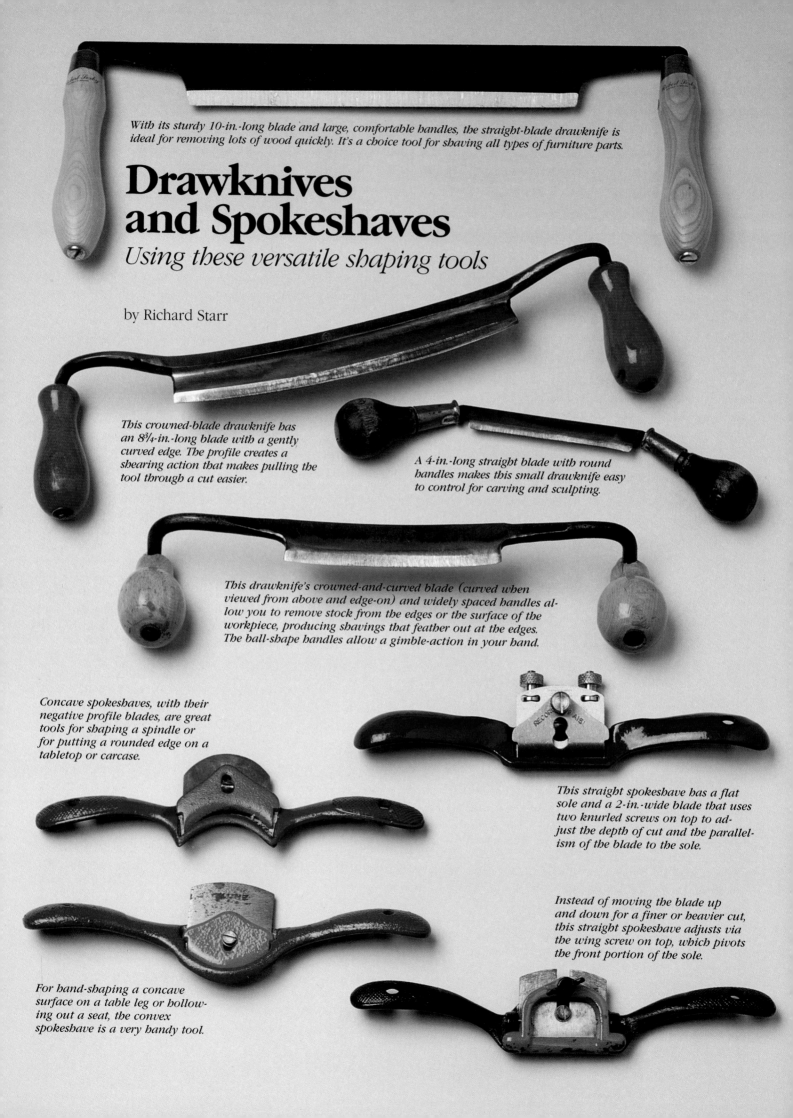

With its sturdy 10-in.-long blade and large, comfortable handles, the straight-blade drawknife is ideal for removing lots of wood quickly. It's a choice tool for shaving all types of furniture parts.

Drawknives and Spokeshaves

Using these versatile shaping tools

by Richard Starr

This crowned-blade drawknife has an 8¾-in.-long blade with a gently curved edge. The profile creates a shearing action that makes pulling the tool through a cut easier.

A 4-in.-long straight blade with round handles makes this small drawknife easy to control for carving and sculpting.

This drawknife's crowned-and-curved blade (curved when viewed from above and edge-on) and widely spaced handles allow you to remove stock from the edges or the surface of the workpiece, producing shavings that feather out at the edges. The ball-shape handles allow a gimble-action in your hand.

Concave spokeshaves, with their negative profile blades, are great tools for shaping a spindle or for putting a rounded edge on a tabletop or carcase.

This straight spokeshave has a flat sole and a 2-in.-wide blade that uses two knurled screws on top to adjust the depth of cut and the parallelism of the blade to the sole.

Instead of moving the blade up and down for a finer or heavier cut, this straight spokeshave adjusts via the wing screw on top, which pivots the front portion of the sole.

For hand-shaping a concave surface on a table leg or hollowing out a seat, the convex spokeshave is a very handy tool.

Drawknives and spokeshaves have always been tried-and-true tools for riving and shaping green wood for folk crafts and rustic furniture. But they're also great tools for many jobs in fine furniture or cabinet shops because you can shave wood with efficiency and a fluidity of motion that makes you feel as if the tool is an extension of your own hands. Drawknives excel at all sorts of jobs that require fast stock removal, such as roughing out tapered legs prior to handplaning them smooth. Spokeshaves are better suited for chamfering the edge of a table-top, rounding the armrest of a chair and other finer shaping or smoothing jobs. Regardless of what kind of woodworking, carving or sculpture you do, I'll bet there are plenty of uses for both tools in your shop.

Comparing a drawknife to a spokeshave is like comparing a chisel to a plane. The drawknife's bare blade allows you to control the thickness of the shaving, but as with a chisel, you must carefully guide the tool to keep the cut smooth and prevent the blade from digging in. Once you master a drawknife, you'll be able to hew away huge quantities of wood, as well as slice off thin shavings. Unlike a drawknife, a properly set spokeshave can't dig in too deeply or split the wood because its blade is enclosed in a sole—like a handplane. And the distance that the blade protrudes beyond the sole dictates the depth of cut. Spokeshaves can do much the same work as drawknives, but they are somewhat easier to use. Further, with certain specialized spokeshaves that have shaped soles, you can create effects that would be difficult with any other tool. Even if you have already used a drawknife or spokeshave, there are many different styles you should be aware of, as well as safe methods when using the tools and techniques for sharpening them. Let's look at drawknives first.

Drawknives—A hundred years ago, dozens of specialized drawknives were made for many trades, including boatbuilding, timber framing and coopering. The various drawknives differed mostly in the size and shape of the blade and the shape and position of the handles. Many of these knives are still manufactured today, and they are readily available from most mail order tool supply companies. Also, you can often find good, older tools at flea markets, auctions or antique tool dealers.

The handles on drawknives are designed to make specific jobs easier (see the photos on the facing page). Cylindrical handles, found on many larger drawknives, fill your whole hand and help you get a good grip to control a large blade while hogging off a lot of wood. Smaller drawknives often have ball-shape handles that aren't practical for heavy work, but really shine for carving. The grip is like a ball-and-socket joint: You can quickly swivel the blade into almost any position, even push the tool instead of pull it, to deal with changing grain direction. Regardless of style, all handles must be securely fastened to the knife. It's best if the tangs come all the way through the handle and are bent or peened over, preferably through a metal cap or washer on the end of the handle. A ferrule where the blade joins the handle reinforces a heavy drawknife and prevents the handle from splitting.

Another consideration in choosing a drawknife is the position and angle of the handles with respect to the blade. This relationship affects your hand position and, therefore, your comfort and control while using the tool. A drawknife must fit your work style just like a good shoe fits your foot: You should try a knife in every position you expect to use before you buy it. For all-around work, bent handles offer a more natural hand position as you draw the knife toward your belly. However, if you are inclined to use the tool with the bevel down, as I am, deeply bent handles may point upward and be uncomfortable to hold and

tiring to use. If you work a lot of green wood, you may prefer handles that are level with the blade. They provide better control with heavy cuts because the tool is less likely to twist upward as you pull. Carvers and sculptors often choose drawknives with so-called "dropped" handles, where the handles are below the plane of the blade. These offer more control in precision work because the hand position allows you to twist the blade up and down easily.

Blade designs—The shape of the blade determines the cut the tool will take. A straight-edge drawknife is a good all-purpose tool, useful for shaping and surfacing. A crowned blade appears straight when you look edge-on, but curves forward when viewed from above. This blade can take a wide shaving that gets thinner at the edges and leave a smooth surface relatively free of marks from overlapping cuts. Another design is the crowned-and-curved blade, which dips in the middle when viewed edge-on. Like a crowned blade, a crowned-and-curved blade takes shavings with feathered edges, but it is better for shallow carving and hollowing a surface, for say shaping the backrest of a seat. Another kind of drawknife, the inshave, has a thick, U-shape blade that's great for hollowing out a solid-wood chair seat.

Working safely with a drawknife—Although it may appear dangerous at first glance, a drawknife's long, exposed blade is relatively harmless, if you follow a few simple precautions. I've been teaching woodworking to children for more than 20 years and I have no problem putting a drawknife in a kid's hands. The tool is actually much safer than a carving knife. Most drawknife cuts occur on the back of your free hand when you lift the tool off the wood to brush away shavings or to adjust your work; therefore, the first rule is to be extra careful when one of your hands is not on a handle. Put the tool away as soon as you are done with it, preferably in a rack made from a scrap strip of ¾ stock with crosscut slots about 1½ in. apart to hold each knife blade down. The rack protects the blades and separates the tools. Also, never leave a drawknife in a jumble of tools. It's a bad risk for your hands and not so good for the blade either.

Beginners often worry that they will cut their bellies as they shave toward their bodies. However, this isn't a problem as long as you keep your body at a reasonable distance from the work. If you hold your work in a shaving horse, make sure your knees are clear of the drawknife's path. When using very small drawknives, grind the corners of the blade edge blunt, to prevent cut thumbs.

Using a drawknife—Unlike a handplane's or spokeshave's housed blade, a drawknife's long, open blade allows many different cutting possibilities. The easiest way to take a shaving is to angle the drawknife's blade and pull with the blade skewed relative to the workpiece. In this manner, shavings come off in corkscrews, and the shearing action is less likely to tear the wood than if you pulled the blade straight through. To cut dense woods with roed or curly grain, it's best to take a slicing cut, moving the knife sideways while pulling it, as though you were slicing bread. Place your stronger hand on the handle near the leading edge of the blade and draw the knife across the wood as you pull. It's a natural and comfortable motion, and using the entire length of the blade keeps the edge from dulling in only one area.

A drawknife's blade can be used with the bevel up or down. For most work, I prefer keeping the bevel down, facing the wood, because I can easily adjust the depth of cut by rotating the handle ends up or down. However, the blade can be hard to control and tends to come out of the work when the drawknife is pulled hard. If this occurs, flip the tool over and work with the bevel up, away from the stock.

Pulling a drawknife makes the best use of your muscles, hence the name *draw*knife. But many times you'll want to push it instead. Pushing lets you exert more force by putting your weight behind the drawknife, especially if the stock is held vertically or at a steep angle. Although pushing a drawknife with precision may take a little practice, it's worth mastering. If you shape curved surfaces, as when carving a wooden spoon, changing grain directions may require alternating cuts in several directions.

If the grain in the workpiece is straight and clear, you can split off large chunks of wood by starting a deep cut, and then twisting the blade by raising the ends of the handles (see the left photo below). This uses the back edge of the blade as a fulcrum and gives you considerable leverage. If a split starts running out of control, you can stop it by shaving the waste above the split or pushing the drawknife and shaving back toward the open end of the split. When shaving green stock, be sure your stock is well secured in the vise or shaving horse.

Sharpening drawknives—As with all other tools, drawknives work best when they are kept razor sharp. Unfortunately, even a straight drawknife blade can be difficult to sharpen because the non-removable handles tend to get in the way. Probably the easiest way to keep a drawknife cutting smoothly is to touch up the edge every once in a while with a hand stone. I prefer a round Norton axe stone (Norton Co., 1 New Bond St., Worcester, Mass. 10615-0008), which has a groove around its edge that keeps your fingers clear of the blade. To sharpen, hold the knife like a fiddle, with the bevel up and one handle nestled in your shoulder, as shown in the right photo below. Since the middle of the blade does the most work, you need not sharpen the whole length of the blade every time you touch it up. Touch up the back of the blade as well, espe-

cially when it's pitted or nicked. It's worth noting that while the backs of most drawknife blades are dead flat (like a chisel), some woodworkers prefer to dub a small counterbevel (5° to 10°) on the flat side. This counterbevel can make the tool a little easier to control when working bevel up, and it makes the edge easier to touch up because you don't have to stone the entire flat side unless it's really bad. When the edge has its share of nicks, it's time to regrind the bevel. Drawknife blades, like chisels and plane irons, are single-beveled tools ground at an angle on one side and usually flat on the other. This bevel is typically between 30° and 40° on a new drawknife, and I usually maintain this angle and the original shape of the blade when I regrind.

Unfortunately, when grinding the edge of a full-size drawknife, the handles usually won't clear the motor on a bench grinder. One solution is to dress the wheel's face at an angle so you can grind with the handles out of the way. Just don't create a sharp peak on the face of the wheel, which may cause the wheel to fracture in use. A stationary belt grinder, or a belt sander held upside down in a vise, also works very well, especially on curved or crowned blades that are a challenge to grind to shape. I start with a 60-grit belt, and then hone with the axe stone and finish with a cloth buffing wheel charged with emery compound.

Spokeshaves—In my school shop, kids who have trouble learning to control a drawknife, or lack the strength to do heavy work with one, can usually accomplish the task more easily (but not as quickly) with a spokeshave. A sharp and well-adjusted spokeshave can skim a crisp, even shaving almost automatically, leaving a clean, smooth surface. Spokeshaves can be used for many shop tasks, from chamfering, trimming a door and wood sculpting, to more traditional tasks, such as shaving spindles. The tool is usually smaller and lighter than a drawknife because the blade is shorter, thinner and removable, not to mention replaceable.

Left: A large, straight-blade drawknife is tops for quickly hogging away large amounts of stock, especially in green wood. With a workpiece secure in the shaving horse, the author twists the knife as he pulls it through the cut, using leverage to split off the waste. Above: Holding the drawknife in his arms like a fiddle, Starr uses a round axe-sharpening stone to touch up the edge.

A spokeshave is actually a very short plane with handles on its sides. The blade is enclosed in the body of the tool, protruding through the sole just far enough to take a shaving. A single screw usually holds the cutter in place. To adjust the depth of cut, you loosen the screw and tap the blade in or out, for a lighter or heavier cut. Some spokeshaves feature a lever cap, which presses down on the blade just behind its edge, that stiffens the blade to prevent chattering, like the cap iron of a handplane. Spokeshaves made by Stanley and Record have two adjusting screws on top that make setting the depth of cut a matter of simply turning the screws on top.

Different kinds and shapes—Like drawknives, spokeshaves traditionally were specialized tools that are still available in a variety of styles and shapes. Most spokeshaves have straight blades anywhere from 1 in. to 2 in. or more in width, with either straight handles or raised handles shaped like gull wings. Straight handles make it easier to take heavier cuts while keeping the sole flat on the work. Raised handles keep your hands clear when shaving on a flat surface, but the tool has a tendency to chatter and roll as you cut. Therefore, place your thumbs on the front of the tool just above the blade, to stabilize the tool.

My favorite straight spokeshaves have adjustable throats, for more sensitive control of the cut. Unlike a smoothing plane's adjustable throat that doesn't change the depth of cut when it's set, an adjustable-throat spokeshave increases the thickness of the shaving as you open the throat and expose more blade. Conversely, closing it down yields a very fine cut, which is great for curly grained woods. With this single control, you can adjust the cut without moving the blade up and down. I really appreciate this feature when, for instance, I chamfer the edges of a round stool, as shown in the top photo at right. As I work around the circle, I can set a deep cut when working parallel to the grain, and then adjust for a very fine shaving when I come around to the endgrain.

Spokeshaves also come with concave- and convex-shape blades. The hollow or half-round spokeshave is concave across the blade. The tool does a nice job of cleaning up the facets left after roughing out the workpiece with a drawknife, producing a smooth, evenly rounded surface on a spindle or rounded chair part, as shown in the bottom photo at right. Unfortunately, the short sole makes the tool hard to control and the blade has a tendency to dig in and tear the edge-grain when, for instance, rounding the edges of a tabletop or carcase side. The radius spokeshave has a convex-shape blade with about a 3-in. radius, and is good for shaping shallow grooves and cleaning up other concave surfaces, such as the seat of a chair that's been scooped out with an inshave. Like the hollow spokeshave, the radius shave can be hard to control and is especially subject to chatter if it's not really sharp and pressed down firmly during cutting.

Modifications—It's possible to modify adjustable-throat spokeshaves for better performance and cutting control. First, remove the D-shape adjustable sole and, with a flat file, slightly undercut the throat, and round and smooth the inside edges. This reduces the tool's annoying tendency to jam with shavings. For finer adjustments, and shavings of even thickness across their width, the throat must be ground evenly across the sole. Mount the blade in the shave and temporarily pin the adjustable sole back in, without the springs. Then, adjust the blade's edge so it is parallel with the adjustable sole when viewed from the front, and check the throat opening for evenness all the way across. If it is not even, use dividers to scribe a line on the adjustable sole, and then file to the line. Finally, reassemble the spokeshave with the springs

A straight spokeshave is a great tool for quickly beveling the underside of a table-top or, as shown above, a stool seat. The author first marks the grain direction, and then cuts the bevel by either pushing or pulling the tool. The half-round spokeshave is the perfect tool for rounding and smoothing the surface of a chair leg after it's been roughed out with a drawknife (right). The edge of the spokeshave blade is ground to a slightly larger radius than the sole.

in place. Each time you replace the blade after sharpening, adjust the throat to its smallest setting, lock the blade in place slightly above and parallel to the sole, and then adjust the throat setting for the desired cut.

Sharpening a spokeshave—Sharpening the blade on a straight spokeshave is identical to sharpening a small plane blade. If you have problems holding the small blade during grinding, use a pair of locking-jaw pliers. Sharpening the blade on a half-round or radius spokeshave is a tougher matter. Besides the difficulty of sharpening the curved edge, the profile of the blade doesn't even match the sole because the blade passes through the sole at an angle. Fortunately, you don't need to grind a perfect match. Instead, grind so that the blade's curve is more gradual than the sole's, so that the blade protrudes only at the center of the sole, which produces shavings with feathered edges. Dress an old grinding wheel to fit the shape of the curve and occasionally check the blade profile by setting the blade in the tool and sighting from the front. □

Richard Starr is a teacher and the author of Woodworking with Kids, *published by The Taunton Press, 1982.*

The Socket Slick

by Michael Podmaniczky

I can remember the first time I ever read about a slick. It was about 12 years ago, and I hadn't a clue to what the author was talking about. Six months later, I asked an old boatbuilder friend about the giant chisel hanging in his shop. The thing looked as if it had been made by one of those novelty companies that sells Crayola crayons the size of cordwood. "That's a slick, you idiot." Already embarrassed, I asked, "What do you do with it?"

He picked it off the wall, tucked it under his arm like a firehose and took a paper-thin, 3-ft.-long shaving off the edge of a piece of 1-in.-thick pine. "But I can do that a heck of a lot easier with my jack plane," I said. "Sure you can, if the work's clamped to the bench," he replied, "but what if you can't get at it with your plane?"

He had a point. In tight spots, this bull of a paring chisel becomes indispensable. Handled, these chisels can be between 2 ft. to 3 ft. long, with a 2½-in.- to 4-in.-wide blade. Usually boatbuilders have these brutes for easing tight plank edges when the plank is already hung on the boat and they don't want to take it back to the bench for fairing. Though boatbuilders make particularly good use of the slick for making the big curved pieces that go into a boat, almost any woodworker could find a use for one.

If the bottom of a cabinet door binds and there's no clearance for your plane below the door (and you don't want to unhang it), try a slick. Taking a whisper off an installed drawer runner is virtually impossible with a plane, but a slick eases into this kind of hard-to-get-at spot with quickness and precision.

Different from big framing chisels, slicks are slightly bent at the socket so they can lie flat on their backs for smoothing large surfaces without the handle getting in the way. For this reason, you shouldn't hammer on the end of a slick, because mallet blows do not transfer directly in a line from handle to cutting edge. You could even break the handle. Besides, remember how this tool is held: under the arm. And the handle is quite long, often decoratively turned, so you wouldn't *want* to hit it. I'm always disappointed when I see a slick rehandled with a splintered piece of scrap and beat up with a claw hammer.

The only new slicks I've seen are available from Woodcraft Supply in Woburn, Mass., but older ones regularly turn up at flea markets and yard sales, often in the abused condition mentioned above. As with any chisel, the one thing to avoid is a used slick with a pock-marked or corroded sole, because each little pit will translate to a chip in the cutting edge. Look for the flattest sole possible in a used slick, and don't expect much from a new one, because their surfaces are belt-sanded instead of surface-ground.

Although every job may require a slightly different grip, the usual way to hold a slick is to tuck the butt end of the handle under your arm. For real meat-and-potatoes work, wedge the end high in the armpit, where the whole upper body can get behind it. For more delicate work, wedge the handle lower down, between the elbow and the area just below the ribs. If you are good, you can reach way out with the same hand, grabbing the side of the blade for one-handed paring. But it's easier if you choke up and hold the socket instead and grab over the top of the blade with your other hand. Don't hold the slick like it is a big, straight-edge turning chisel, because it is not. Your upper

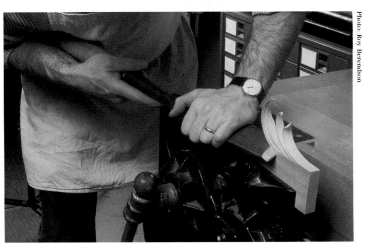

Despite its cumbersome appearance, the socket slick allows a delicate shaving to be taken, even in situations where it's impossible to use a plane.

body provides the "third point" of contact for the slick that the lathe tool rest does for the turning chisel. This three-point grip on the long slick is what gives you amazing control.

To use the slick, lay its flat sole down on the work and try some slicing motions, without cutting at first. Your under-the-arm grip should provide the power and stability, and your lead hand the control. Now shrug your shoulder a fraction until the blade begins to bite, and practice long paring cuts. If the edge starts to dig in, just lower your shoulder until you get a fine shaving and the blade obeys your motions. It will feel much like a sheering cut on the lathe, where the tool cuts and rides on the bevel at the same time. In the case of a slick, the bevel is up and the contact between the sole and the work provides the guidance.

One drawback is that, unlike a plane, which can deal with rowed or curly grain, the slick can't help but lift or tear it. Before putting slick to wood, carefully check how the grain is running and try to approach from the most kindly direction.

I sharpen a slick just like any other chisel, and because it's pushed instead of struck, you can sharpen it to a fine edge—like a paring tool. Hollow-grinding the bevel first will reduce the amount of material that needs removal during honing. You may find it easier to bring the sharpening stone to the edge instead of trying to keep the bevel flat while supporting the massive blade. Just rest the slick's butt on your knee, lay the sole against the workbench (with the bevel facing you) and rub the stone across the edge until it's sharp.

Although a slick is about the size of a baseball bat, it can be stored quite compactly: The handle just slips out of its socket, because the slick is used quite gingerly and doesn't need a fused fit between blade and handle. But keep in mind the story of the guy who finished paring and let the tool hang down at his side with a jerk. Good-bye baby toe. □

Michael Podmaniczky is a contributing editor to Fine Woodworking *and a furniture conservator at the Winterthur Museum in Winterthur, Del.*

Birds of a feather: in foreground from left to right, AMT, Lion and Grizzly. While differences are minor, parts are not interchangeable among the three machines, whose common *ancestor sits in the background, stamped Lion Universal Cutter No. 4, Pootatuck Corp., Shelton, Conn. The design has been virtually unchanged since the early part of this century.*

Miter Trimmers

Slicing cuts for picture frames and trim

by Jim Cummins

As soon as I received two of the three guillotine-type miter trimmers on the market, I jumped at the chance to have some fellow woodworkers try them out. We all sliced up an assortment of woods and molding scraps until the chips half-filled a shop-vac. "Hey, that's great!" was heard more than once. "It doesn't take any force at all; how can it cut like that?" "It cuts smooth as glass and it's *quiet,* too." The machines looked almost identical in every feature and adjustment, and both sliced wood about the same. Yet after a few cuts on one machine and a few cuts on the other, each volunteer would generally pause, step back, then point decisively and say: "I like *that* one better." That *one* was the venerable, American-made Lion, which is the obvious inspiration for the two contending imports from Taiwan. These three machines are so alike that whether the Lion can survive the invasion depends, I think, on people's sensitivity to some subtle factors. I hope these will be clear by the end of this article.

With that aside for the moment, I have no doubt that a miter trimmer would be a handy tool to have around if you do a lot of applied moldings for interior trim, cabinets, clocks or what-have-you. In fact, trimmers have some curious uses that don't quickly spring to mind. Wood technologists find the cut is clean enough to allow endgrain analysis for wood identification. Telephone companies use them for slicing plastic cable housings during inspections. But of course the main market is finish carpenters, cabinetmakers, part-time frame shops and individual artists. I say part-time framers because if you're serious about making picture frames or doing much other commercial mitering, you'll want a full-size, foot-operated $1,500 chopper. This article focuses on trimmers, but if you're intrigued with the idea of a chopper, literature on the two best-known machines, both made in Denmark, is available from S&W Frame Supplies, 120 Broadway, Garden City Park, N.Y. 11040, (516) 746-1000; and Juhl Pacific, 7585 Equitable Drive, Eden Prairie, Minn. 55344, (612) 937-3200.

I bought my Lion used for $25, 20 years ago, intending it to be only a backup for my chopper. The rusty, paint-spattered machine had a broken handle, which had been fixed by wedging the

Moldings must be rough-cut to size before the trimmer can start to work. The secret to perfect joints (here with the Grizzly) is to finish up with a series of light slices.

The Lion trimmer has an optional length gauge ($50) that can be adapted to fit the other machines by drilling mounting holes in their beds. While it saves pencil-marking each length, perfect cuts can be made without it.

Moldings that tend to tip or tear out when cut normally may be sliced using the Lion's optional top trimmer ($38), which also allows compound miters. Note that the same results can be achieved with a shopmade angled block.

pieces into a length of pipe. And one of the wings had the lip cracked off the front edge, a result of overtightening the locking screw. Despite this, the trimmer still works fine at 45° and 90°, the only drawback being that it can't be locked at other angles without using a C-clamp. The foreman of my picture-frame shop, Mike Densen, uses it even more than I do and finds it the ideal tool for slicing strippings, which are unrabbeted frame moldings that have to be individually, and perfectly, fitted around a canvas. He also reaches for it whenever we have to frame work at a customer's home (some pictures are too big to move easily). Densen's first experiences with a Lion came long before he ever worked with me; the trimmer was the tool of choice for fitting window trim when he worked for a contractor back in the early 1960s. "Nothing can touch it for a joint that *fits,*" Densen maintains.

Operation—Unlike the usual fuzzy sawcut, a miter trimmer works like a giant paring chisel, slicing miters or cleaning up endgrain. The trimmer's two knives—one for left-hand cuts, one for right-hand—are fastened to a carriage that slides in grooves in the back of the cast-iron bed. The knives are powered by a hand lever that turns a cast-iron gear wheel. As the knives cut, they apply pressure that squares the work down against the bed and against a fence, or wing, at each side; clamping the work is usually unnecessary. The wings butt up against adjustable stops at 45° and 90°, or they can be clamped at any angle between. When trimming a room that is not quite square, it's easy enough to shim the moldings slightly askew against the wings to change the angles slightly and achieve perfect fits.

The photos show the essentials of how a trimmer is used: Work is precut slightly longer than final size using tablesaw, handsaw or whatever means is convenient, then a series of thin slices on the trimmer brings the ends to a perfect miter at the correct length. It's recommended that the trimmer be screwed down or clamped, which is probably necessary if you are taking heavy cuts in wide moldings, but I've never clamped mine.

You can stand (or kneel if you're working on-site on the floor) directly in front of the tool, working the lever to the left and right as necessary, or you can stand at one end, as I usually do. This position is less fatiguing, because you use your stomach and back muscles to pull or push the lever. I make the pull cuts first on all pieces, mark the lengths on the other ends, then make the push cuts last. By standing at the end of the machine, I have a clear line of sight down the knife as it approaches the pencil line, which is difficult to gauge when in front of the machine, particularly if the molding is rabbeted and the pencil line is in the rabbet.

The Lion accepts an optional length gauge that might be useful (see the middle photo at left), but I've never felt the need for it. Also, directions for using the gauge call for very accurate precutting, and I'd rather let the quality of the wood determine how accurate I have to be at the roughing stage. For example, you can take very heavy cuts in pine. When mitering a 2-in.-wide clamshell molding flat on the bed, anything up to an inch long can be speedily hogged off in one chop, then a couple of finer slices can be taken to ensure a straight, glass-smooth surface with no tearout. Fussing much with measurements at this stage is more time-consuming than profitable. Hardwoods are another story. Trying to take a 1/16-in. slice in maple may be too much, so here it's a good idea to make accurate rough cuts at the proper angle.

Another thing, quickly learned through experience, is that there must be a certain minimum thickness to the shaving; otherwise, the work will slide away from the knife. This minimum thickness varies from wood to wood. As you approach your pencil line in a series of slices, you have to leave just the right amount of wood for the last cut. Too far from the line, and you won't get the cleanest cut possible; too close, and the knife may enter the work all right, but it will ride out of it before the cut is completed, ruining the cut's accuracy. Shaving thickness is especially important when cutting very hard woods, where there may be little difference between the maximum and minimum shavings possible.

Some moldings are difficult to cut because their shapes leave poor bearing surfaces against the bed and wing; under cutting pressure, they tend either to tilt or to slide. Other moldings may tear out when cut in the usual way. As a cure, Pootatuck makes a "top trimmer" for the Lion that changes the orientation of the molding, as shown in the bottom photo on the facing page, so that its best bearing surface may be used. Another idea is to make an angled block to back up troublesome moldings so they will be sufficiently supported when cut at the normal wing position.

Safety and maintenance—If your hand should brush against a knife, you'll draw blood so easily you may not even feel the cut until it is very deep. These machines weigh about 26 lbs., and the new models all have a simple but very effective carrying handle to keep hands out of the danger zone. I've cut myself twice on my old model—once badly, when I picked it up by grabbing the two projecting knife guards, not realizing that the knife was all the way to one side. Another time, I picked it up by the guards and the handle swung to one side under its own weight, forcing the knife's top corner hard enough into my hand to gouge it.

For best results, knives should be kept razor sharp. You can periodically refresh the edge by honing a secondary bevel using regular benchstones, working off the burr by honing the knife's flat side flat against the stone. The process is much like chisel sharpening, as described on pp. 105-109. However, I advise you to send knives off for grinding when the secondary bevel gets too wide for practical honing. It's not a good idea to grind them yourself, because there's too much danger of overheating the steel. AMT and Grizzly suggest finding a local sharpener to do the job—anyone who sharpens jointer and planer knives can do this work. You can send Lion knives back to the factory. Pootatuck sharpens 16 pairs at a time on a Blanchard grinder. To ensure a fast turnaround, usually next-day, they exchange knives. When a customer's knives arrive, they are measured for width, $\frac{1}{16}$ in. is deducted as a sharpening allowance, and a pair that size is shipped out from stock. The cost is about $20 postpaid, but these tools don't dull all that fast. Commercial picture framers average close to a year between sharpenings, Pootatuck says. Their most regular customer is a millwork shop that sends knives back two pairs at a time every six months or so.

In fact, I have had my knives reground only twice so far, and I even spoke with one Lion owner who has been hand-honing the same set of knives for 30 years. These machines are somewhat tolerant of abuse and neglect. In a torture test, slicing particleboard, the imported knives and the Lion knives dulled at about the same rate. Afterward, they still cut wood accurately but did not achieve the glass-smooth surface.

All told, trimmers are easy to learn to use and maintain. Their lifetime is practically unlimited, and they may prove handier than expected: They make outstanding endgrain chamfers, for example, and can be coaxed into nibbling corners round. But now that you may want one, how do you choose which to buy?

Rating the tools—The Lion is made in Claremont, N.H., and is sold for about $250 by Pootatuck Corp., P.O. Box 24, Windsor, Vt. 05089; (802) 674-5984. It may also be purchased from a number of mail-order houses. AMT (American Machine & Tool Co., Inc.,

Fourth Ave. and Spring St., Royersford, Pa. 19468; 215-948-3800) introduced their Taiwan copy two years ago for about $150. Grizzly (Box 2069, Bellingham, Wash. 98227; 206-647-0801 or 2406 Reach Road, Williamsport, Pa. 17701; 717-326-3806) followed with theirs just last November for $120.

Is the Lion worth $100 more than the AMT and $130 more than the Grizzly? Maybe yes, maybe no. The question boils down to a series of gives-and-takes. To help you make up your mind, here are some impressions:

Woodworker Larry Green of Bethel, Conn., bought an AMT trimmer two years ago. He had been bandsawing mitered boxes, then tediously handplaning the miters smooth. He thought the AMT would save that step and be more accurate in the bargain. Having seen and used a Lion since, he says he wishes he had bought the Lion instead. Green's main complaint with the import was the condition of the knives, which were incompletely ground, leaving a rough and pitted inclusion on the cutting edge. AMT has a good reputation for dealing with defects, but Green wanted to get on with his work. So instead of sending the tool back, he painstakingly reground the defective knife himself, which took the best part of a Saturday afternoon. He also notes that his machine's main casting shows severe pitting and inclusions, cosmetic defects that trap dirt and may also prove potential breaking points in the iron.

The AMT we borrowed from the importer had very minor pitting, and its knives were razor sharp. But the knife carriage had noticeable play in it and the action wasn't as smooth as the Lion. A $100 difference? To my eye, not if judged pound for pound, nut for nut, spring for spring. But such subtle differences do begin to add up, at least in my mind.

The Grizzly arrived in excellent shape. Castings were clean, and knife movement was a little smoother than the AMT. In fact, it was so good that my suspicions were aroused: How could something as nicely finished as this possibly sell for only $119.95 postpaid?

I asked another editor to order one off the shelf and have it shipped to his home address. It arrived in a week, and to my surprise, was almost as nice as the one we'd borrowed. Minor shipping damage cracked one wing nut, whereby the "brass" revealed itself to be plated pot metal. There was inconsequential pitting along the front of the casting, one of the knives was slightly off-line (shimming would fix it), the knives had a couple of minor chips and the handle wouldn't seat fully in the slot in the gear (just like the first one, whose handle has fallen out a couple of times; the mis-fit is visible in the top photo on the facing page). The importer had clearly looked over the machine we'd borrowed, cleaning up the Cosmoline shipping grease and possibly honing the knives, but you can't blame a company for trying to put its best foot forward.

As noted earlier, everyone who compared the machines preferred the Lion, not just for its slightly neater castings and general look of quality, but for its clearly smoother action and precise feel. The other machines could be made to work about as well, but it would take some time with a file, some time to hone the knives, and a trip to the hardware store to replace cheap screws and fittings. That may well be the route a lot of woodworkers will choose; the price war is clearly on and the imports give a lot for the money. My personal vote, however, still goes to the Lion. Price differences soon depreciate away and are forgotten, while a manufacturer's initial attention to quality affects a tool's whole working life, and hence the satisfaction of owning and using it. □

Jim Cummins is an associate editor at Fine Woodworking. *His frame shop is in Woodstock, N.Y.*

Making and Using a Northwest Coast Adze

A fast cutter that also finishes

by Gregg Blomberg

Gregg Blomberg's gutter-style adze with yew handle finished with shark oil. Adze is shown ¾ of actual size.

When Captain Cook visited the Northwest Coast of North America in 1778, he was impressed by the woodwork done by the native American craftsmen—carved and painted totem poles showing family crests and mythical creatures, canoes, masks, chests, boxes and other items. The tools used by the Indians were basically the same as those found today: the adze and the crooked knife. The Indians had both D-adzes and elbow adzes, but in this article I'll concentrate on the elbow adze. Today's wood sculptors and carvers, even those who don't carve in the Northwest Coast tradition as I do, have discovered that properly designed adzes are precise tools, capable of repeatedly removing paper-thin chips.

The most crucial element of elbow adze design is what I call Holm's Constant, after Northwest scholar, author and artist Bill Holm, who first noted it: "The edge of a hand adze blade must be at right angles to the first finger," as shown in the drawing on the facing page. If you follow this rule, regardlesss of the angle of the haft or the length of the blade, the edge will crisply enter and exit the wood, turning a chip as it goes. Vary this angle much and the adze digs in or requires an unnatural swing to get the edge to cut.

In practice, Holm's Constant will vary somewhat depending on wrist length, natural stroke and actual blade shape, but by following these instructions you'll be able to make a first-rate tool. The two common types of elbow adzes are the shaping adze, for roughing out and hollowing, and the surfacing or texturing adze, for producing the final, evenly textured surface. The two adzes are similar, except that the haft of the texturing adze is cut away between the head and grip to give the tool extra spring for popping out chips. This springiness also reduces shock to the wrist and elbow. The surfacing adze has an acute profile, and the point on the haft to which the blade relates at 90° shifts upward somewhat, closer to the head, than on a shaping adze.

The first step in making a Northwest-style adze is to find a crook with a suitable elbow shape for the type of adze you want. Almost any hardwood tree will do. I've used yew, maple, apple, plum and alder. The crooks can vary quite a bit and still be functional.

If you choose a crook with an angle that's too acute for a shaping adze, even though you've satisfied Holm's Constant and the tool cuts well, its head will bang into the work if you try to carry the stroke through. This is true to some extent on all Northwest-style adzes and can help stop a dangerous understroke. There is no banging of the adze against the work in normal cutting. The eye and hand automatically coordinate to use the energy for the actual cut, and there is no carry through. Of course, if the crook is quite steep, you can fudge a bit and carve some of the angle out of it. A crook too acute for a shaping adze often makes a perfect finishing adze.

Select a crook that will allow you to lay out the head of the adze parallel with the tree trunk or main branch. The secondary branch will become the handle. Cut the haft blank as shown in the drawing, then make or buy your iron. Most likely, you'll choose either the straight or gutter configuration shown. The gutter blades are better for cross-grain cutting and hollowing; straight blades are used for shaping and texturing.

I usually begin with 1¼-in.-wide 1084 steel, either ³⁄₁₆ in. or ¼ in. thick, about 6 in. long. I prefer plain high-carbon steel for edge-holding in wood. Carbon steels from C1070 to C1095, W-1 or 0-1 steel (available from local industrial supply houses and MSC Industrial Supply Co., 151 Sunnyside Blvd., Plainview, Long Island, N.Y. 11803) will work. I think the water-hardening steel has better edge-holding abilities than oil-hardening steel. Probably the most important source for adze irons has been old files, but I dislike them because their high carbon content tends to make them brittle. It's important to fully anneal these steels, especially file steel, to relieve all internal stresses before final heat-treating.

When heat-treating the iron, quench in warm light oil and tem-

From *Fine Woodworking* magazine (March 1987) 63:58-60

Author Blomberg roughs out a coyote forehead mask with his adze. The mask, which will be attached to a coyote hide, is similar to ceremonial masks traditionally made by Northwest Coast Indians. The key to making accurate cuts with the adze is to brace your arm against your body and take many light cuts with the razor-sharp tool, rather than fewer, more forceful strokes.

per slowly over a hot plate to a medium straw color. (For another method of heat-treating, see p. 49.) The angle of the blade bevel should be from 20° to 30°, no matter how it's shaped; 25° seems best for edge support and easy entry of the blade into the work. A heavy adze used for hogging may benefit from the steeper angle since a low angle may tend to "stick" when driven into the wood. When hollowing beyond the normal stroke, the adze is often used for "scoring" from each side, making a number of cuts and breaking out the chips. If the adze sticks, a twisting motion at the end of each stroke frees it. Hone your iron razor sharp. The gutter blades must be sharpened from inside the bevel with slip stones. In fact, resharpening is usually done on the inside of the blade so as to not change Holm's Constant.

Once you have your iron in hand, draw your adze profile on the haft blank. Lay the iron on the blank and play with the relationships using a square. You want a layout that satisfies Holm's Constant, seems balanced and is attractive. Then cut out your haft. Shape the haft with a crooked knife or a rasp, and secure the blade to the top of the adze with a stainless steel hose clamp. Slide the iron back and forth, trying different positions. The hose clamp will hold the iron so tightly that you may not want to notch the haft until you've had a chance to work with the tool for a while. Once you've found the position you like best, mark and cut the notch, being careful not to change the angle. The ¼ in. or so difference in depth, caused by lowering the iron into its notch, won't alter the action noticeably. I coat the iron with a thin coat of nondrying Prussian blue (available at industrial suppliers) and try it in place on the haft. The blue marks the high spots that need to be carved away. Repeat the paint-and-carve sequence until the pieces fit snugly. In some combinations, it may be necessary to trim the butt end of the iron. If it's too hard to hacksaw, grind it or use a metal cutoff blade in a Skilsaw.

Once the notch is cut, hose-clamp the iron into it and try cutting. The wrist and forearm provide the driving force, while the elbow is braced against the side for added control. Working with a natural wrist motion, you should see the blade enter and leave a flat surface, turning a chip on the way. The adze should be perfectly tuned at this point, but if you're having trouble reaching the wood, re-

Elbow adzes

1. Preparing crooks

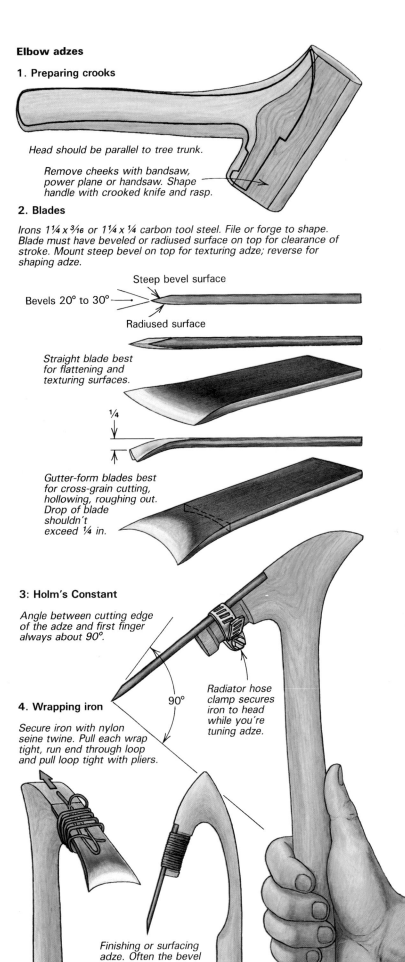

Head should be parallel to tree trunk.

Remove cheeks with bandsaw, power plane or handsaw. Shape handle with crooked knife and rasp.

2. Blades

Irons 1¼ x ³⁄₁₆ or 1¼ x ¼ carbon tool steel. File or forge to shape. Blade must have beveled or radiused surface on top for clearance of stroke. Mount steep bevel on top for texturing adze; reverse for shaping adze.

Steep bevel surface

Bevels 20° to 30°

Radiused surface

Straight blade best for flattening and texturing surfaces.

¼

Gutter-form blades best for cross-grain cutting, hollowing, roughing out. Drop of blade shouldn't exceed ¼ in.

3: Holm's Constant

Angle between cutting edge of the adze and first finger always about 90°.

90°

4. Wrapping iron

Secure iron with nylon seine twine. Pull each wrap tight, run end through loop and pull loop tight with pliers.

Radiator hose clamp secures iron to head while you're tuning adze.

Finishing or surfacing adze. Often the bevel is on only the top of the blade, the haft is cut away to allow it to spring, popping out the chip.

duce the angle of the blade to the haft (make it less acute), shorten the iron, or grasp the haft higher up. Conversely, if the adze tends to bite and stick in the wood, increase the angle, substitute a longer iron or grip the tool farther down the haft. Once your adze is tuned, you can replace the hose clamp with a wrapping of seine twine used by commercial fisherman, or some other strong, thin line, as shown in the drawing on the previous page.

In use, the surfacing adze has a distinct feel and action. You'll find that you naturally adjust your wrist angle, and the position of your grip on the haft, so that the adze strikes the wood near the outside of its cutting range. Upon entering the wood, the cut-away haft springs inward, popping out the chip. The force must be strong enough to cause the haft to spring. If using this tool seems like hard work, your haft probably isn't springy enough.

The surfacing adze cuts at an angle of up to 45° to the grain of the wood. Use light, rapid strokes. A sharp blade is an absolute necessity—I strop often as I work. It's a constant challenge to keep the cuts regular as I work around curves, knots and squirrelly areas. Laid down in a regular pattern, the resulting texture is attractive, and considered by some a hallmark of Northwest Coast work. □

Gregg Blomberg operates Kestrel Tool in Lopez, Wash., and has published monographs on making elbow adzes and kerf-bent boxes. For more information about adzes and crooked knives, and tool making supplies, write him at Rt. 1, Box 1762, Lopez, Wash. 98261. Catalogs are $1, refundable with first order.

Getting the hang of an ancient tool

by Simon Watts

The adze is one of those Stone Age survivors that's too useful to become extinct. It is deceptively simple—a free-swinging iron with a very sharp cutting edge that resembles a garden hoe. In expert hands, an adze can remove wood with precision, but a novice can lame himself for life with one hasty swipe.

Since it looks ancient and requires so much skill, the adze enjoys a certain mystique among the new breed of boatbuilders. You often see an adze hanging on the wall, like a kind of diploma, while the electric buzz plane does the work.

In the days before powered machinery for squaring beams, the adze and hewing ax dressed out large timbers. The conspicuous marks left by these tools are easily recognizable in Colonial house frames and wooden ships. One of the most common adzes in this country was the long-handled railroad adze, which had a 4-lb. to 6-lb. head forged with a maul head opposite the straight blade. The cutting end dressed down the ties; the maul end drove the spikes that fastened the tracks to the ties. These tools were only for rough work because the corners of the blade inevitably dug into the wood grain and tore it up.

A curved adze, which resembles a ½-lb. to 1½-lb. carving gouge, has a straight or bent blade and is usually mounted on a handle short enough to be used one-handed. Thus, it's well-suited for roughing out large sculptures and for hollowing chair seats, canoes or bowls. It removes wood quickly, but leaves conspicuous tool marks. As with any adze, it works best in green or partially dry wood.

In the mid-19th century, American tool makers combined the straight and curved profiles to produce the lipped or shipwrights' adze, which was more versatile than any of its predecessors. Its blade is slightly curved, and each corner turns up sharply to form a lip that won't dig into the wood. When used across or diagonal to the grain, the sharpened lip shears off the wood fibers before they can tear out. In skilled hands, the lipped adze can remove great quantities of wood, as well as dress down a surface so that the individual strokes are barely visible. Thus, it's ideal for smoothing timbers or floors and trimming boat keels and ribs, especially in tight places and on curved surfaces.

It takes years of practice to master the lipped adze. It can also be outright dangerous. When working at floor level, dressing down a new deck or standing on a log being squared, the worker swings the blade toward his own feet. Apprentices were advised, facetiously perhaps, to stand in a couple of nail kegs until they got the hang of it. To see how a modern worker uses an adze, I visited Bob Darr, director of the Center for Wood Arts in San Rafael, Calif., who claims the adze is his favorite tool. Darr encourages his students to use the lipped adze because of its versatility, but the principles apply to other

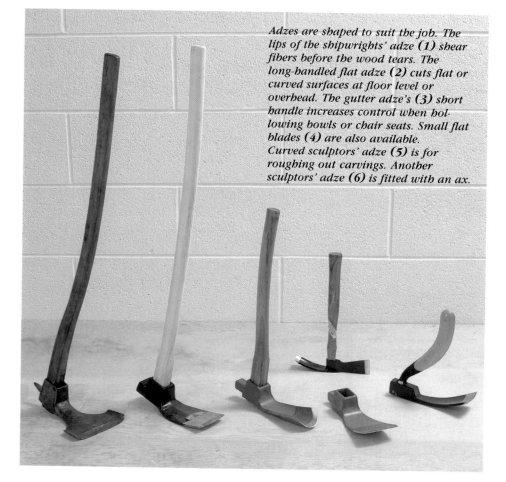

Adzes are shaped to suit the job. The lips of the shipwrights' adze (1) shear fibers before the wood tears. The long-handled flat adze (2) cuts flat or curved surfaces at floor level or overhead. The gutter adze's (3) short handle increases control when hollowing bowls or chair seats. Small flat blades (4) are also available. Curved sculptors' adze (5) is for roughing out carvings. Another sculptors' adze (6) is fitted with an ax.

From *Fine Woodworking* magazine (March 1987) 63:60-61

types as well. Students at the school use adzes to shape keels, cut the long notches or rabbets for planking and dress down sawn frames to correct bevels.

To demonstrate how to use the lipped adze, Darr set up a 6x12 block of Douglas fir and drew a couple of guidelines on adjacent faces. The general strategy is to cut across the grain, or along a diagonal. Cutting parallel to the grain may tear up slivers, if the wood fibers happen to be slanting the wrong way. (Incidentally, the process isn't called "adzing," but rather "dubbing" and the workers are called dubbers, perhaps because of the characteristic sound an adze makes). He stood about 2 ft. from the timber, gripping the tool with both hands. Then he began chopping notches in the wood, a process called "leading in." He continued taking successive bites at several spots until the blade of the adze just touched the line. Keeping his body in the same stance, Darr swung the adze head in an arc from about his elbow. "It's like you have a third arm," he remarked. After leading in at a couple of spots farther along, he dubbed off the wood remaining between the openings, smoothing the chamfer. Heavy flakes of wood, ½ in. to ¾ in. thick, fell until the ground was covered. As he approached the lines, the shavings became finer, until they barely floated down.

Before an adze will work well, you may have to adjust the blade a little. The angle between the cutting edge and the handle, the "hang" illustrated in the drawing, is critical. If the hang isn't right, the tool will glance off or dig into the work as shown. A lipped adze with a 34-in. handle normally has a hang of ⅝ in. to ⅞ in. To adjust the hang, trim the front of the handle where it fits into the head, until the head can be tilted to the proper angle, then lock the head in place with a wooden or metal wedge inserted between the front narrow edge of the handle and the head. If the handle projects through the head, it must be trimmed off flush or it will strike the work surface with a jolt.

I've found that the short-handled adzes are easier to learn how to use. Experienced workers generally prefer short-handled adzes for rough work. Longer handles are common on adzes used for finishing and for work at floor level—three feet is about right for the average male. The long handle can also be used effectively at waist height or overhead.

Adzes are usually sharpened with a file, rather than an abrasive wheel, which could require removing the head from the handle. Darr clamps his adze in a vise, so the cutting edge is parallel to the ground and facing him, then files and hones the edge, as shown in the photos at right. Fil-

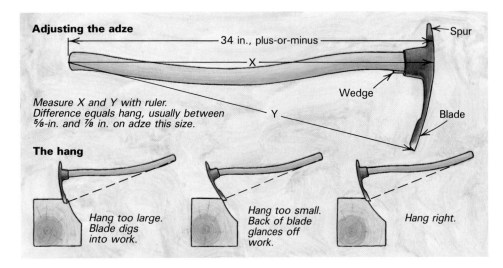

Adjusting the adze

34 in., plus-or-minus

X

Spur

Wedge

Blade

Measure X and Y with ruler. Difference equals hang, usually between ⅝-in. and ⅞ in. on adze this size.

Y

The hang

Hang too large. Blade digs into work.

Hang too small. Back of blade glances off work.

Hang right.

A razor-sharp adze precisely cuts to the line drawn along a Douglas fir beam. The spur shown is often used as a built-in nail set. A worker can quickly sink a nail below the surface, out of harm's way, then continue cutting.

A mill file is used to joint the edge of the adze, and round the corners of the blade slightly so the center cuts into the wood first. The inside corners are sharpened with a round file, rotated slightly on each stroke to prevent grooving.

After establishing the 25° bevel and sharpening the edge with a flat mill file, Darr hones the back of the adze with a medium India whetstone, following with a flat, medium Arkansas stone.

ing takes about 15 to 20 minutes, but unless you hit a nail or otherwise damage the edge, you won't have to do it very often. Honing, three or four times a day when the adze is in constant use, is the best way to maintain the edge. Darr also believes the edge lasts longer if you cut rather gently for the first few strokes, until the edge is slightly burnished. Then it will withstand heavier use without damage.

Due to the decline in wooden shipbuilding, shipwrights' adzes are no longer produced in this country, although German imports do occasionally turn up in mail-order catalogs. Other types of adzes are readily available. Darr advises anyone wanting a good lipped adze to try to find one secondhand. The best names are Collins and White. Make sure repeated filings haven't removed too much metal. A new lipped adze should have at least 2¾ in. of blade. If more than an inch is gone, you probably don't want it. Whether it's worth your time to find an adze and learn to use it depends upon your attitude toward wood and what work interests you. If you enjoy mastering ancient skills and prefer working the wood, instead of processing it by machines, then an adze may be the challenge you're looking for. □

Simon Watts lives in San Francisco and teaches wooden boatbuilding in seminars throughout the country.

Sources of supply

Secondhand lipped adzes can be ordered from the Wooden Boat Shop, 1007 N.W. Boat St., Seattle, WA 98105. Prices range from $55 to $85, depending on brand. Lipped adze irons are available from Kestrel Tool.

Short- and long-handled adzes are available from Garrett Wade Corp., 161 Avenue of the Americas, New York, NY 10013; Lee Valley Tools, 2680 Queensview Dr., Ottawa, Ontario K2B 8H6; Woodcraft Supply Corp., 41 Atlantic Ave., PO Box 4000, Woburn. MA 01888; Frog Tool Company, 700 W. Jackson Blvd., Chicago, IL 60606.

Grinding Wheel Primer
Choosing the best wheel for your steel

by Jerry Glaser

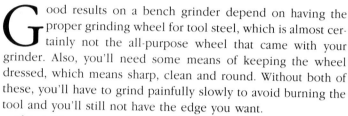

Good results on a bench grinder depend on having the proper grinding wheel for tool steel, which is almost certainly not the all-purpose wheel that came with your grinder. Also, you'll need some means of keeping the wheel dressed, which means sharp, clean and round. Without both of these, you'll have to grind painfully slowly to avoid burning the tool and you'll still not have the edge you want.

About 25 years ago, I was really frustrated with grinding. The wheel on my power grinder seemed as likely to burn the steel as sharpen it. The wet sandstone wheel I had bought as a cure was almost worthless. Then one day at work I happened to notice that the guys in the tool room were grinding with white wheels, not gray, and I started asking questions. (The company I work for uses half-a-million dollars worth of abrasives a year, for grinding everything from turbocharger parts to bronze bushings. The wheels range anywhere from 3 in. on up to monsters 30 in. in diameter and 6 in. wide.)

Notice the chart on the facing page. All American-made grinding wheels are marked, on the paper washer at the side of the wheel, with a series of letters and numbers that tell you the wheel's characteristics. This code covers the type and coarseness of the abrasive (the hard grains in the wheel that actually do the grinding) and the type and concentration of the material used to hold the grit together, called the bond. There isn't room in a magazine article to cover all the grinding wheel variations (and I admit that in some places I'll be simplifying things), but here's what you should know about choosing a wheel for grinding woodworking tools.

Let's cover the simplest thing first, the bond type, which can be V, S, R, B, E, or O. For our purposes, you can forget any bond type but V, or vitrified, which means that the abrasive particles are held together by ceramic material fused in a furnace—the other bonds are mostly for high-speed cutoff wheels and other industrial applications far removed from tool grinding. A vitrified wheel is similar to glass or china, which makes it waterproof (and oil proof), allowing it to be cooled if you are so inclined. It is perfectly safe to use a misting or spraying system when grinding, but don't allow a wheel to sit with one edge in water; enough may soak in to leave the wheel dangerously unbalanced the next time it's turned on.

The next symbol to consider is the type of abrasive. Diamond and the new cubic boron nitride are out of this discussion because of their cost, at least five to ten times more than the standard abrasives, namely silicon carbide and aluminum oxide. Silicon-carbide (C) wheels may be green or black in color. They are used for grinding cast iron, brass and aluminum, and the green ones can sharpen carbide tools. They are not a good choice for tool steel, however, because the individual grain particles lose their sharp edges in use, and the dull grit generates heat without removing steel. In contrast, aluminum-oxide (A) wheels remain sharp because the individual grit particles fracture and chip in use, constantly exposing new cutting edges.

There are a few different kinds of aluminum oxide, distinguished by color. The familiar gray wheel, the one that comes with the grinder, is not a bad choice for all-purpose grinding. But the other aluminum oxides, which are white, off-white, or pink are a better choice for tool grinding because the grains fracture more easily—the wheel grinds cooler, stays sharper and requires less frequent dressing to keep it clean of embedded steel particles.

If you're looking at wheels on the shelf, you can see the color. If ordering sight-unseen from a catalog, look for a qualifying number ahead of the A in the code—Norton's white wheels (off-white, actually) are called 32A, for example, and Bay State's are called 9A. Any of these pink or white wheels is an excellent choice for both carbon steel and high-speed steel.

The remaining part of the code—the grain size, the structure and the bond grade—is more complicated because each is interrelated with the others.

The *grain size,* ranging from 10 up to 600, refers to the size of each particle, and is the same grading used for sandpaper: Grain particles are sorted by passing them through a series of screens with larger or finer openings. Other things being equal, the large grains in a 36-grit wheel remove steel more quickly and with less heat than the finer grains of a 100-grit wheel, but the tool's surface will be rougher and require more honing before it can be used.

The *structure* of a wheel refers to how much open space there is between grit particles, and is designated by a number ranging from 1 to 15. The higher the number, the more space between particles. Wheels in the 5-to-8 range are all good for grinding tools. Generally speaking, if two wheels are the same grit size, 60 let's say, an 8 structure will grind faster than a 5, and will run a little cooler. But the denser 5 wheel will grind a smoother surface. Thus, structure tends to "modify" grit size—a dense 60-grit wheel acts like it has finer grit, and an open one acts coarser.

The *bond grade* of a wheel, ranging from A to Z, tells you how much bonding material is in the wheel. The less bonding material, the faster the wheel will shed grains from the surface during grinding, and the more self-cleaning and self-sharpening the wheel will be. Harder wheels hold each grit particle longer, and thus have a longer life. Wheels in the H to M range are all good for grinding tools. The H (softer) wheel will wear out faster, but

From *Fine Woodworking* magazine (November 1986) 61:52-54

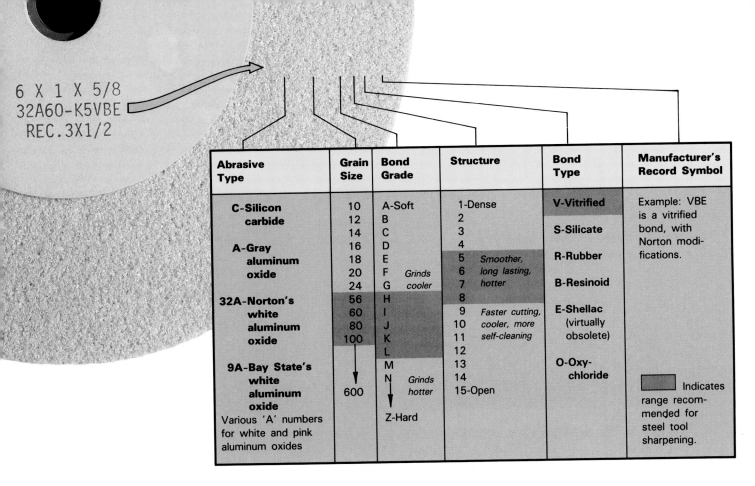

6 X 1 X 5/8
32A60-K5VBE
REC.3X1/2

Abrasive Type	Grain Size	Bond Grade	Structure	Bond Type	Manufacturer's Record Symbol
C-Silicon carbide	10	A-Soft	1-Dense	V-Vitrified	Example: VBE is a vitrified bond, with Norton modifications.
	12	B	2		
	14	C	3	S-Silicate	
A-Gray aluminum oxide	16	D	4		
	18	E	5 *Smoother,*	R-Rubber	
	20	F *Grinds cooler*	6 *long lasting,*		
	24	G	7 *hotter*	B-Resinoid	
32A-Norton's white aluminum oxide	56	H	8		
	60	I	9 *Faster cutting,*	E-Shellac (virtually obsolete)	
	80	J	10 *cooler, more*		
	100	K	11 *self-cleaning*		
		L	12		
9A-Bay State's white aluminum oxide		M	13	O-Oxy-chloride	
	600	N *Grinds hotter*	14		
			15-Open		
Various 'A' numbers for white and pink aluminum oxides		Z-Hard			

Indicates range recommended for steel tool sharpening.

it won't clog as quickly and will grind cooler than the M wheel. Bond grade modifies grit size in the same way structure does—a hard, 60-grit wheel cuts finer, and hotter, than a soft one.

So, what's the best wheel for you? As a woodturner, I do a lot of grinding of both carbon steel and alloy steel, and I use a Norton 32A60K5VBE grinding wheel. Disregarding the 32A (Norton's white aluminum oxide) and the VBE (vitrified, the BE is a Norton code and pretty much immaterial to us), the important part is 60K5. Because I spend a lot of time at the grinder, I like a 60-grit wheel. It removes metal quickly and coolly, yet leaves the tool smooth enough to hone easily. I could probably get used to a 54-grit wheel just as well, but wouldn't want to go much coarser and still hone by hand.

I also like a dense wheel (the 5) because it lasts. If you want a wheel like mine, your best bet is to shop at your local industrial-hardware or machine-shop supplier (larger Yellow Pages often have a separate listing under "Abrasives"). Specify the wheel diameter and arbor size to fit your grinder.

I find my wheel ideal for lathe tools, but someone with less practice grinding might prefer a softer, more open wheel that would be less likely to overheat the tool. If so, you don't have to look far. Woodcraft Supply (P.O. Box 4000, Woburn, Mass. 01888) sells a 9A60J8V5 wheel in 6 in. and 7 in. diameters. The wheel is made by Bay State, and 9A is their code for white aluminum oxide. Woodcraft also sells 6-in. and 7-in. wheels of 9A100I8V, which should be good for very fine grinding of small carving tools and the like. Prices range from $23.50 to $33.50 (depending on the size), which is about what I'd expect to pay for a well-made wheel. But you might consider shopping around locally to see if you can get a better bargain—now that you understand the code, you might find a very usable wheel on sale for half what it's really worth.

I advise against buying an inexpensive imported wheel, which is likely to contain a percentage of low-cost, low-performance abrasive, such as flint.

Mounting and dressing a wheel—As mentioned earlier, a vitrified wheel is glass-like, and a new one should always be tested for cracks. Put a dowel through the hole to suspend the wheel, then tap the side with a small piece of hardwood. A good wheel will ring. A cracked wheel will sound dull, like a cracked baseball bat. The drawing below shows how to mount the wheel.

All grinding wheels are labeled with the maximum safe speed, but this is not likely to be a factor unless you're working with a shopmade grinder that has been set up with an unsuitable pulley combination or fitted with a too-large grinding wheel. The usual commercial grinder has protective shrouds that limit wheel size, and the motor speed is chosen accordingly.

The first order of business when you turn a grinder on is to stand to the side for a minute or so, to be sure that the wheel is not going to fly apart. Obviously, any guards and side shrouds should be in place before running the machine.

Once the wheel is mounted, it will have to be dressed true to the arbor. A wheel running out-of-round will cause the tool to bounce around and make smooth grinding impossible. Dressing, which means scraping or chipping away the high spots while the wheel is turning, is the cure. Dressing is also used to rejuvenate a wheel that has become dull or clogged with metal particles; it trues the surface of a wheel that has become rounded or grooved, and can also shape the profile of a wheel for special jobs, like regrinding the flute of a gouge.

There are basically four dif-

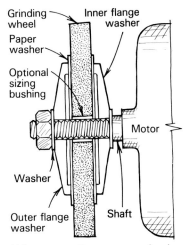

When mounting a new wheel, clean the shaft of grit and remove any paper-washer residue from the flange washers. Do not overtighten nut.

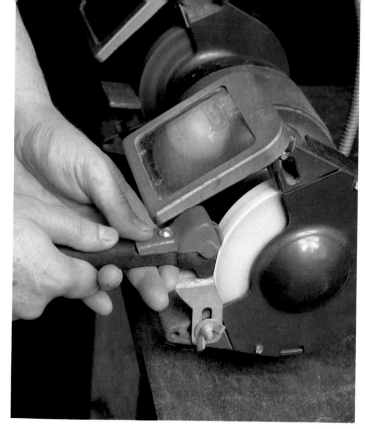

Norton's 60-grit wheel, off-white in color, with a variety of wheel dressers (shown counterclockwise from top): a star wheel, a single-point diamond, a Norbide stick and a plain abrasive stick.

ferent tools that can be used to dress a wheel. The simplest and least satisfactory is nothing more than an old piece of coarse grindstone or the coarse abrasive sticks sold for the purpose. The second type is the star-wheel dresser, which chips away at the surface of the wheel removing large quantities of grit quickly. Then there are diamond dressers and finally boron-carbide sticks (Norton calls theirs Norbide), both of which are hard enough to wear the wheel down. All of these dressers should be available at the nearest industrial hardware supply house.

The star-wheel dresser is the best tool for the initial dressing for the simple reason that its mass, width and fierce chipping action make it easy to get the wheel true. The usual diamond dresser, in contrast, cuts at a single point, and must be rigidly controlled in a straight, square path across the wheel to work effectively. If your grinder has a tool-holding setup that will accomplish this, then a single-point diamond dresser will work fine, but otherwise, a diamond dresser may leave a wheel grooved and more out-of-round than it was to start with. You can buy multi-point diamond dressers, which are easier to use, but these are expensive and a star wheel costs less than $10.

To dress a wheel, support the star-wheel dresser against the tool rest and bring the star wheels into full contact with the rotating grinding wheel. Then sweep the dresser across the face of the grinding wheel using only a light force to push the two together. After a couple of passes the wheel should be running true. Wear safety glasses and a face mask during the operation. The peripheral speed of a grinding wheel can approach 60 MPH, and dressed-off grit particles will be traveling at this speed.

A star-wheel dresser tends to open up a wheel, leaving the surface rougher than it will be after you've ground a few tools on it. This is because some of the freshly exposed grit has higher cutting edges than the other particles. The effect can be a good thing because the wheel will run cool, but the wheel will also cut a little coarser. For a finer grind, re-dress the wheel very lightly with a diamond or a carbide stick.

As a last note, most wheels are marked "Do Not Grind on Side." There are a few reasons for this: First, it's less efficient to grind on the side of a wheel because the surface speed is less than on the face. Also, when the side of a wheel becomes glazed and clogged it is much more difficult to dress. Another problem is the danger of grooving or undercutting the wheel, which might weaken it to the point where it could shatter. Occasional light grinding on the side of a wheel shouldn't cause problems, but my general advice is to avoid it unless there is no other choice. □

Bottom photos show Bay State's 100-grit wheel before and after dressing. At left, after much grinding of lathe tools, the wheel is worn concave with some embedded steel particles, which cause excess heat. Top photo shows the initial coarse dressing with a star wheel; center photo shows final truing with a Norbide stick.

Jerry Glaser is manager of manufacturing engineering at Garrett Automotive Products Co., in Torrance, Calif.

Podmaniczky's favorite sharpening setup is the Multi-Stone (rear), a set of three stones mounted so they can revolve through an oil bath to keep them clean. His boxed stones, bought 15 years ago, are a medium-grit India (right) and a hard black Arkansas.

Sharpening With Oilstones
No jigs, no gadgets, no nonsense

by Michael S. Podmaniczky

There are legions of would-be woodworkers who think that the edge that their new chisel arrives with is forever. I know because I've met some of them. But charity and understanding are needed rather than contempt; after all, I hate to think what I will do the first time I have a masons' trowel in hand, or at which end of the cobblers' bench I would sit down. No, this sort of thing is not at all inherent and must be learned like everything else.

In fact, without a good grounding in sharpening procedures, nothing else that follows can be properly done, and that includes, well, everything. I hate to think how many beautiful projects have been discouraged because the tools just didn't perform as expected. Sharpening is so important that it must eventually become second nature to the wood craftsman. We will discuss the various steps necessary to take a chisel or plane iron from dull to sharp: establishing the bevel on the bench grinder and sharpening on the various stones, from coarse to fine. While this is a step-by-step procedure, I hope that in due time those steps will blend together in your subconscious so that there will be no more thinking, only doing.

Before doing, however, must come knowing. What exactly does "sharp" mean? We know the ideal, a perfect wedge of steel, tapering down to microscopic nothingness. Unfortunately, whether in foreign policy or tool handling, ideals are easier to imagine than to attain. When steel is pushed across even the finest stone, bits of metal are worn away and microscopic serrations are formed on the edge—these correspond in dimension to the grit of the stone. What we try to do is minimize the size of the serrations and maximize their regularity.

Most edge tools are pushed through the wood, and consequently require the finest serrations so as not to drag on the wood fibers. For this, a progression of stones is used, ending with the finest grit possible. A knife, drawknife, or other tool that is used in a slicing motion, such as (forgive me) a steak knife, works best with slightly greater, but still regular serrations on the edge. In this case, the progression through stone grits can stop short of the finest. Our task is to be able to consistently produce the edge we need for the best woodwork possible.

As I have said, this should be second nature, so I'm afraid that that means out with all the paraphernalia pushed by the tool

From *Fine Woodworking* magazine (November 1986) 61:55-59

catalogs to "help" with sharpening—jigs, holders, rollers, etc. You are perfectly capable of doing without all of that. There are, however, a few things you can't do without, such as benchstones, so let's discuss them first.

I don't much care for Japanese waterstones. One reason is that waterstones wear hollow much faster than the harder oilstones and must be regularly dressed in order to keep them flat.

I use oilstones, and feel that the best way to go, if you can afford it, is the Norton Multi-Stone. It holds a medium Crystolon stone, which you will use about once a year, a fine India, and a hard, black Arkansas (pronounced ar*kanz*as), both of which you will use almost every time you sharpen. These three stones are mounted on a shaft so they can be revolved through an oil bath to keep them clean.

Like the grinding wheel, benchstones are made up of many sharp micro-particles, bonded together in such a way that they cut steel until they are dull, and then wear away from the stone. Man-made Crystolon, a Norton trademark, is "soft," with large (relatively), loosely bonded particles; it cuts rapidly and wears down just as quickly. It's really only useful if you don't have a bench grinder and have to remove a lot of meat by hand. India (also a Norton trademark) is a bit finer grit and stronger bond (i.e. harder); it's the best all-around stone, well-made and well-wearing. Natural Arkansas stones can be purchased from coarse/soft to fine/hard, but with high-quality man-made stones available for most of the range, I stick with the top of the line—hard and black. These are the stones that surgeons sharpen scalpels with.

If you can't go the Multi-cost (about $175, from Woodcraft Supply, Box 4000, Woburn, Mass. 01888), buy the Norton combination stone (Crystolon on one side, fine India on the other),

and a separate, hard black Arkansas. Spend some money for a change: buy a bit of really nice exotic wood and make a couple of nice hinged-top boxes for the pair of them. This will keep them clean and give you the pride and confidence necessary to keep up a well-sharpened set of tools.

This brings me to another reason why I don't like waterstones. They are said to cut faster than the oilstones that we of Western tradition are used to, but this is a bit misleading. For one thing, the Japanese grit-numbering system is very different from the American. For example, a 1200-grit Japanese stone is roughly the equivalent of a 550-grit oilstone (about the grit of a soft Arkansas stone), and a 6000-grit Japanese stone is about the same as a hard Arkansas stone (our 800- to 1000-grit). If you compare the speed of cut between a 1000-grit Arkansas stone and a 6000-grit Japanese stone, you'll find that they are about the same and that they give an equivalent finish to the steel.

The other thing that affects cutting speed is the fluid used to keep the stone clean. A stone should be flooded with an appropriate liquid during sharpening in order to float particles of steel and stone away and prevent the abrasive from clogging up. Natural Arkansas, and most man-made stones, require the use of oil, other man-made stones require water. The problem is the common understanding of what is meant by "oil." I have actually heard responsible people say that the oil is used to *lubricate* the stone, so they use heavy, viscous oil (sometimes even marketed as "honing" oil) and it does indeed lubricate. Unfortunately that is the last thing one wants. We want friction, we want to abrade, so it's no wonder that waterstones seem to cut faster; there's less lubrication with waterstones, mostly abrasion.

I use a very light oil. Kerosene and fuel oil are about right, but I discovered a few years back that WD-40 not only has a good viscosity, it also doesn't smell bad on my hands. Unlike the use of water, residue on the tool inhibits, rather than promotes, rust. Buy WD-40 in the half-gallon jug and use it for everything except salad dressing. For your kitchen stone, try a little liquid dish-washing soap as a lubricant, or better still, Norton's honing oil, which is a highly refined mineral oil and safe to use around food.

The other stone you should be concerned about is the wheel on your grinder. There are volumes written on abrasive wheels (see "Grinding Wheel Primer," pp. 102-104). The different types of stones do different jobs and produce different finished surfaces, but since I put the important, finished edge on with benchstones, I just use what works for me, the white aluminum-oxide wheels sold by Woodcraft Supply. They wear down faster than gray wheels, but have less tendency to burn.

Given the lack of extended operation any of us will ever ask of our grinder, it's not necessary to go overboard buying one. Just be sure that it's well-anchored to your sharpening bench, and that there is plenty of room around it. I discard the tiny tool rests that are usually supplied with grinders and fabricate my own. The drawing at left shows my setup, which is versatile yet easy to make. It's merely a loose wooden rest held in position between two uprights by wingnuts and threaded rod. As shown in the detail, the tool rest can be used for sharpening jointer and planer knives. I clamp a metal ruler to the rest and run the knife along it. For fine adjustment, you can simply pivot one end of the ruler; it doesn't have to be exactly parallel to the face of the wheel.

Putting tool to stone—A plane iron is ground at approximately 25°, but a free-handed tool, such as a chisel, can be ground to a range of angles depending on the circumstances. A very fine angle, say 20°, will cut very nicely, but unfortunately will also break

Shopmade grinding guide

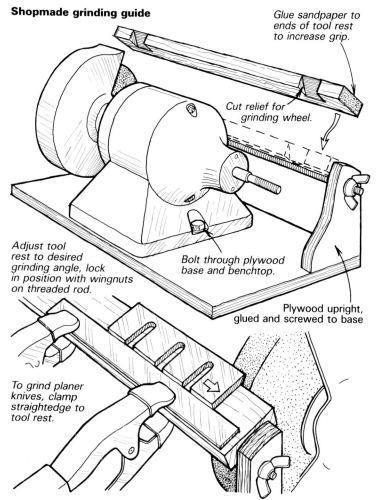

Glue sandpaper to ends of tool rest to increase grip.

Cut relief for grinding wheel.

Adjust tool rest to desired grinding angle, lock in position with wingnuts on threaded rod.

Bolt through plywood base and benchtop.

Plywood upright, glued and screwed to base

To grind planer knives, clamp straightedge to tool rest.

The other side of the edge

All the time in the world spent sharpening a bevel won't give you a sharp tool if the back of the edge is scratched, rusty or pitted. These imperfections cut into the edge from the back side. Just as a nicked jointer knife leaves its trail on the work, so does a chisel with a dull back.

Sharpening a bevel takes but a few seconds, for there is very little metal to be removed. Flattening and sharpening a back, however, is a long job. Here are a couple of extensions to the basic sharpening stones, which I learned of several years ago from Robert Meadow, of West Saugerties, N.Y., that can help bring your chisels to their full potential.

The first is a diamond plate, made by Eze-Lap, P.O. Box 2229, Westminster, Calif. 92683. The main virtues of the plate, which sells for about $55, are that the entire surface is covered with diamonds and that the plate is dead flat, which provides a reference surface—when the scratch pattern is even across the width of the chisel, then the chisel itself is flat.

You *could* stop right here. The flat back, by itself, will make your chisel a superior tool. You'll be able to pare with it flat, the edge will be straight, and the corners will be sharper than ever before. But you can still improve things.

Move to your coarse stone and make a few passes to see the new, finer, scratch pattern superimposed over the old. Use each stone in the series to remove the previous stone's scratches.

After the Arkansas stone, the final step is to buff the chisel back by pulling it across a hardwood block coated with rottenstone, a fine abrasive available in paint and hardware stores. To make the block, mix rottenstone with water and apply it as a thick paste. When the paste has dried, use the block as a strop, working away from the chisel edge, not into it, on both back and bevel. The photo at right shows the results, and I only wish chisels came like this in the first place.

The photos also show a new diamond-sharpening system developed by Robert Sorby in England. It consists of a flat ceramic tile and an aerosol can of diamond particles in a lubricating fluid. You spray diamond on the tile, then use it much like a regular sharpening stone.

There are three grits—medium, fine and super-fine—covering the range that compares with oilstones from coarse up to about fine India. At least, that's the way the cutting speed and polish seem to me. Each grit and its accompanying tile costs $53.50 (from Garrett Wade, 161 Ave. of the Americas, New York, N.Y. 10013).

Initial tests showed that it flattened chisel backs faster than anything. Further test-

The strong point of Robert Sorby's aerosol diamond slurry is the flatness it gives to the backs of chisels and plane irons. The diamond can also sharpen carbide router bits.

To extend the range of the typical sharpening stones, you can use a diamond plate for initial flattening, and a wooden block coated with rottenstone for final polishing. Mirror-like results are shown at right.

ing by woodworker Frank Klausz and his five-man crew in Pluckemin, N.J., suggested that the system wasn't at its best in all-around shop sharpening work. The slurry becomes black with metal particles almost instantly, requiring a woodworker to wash up before continuing work. The same metal particles quickly clog the lubricating fluid and slow the cutting action, tempting the user to spray another shot of expensive diamond on the tile. When Klausz ran out of spray, he figured the cost at $1 per tool, and was so unimpressed that he asked me to check with Sorby for their side of the story.

Sorby's technical spokesman, Tony Walker, said we had somewhat missed the point. After the first few sprayings, the tile should be used dry, until the diamond re-

maining on it ceases to cut. This cutting action may be slower than with fresh, wet diamond, but it will still do the job at a reasonable pace. The advantages of the tile are that it stays flat, like the diamond plate mentioned above, and that it can be used to sharpen high-speed steel tools with just a few light strokes. (High-speed tools, popular with woodturners, are notoriously difficult to sharpen with the softer abrasives found in regular honing stones). Also, Walker went on, the tile can be used to hone the flat faces of a carbide router bit. A couple of strokes each time you use the bit will keep it like new.   □

Jim Cummins is an associate editor of Fine Woodworking.

down most quickly. A blunter instrument, say 40°, won't break down as fast, but requires more muscle to drive into the work ("Hand me the commander!"). This all works out in practice, since the lovely carving and parting tools you use on fine work are hard enough to take a fine edge, and you would seldom put a mallet to them. Your mortise chisels or drawknife, at the other end of the spectrum, are made from softer, tougher steel, and therefore need a blunter edge, which in turn stands up longer to the abuse you'll deliver when using them.

As a matter of fact, those tools at the rough-and-tumble end of the tool kit—hatchets, axes, some drawknives, some adzes—can often be sharpened with a file to a slightly rounded, blunter edge, giving that edge longer life.

Adjust the tool rest on the grinder to the desired angle and begin removing steel, passing the blade back and forth across the face of the stone, keeping the forefinger of your holding hand tucked underneath and riding against the edge of the tool rest. This regulates constant but light pressure on the stone, which will hollow grind the tool bevel—producing in profile a concave bevel the same radius as the wheel—and removing steel much faster than you would be able to on the handstones. Light but firm—don't press down or hold the tool in one spot, or you'll burn the edge and ruin your day.

When you feel the tool heating up, remove it from the wheel and hold it in the draft of the grinder until it cools down. A lot of people cool the tool by dipping it in water from time to time as grinding proceeds, but I was once told by a blacksmith that such

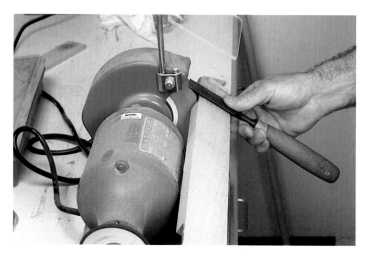

As a guide, Podmaniczky runs his forefinger along the front of his shopmade tool rest (see figure 1). Next, working at the ends of the stone, he hones the chisel with a circular motion, about as fast as you'd stir a cup of coffee. The grip maintains a steady angle and balanced pressure directly on the cutting edge.

treatment, if repeated often enough, can subtly affect the steel. I have quenched with water many times when I was in a hurry, but I don't feel comfortable with the practice.

Remember, if you blue the steel, the edge is shot, so you might as well start over. Don't try just lapping the blue surface oxidation off on a whetstone—it's a waste of time, because the steel underneath is still burned and softened. Set the angle of the tool rest to 90° and grind the tool edge blunt, square to the face of the wheel, until you are past the burned material (or the chip you took out of it when you dropped it on the cement, or hit that nail that wasn't there . . .). Reset the rest to the angle you are working on and resume grinding the bevel.

Never grind to a featheredge—It's almost impossible not to burn the steel if you allow it to get too thin; the heat just has nowhere to dissipate. As you grind, stop every so often to look at the bevel. The area that's cleanly ground will slowly increase as the area along the edge that had been previously hand stoned decreases. When your grinding is about a shy ¼₄ in. from the edge (or just touching the blunted edge you put on in the last paragraph) stop and move to the benchstones to finish removing metal right out to the edge.

Slosh the fine India with oil, or if you're using a Multi-Stone, give it a turn through the oil bath, and you're ready to go.

The next step is the dealer's choice: grip your tool. I'm afraid that there's no "one way" to do it. At one extreme is Ian Kirby's interlocking-fingers golf grip (which I have never been able to master), and at the other extreme is the three-fingered-with-one-hand-in-your-pocket grip (which I have always liked in a very cold boatshop). Any way that works is the right way. Try holding the plane iron or chisel with the right hand, leaving enough room to place one or two fingers of the left hand on the back of the blade near the edge to distribute the pressure evenly.

The object of this is to be able to set your blade to the stone at the desired angle, and hold that angle throughout the sharpening process, so as not to rock the tool and round the bevel. You'll practice with clenched teeth and white knuckles for what will seem like ages, and one day you'll realize that you can't re-member when you last thought about it . . . you'll be there.

Here's another plus for hollow grinding: Laying the bevel flat on the stone has a solid feel when both the edge and the heel of the bevel are in contact with the surface. Ever so slightly rock the heel off the stone, so that just the edge is in contact . . . and hold it! If you draw the tool back across the stone in this position, scraping oil away, you can then rock back and forth, heel to edge, and watch the little wake of oil form at the edge when the bevel is flat, and then flow away when the heel is picked up. All these little tricks can help you get used to the feel of the tool on the stone.

When you feel that you have a comfy grip, and can hold the angle, start moving the tool around the surface of the stone. Keep constant pressure on the edge with whatever fingers you have up there. A good rule of thumb is: keep the tool off the center of the stone. The natural impulse is to wear away in the middle, scrubbing away stone until there's a shallow dish instead of a nice, flat surface. This is a constant battle when you use waterstones, but even harder oilstones need to be dressed flat once in a very great while. To dress a stone, you can use coarse valve-grinding compound (from an auto supply store) spread on a sheet of plate glass. A few minutes spent rubbing the stone on the glass will flatten even a badly dished surface. Another way is to wet a sheet of coarse wet-and-dry sandpaper and lay this flat on a piece of plate glass (the water should hold it in place; if not,

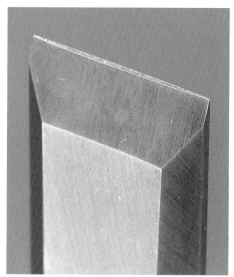

The hollow-ground bevel, directly from the grinding wheel. The old edge has been squared off on the wheel, and the grind stops just behind the flat spot, in order not to burn the steel.

As the edge is honed sharp, the excess metal may come off as a 'wire edge.' This chisel has been deliberately honed with more pressure on one corner than the other to demonstrate the wire.

It's a waste of effort to hone the entire bevel. After four or five more honings, the polished area at the cutting edge will become wide enough that it will be worthwhile to regrind the bevel.

you can tape it down before wetting). But this chore shouldn't be necessary very often, provided that you don't provoke the condition; my hard Arkansas has stayed flat for more than 15 years. "Stay in the corners and the middle will take care of itself," the old guy used to say, and he was right.

Stone the tool at whatever pace feels comfortable. I've seen even experienced woodworkers stone tools in a series of separate, measured straight strokes, stopping often to gaze at the developing edge...like they were grooming their Karma or something. But I got away from that a long time ago (by the time they're on their third stroke, I'm finished). I sharpen in small circles at the ends, or the corners if the tool is small, moving occasionally from one end to the other, working at about the speed I would stir a cup of coffee. Staying in one small area helps me keep that angle without rocking. I'll finish up with a few brisk forward and back strokes the length of the stone in order to align those serrations as regularly as possible.

As the metal wears away, the edge eventually becomes so thin that it can no longer support itself and begins to bend back and away; this is what's called the burr. When you feel it forming across the whole back of the edge, flip the tool over and hold it flat on its back, moving it about the stone until the burr is no longer felt on the back, but on the bevel side of the edge. Repeat both steps and the burr is almost ready to come off as a "wire edge." Draw the tool edge backward across a clean piece of leather, or your palm, first on one side and then the other, or work the burr back and forth with your thumb (carefully) until the wire edge comes off. During the process of forming the burr, it's imperative that the back of the tool is kept perfectly flat on the stone, since any rocking and consequent rounding of the back eliminates the jigging action that a straight edge gives when in use. Try paring with a cheap chisel that has been belt sanded to shape and you'll soon see what I mean.

After the burr has come off, a tool that's going to be used primarily in a slicing manner may be ready for use. Try it and see if it does what you want.

If you need a finer edge, move to the hard Arkansas, and repeat the same operation, only this time rock the tool up a degree or so, so that you are sure you are working right at the edge. You

will see a very fine, but unmistakable, polished line developing out at the business end of the tool. You will probably not bring up much of a burr on the hard stone, but if you do, and are able to work a wire off the edge, give the edge one or two extra passes along the stone in order to straighten out those micro-serrations. Trying to put what amounts to a polish on the whole bevel is time-consuming and unnecessary; after all, it's only the edge that's doing the cutting. A hard Arkansas doesn't take away much material per minute spent working on it, so don't beat yourself to death if you don't have to.

If you're new at this, and if you've been careful to follow the procedure, I can safely say that your tool is sharp, or at least that you'll be pleased with the results. There are a few esoteric ways of "testing" the sharpness you have achieved: Try shaving some hair from your arm *carefully*; lightly draw the edge in a slicing motion across the back of your thumbnail in order to feel if there are any invisible nicks; stand the blade on your thumbnail and see how far you can lower it down before it begins to slide across the surface of the nail; *look* at it. Except for looking, I don't do any of these things under normal circumstances, since, as I said, if everything was done right, the edge is sharp. If for some reason I'm not happy with the way the tool performs, I go back to the stones and freshen it up.

Work away until you notice that there has been backsliding by the tool to its old pre-sharpened tricks—there may be ridges developing on the wood due to tiny nicks or breaks in the edge; the cut surface is no longer clean and crisp—you'll know. For resharpening, stay with the benchstones until you have flattened out most of the hollow grinding on the bevel, or you've begun to round the bevel, or it's taking too long to bring back an edge. In order to bring up the burr, you'll find that you are ever so slowly increasing the angle to the stone with each subsequent sharpening, and it will eventually be necessary to grind again, establishing the hollow and proper bevel once more. You should be able to sharpen a chisel or plane iron in a minute or two, and get about four or five sharpenings per grinding. □

Michael Podmaniczky, a contributing editor for FWW, *works for the Williamstown (Mass.) Regional Art Conservation Laboratory.*

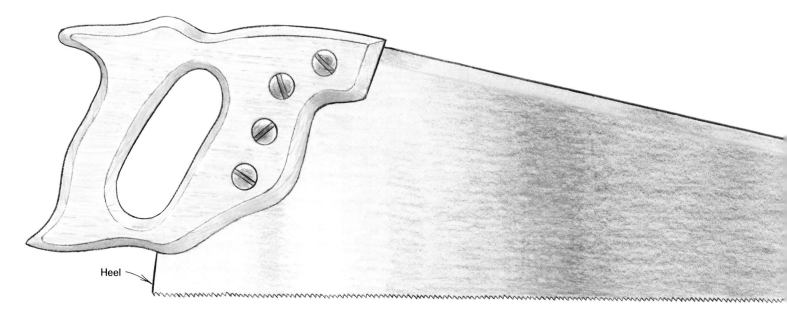

Heel

Sharpening Handsaws
It's a matter of knowing all the angles

by Harold H. Payson

Years ago, a visitor to my father's shop in Rockland, Me., spying the half-dozen or so heavily chewed file handles sitting on his filing bench, paused his conversation for a moment and asked, "You got rats?"

No, my father, Herman W. Payson, didn't have rats in his shop. What he had was the best reputation around for sharpening saws of any kind, especially handsaws—an honor not to be taken lightly. Many of the best ship and house carpenters in our area brought their handsaws to him and returned faithfully, time and time again. The handles on his files were chewed up not from rats, but from years of being lightly "thunked" on freshly sharpened sawteeth to remove the burr left by the file. If removal of the burr showed a tooth not brought up to a sharpened point, then that tooth received another swipe or two with the file until it did.

My dad's heyday was back in the 1930s, in the era before circular saws replaced handsaws as the common tool for cutting lumber on the construction site and shipyard. The handsaw that cut fast and true to the line without binding or rattling in its kerf was much admired and well remembered. Handsaws aren't as widely used as they once were, but that's no excuse for using a dull one or not knowing how to sharpen one properly. A properly sharpened handsaw is handy for jobs where a circular saw is dangerous or just unwieldily to use. If sharpened correctly, they make short work of most cutting tasks; improperly sharpened, they're drudgery to use.

Learning how to sharpen a handsaw isn't difficult, just time consuming. My father developed his reputation for sharpening handsaws over many years, and it took me a year of practice filing before he squinted down the teeth of my best efforts and

declared, "That's as good as I can do." Words I never thought I'd hear. Was it worth it? You bet.

It's rewarding to know that I can remedy a saw's problems myself with little fuss or lost time. I'll never have to put up with lame excuses from a saw-sharpening shop that they can't get around to sharpening a saw until next week. True, I can't match the precision of a saw-filing machine, but why should I? Small variations between teeth don't detract from a saw's cutting ability. A machine-sharpened saw does the job, but a saw sharpened by hand is a pleasure to use.

The problem with saw-filing machines (at least the ones I'm familiar with) is that each tooth is sharpened based on the profile of the tooth ahead of it. A dogged lever drops over each tooth and pulls the saw into position for a swipe of a file. If the saw was newly re-toothed and the teeth perfect, a machine does fairly well. But teeth damaged after hitting nails throw the machine off. The machine will position a tooth for a swipe of the file based on the shape of a damaged or misfiled tooth. The result is a saw with teeth spaced too wide or too close. In the process, some teeth may be filed to oblivion, in which case the saw has to be re-toothed. New teeth are stamped or filed on the saw, and more metal is removed from the blade in the process than a year's worth of sharpening would take.

Incidentally, I feel the same way about saw-filing gadgets as I do about filing machines. A friend of mine bought one that held a file on a slide. The entire contraption slid over the saw and the file was moved precisely back and forth over the teeth to produce any tooth angle wanted. However, it didn't allow you to file

From *Fine Woodworking* magazine (January 1988) 68:72-76

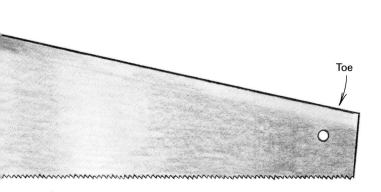

Toe

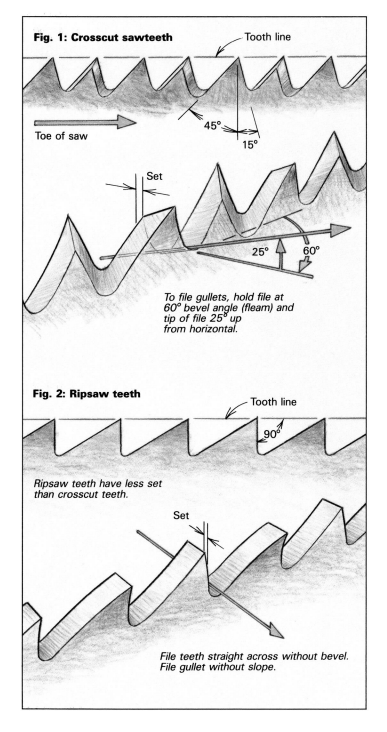

Fig. 1: Crosscut sawteeth

Tooth line

Toe of saw

45°

15°

Set

25°   60°

To file gullets, hold file at 60° bevel angle (fleam) and tip of file 25° up from horizontal.

Fig. 2: Ripsaw teeth

Tooth line

90°

Ripsaw teeth have less set than crosscut teeth.

Set

File teeth straight across without bevel. File gullet without slope.

sloping gullets, one of the chief advantages of hand filing. Also, there was no way of controlling side pressure on the file to correct teeth that were too large.

Before I tell you how to sharpen a saw, I'll outline the basic process. First, the saw is clamped in a saw vise. The teeth are jointed so their tops are flat and at the same height. Using a saw set, the teeth are then set (bent) left or right of the sawblade. The teeth are filed with identical cutting angles. Consequently, the teeth should all be the same in profile, with all their points at the same height. I will describe sharpening rip and crosscut saws, but the same techniques are used on backsaws and dovetail saws.

Don't be overconcerned about tooth pitch or bevels in this process. They are bound to vary slightly when you are first learning—you'll become more consistent with practice. Having said that, here's how to set yourself up for saw sharpening.

The filing bench—My bench is a 10-in.-wide by 5-ft.-long plank, and its top is belly-button height off the floor. For comfortable stand-up saw filing, each bench must be tailored to the filer, however. You can't sit while filing handsaws, you must stand and put your whole body into the stroke of the file, rocking back and forth while using your arms. This gives you better control over the file stroke and makes the job less tiring. I painted the bench-top flat black to ward off unwanted glare.

My filing bench is positioned in front of a west-facing window. My father's bench was in front of a south-facing window—other filers work best with a north-facing window. I don't give a hoot what direction the window faces, I just want all the light I can get as long as it falls on the sawteeth and not in my eyes. What about artifical light? Even when my eyesight was good I couldn't do a decent job under it. I don't recommend it now.

I lower a curtain partially over the window until a comfortable amount of light comes through, and improve the visibility of the sawteeth by tacking up a piece of tar paper above the window apron. When I look across the saw, the black background contrasts with the teeth, making burrs or minor irregularities more apparent.

The filing vise—Position the top of your vise at chest height to allow for proper visibility and arm comfort. While you can buy saw vises through many woodworking catalogues, you can make your own out of scrap wood, as I did. Each half of the vise consists of a vertical leg with a long jaw attached perpendicular to it, to form a "T". The two halves are bolted together with a fulcrum between them. A swinging handle is bolted between the halves, too. As the handle is swung up, an arc-shaped dome on the handle pushes against the vertical leg, tightening the vise. To loosen the vise, the handle is knocked down. The jaws don't have to be the same length as your sawblade, but they should be long enough so you can do significant filing before reclamping the saw. The jaws on my vise are about 20 in. long, and the legs are about the same. The vise legs are set into a notch in the bench and clamped in place. The vise leans away from the filer 10°, which helps the file leave sloping gullets between teeth. A diagonal brace behind the vise makes it rigid against the push of the file.

A final tip about the filing vise: Line the jaw with lead sheet flashing, available from roofing and industrial suppliers. Wrap the lead so it folds over the outside of the jaws and staple through it on the outside so the staples don't mar the sawblade. The lead deadens the vibrations of the file. Combined with the brace behind the vise, this makes for a rock-solid filing vise.

Saws are rated in points of teeth-per-inch, the more teeth per inch, the finer the saw. The type of file you use depends on the

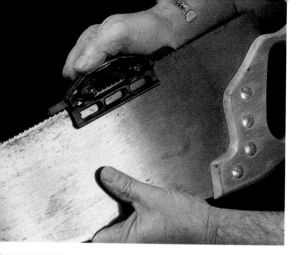

Begin the saw-sharpening process by leveling the teeth with a jointer (left). Though the author is shown using a commercial model, you can make one from a wood block grooved to accept a file. The jointer holds a file level and perpendicular to the sawteeth. Moving from handle to tip, draw the jointer down the blade's length until a small flat is filed at the top of each tooth. A saw set (right) bends alternate teeth to the left or right. Set every other tooth in one direction first, reverse the saw and set the remaining teeth in the opposite direction.

To begin filing a handsaw, clamp the saw in the vise with the handle to your right (above). Using a three-corner file, start at the toe and work to the heel, filing the teeth facing away from you. Reverse the saw, start at the toe again, and file back to the heel. The photo at left shows the 10° slant of the saw vise that contributes to the sloping gullets filed into the sawteeth. Note that a grip is also attached to the file's tip for more comfort and stability. The final step is to lightly dress the side of the teeth with a three-cornered file tipped on edge (right). This step removes burrs on the side of the teeth, making for a cleaner cut. Dressing the sides also removes a slight amount of set and can remedy saws that rattle because their kerf is slightly too wide.

saw's teeth size. A 10-point saw has 10 tips and nine full teeth (not 10 teeth) per inch and is sharpened with a 7-in., extra-slim taper, three-cornered file. All saw-sharpening files are three-cornered and taper slightly along their length. These files get progressively thinner in cross section and are rated as: taper, slim taper, extra-slim taper and double extra-slim taper. A six- or seven-point ripsaw has coarser teeth than a 10-point crosscut saw and thus would require a larger file; a 7-in. slim taper will do nicely for this saw. If you're having trouble deciding which file to use, bring the saw to the hardware store and fit the file between the teeth. Saw files are also available from: Home Lumber Co., 499 W. Whitewater St., Whitewater, Wis. 53190. Be fussy when choosing a file, because

one that is too large for the saw will file one tooth to oblivion while you are concentrating on getting the other one sharp. A file too small will rattle in the gullet, cutting only one side of a tooth when it should be cutting the face of the adjacent tooth as well. Add a wood handle to the file's tang and another at the tip. The two handles provide better control and more comfort than one handle.

Sawtooth jointer and saw set—A jointer is simply a jig for holding a flat-mill bastard file. When drawn along the length of the sawblade, from the handle to the toe, it files teeth down to a uniform height. You can buy a commercially made jointer or make one out of a wood block with a slot cut in it to hold the file.

A saw set is a forming tool that bends the tooth against a miniature anvil. The set in a saw's teeth makes the kerf slightly wider than the saw's body, and hence reduces drag on the saw. There are a couple of different styles of sets, but the one with a pistol grip works the best. Stanley Tool Co. still makes them, and they come with a numbered screw-knob adjustment—available from: Frog Tool Co. Ltd., 700 W. Jackson Blvd., Chicago, Ill. 60606. Mine is numbered from 4 to 16, with each number corresponding to the points-per-inch of a saw. To set the teeth of a 10-point saw, roll the set's knob to 10 until it lines up with the anvil. Hold the saw handle under your arm and, starting at the toe of the saw, place the first tooth leaning away from you between the anvil and the set's punch block and squeeze the set's handle. Set every tooth leaning away from you from there to the handle. This completes one side. For the other side, tuck the handle between your knees and work from the toe again, repeating the procedure.

How much set to use is based on experience; the numbers on the sets act as a guide, but don't go entirely by them. Green wood puts greater drag on the saw and hence requires more set; dry wood requires less set. If the saw is dragging, increase the set.

Watch for saws that are taper ground, their blades are thicker at the teeth than at their back and require less set. This feature was found in the more expensive saws, but is seldom seen now.

Sharpening crosscut saws—I'll explain how to sharpen an 8-point crosscut saw because these are relatively common. First, joint the teeth down. This is done in the handle-to-toe direction until you see flats form on the tops of the teeth and the teeth shine. You can hold the saw in your hand during jointing rather than locking it in a vise.

Set the teeth if they need it. It's possible to set your saw after it's sharpened, just do it carefully so as not to damage any of the cleanly-filed teeth. I have received saws for sharpening with teeth so badly out of shape that both the teeth and gullets had to be rough filed before setting.

Put your saw in the vise with the toe either to your right or to your left. In the photos, the saw has its toe to the left. File the face of the first tooth leaning away from you at the toe. Hold your file with its handle angled back to the saw's grip about 30° to produce sloping sides on the teeth known as fleam. Tilt the file's handle down from horizontal toward you about 15°. The downward slope of the vise, combined with the slope of the file, produces a gullet slope of about 25°. This produces deeper gullets than saws filed on machines where the file moves in a horizontal line, leaving level gullets. I'm inclined to agree with my father, who claimed this aspect of hand sharpening makes a saw cut better, because the deeper gullets chamber more sawdust—the gullets are capable of handling what the teeth bite off.

The profile of a crosscut saw's tooth is best described in this manner: If you drew a line along the tips of all the saw's teeth, and then struck a perpendicular from that line across the width of the blade, each tooth front would have a 15° slope from the perpendicular. Each tooth back would slope at a 45° angle from the perpendicular. If the front angle is more than 15° to the perpendicular, the saw will not cut as quickly. If the angle is less than 15°, then the saw will have a tendency to bite off too much wood and it will chatter.

In addition to the angles of tooth profile, fleam angle affects cutting ability as well. Fleam angle bevels the front of each tooth, giving each a shearing effect. Think of sharpening a chisel as you file each tooth. Too much bevel results in a sharper tooth that cuts faster, but dulls sooner. Too blunt, and it's slow cutting.

In this process, you are filing the front of one tooth and the back slope of another at the same time. Watch the tops of the teeth so you file only half of each jointed flat—the remainder of the flat is filed away when the saw is turned around and the opposite-set teeth are filed. Don't try to bring them to a point the first time across.

When you reach the handle, turn the saw so its toe is to the right and start filing at the toe again. This time bring each tooth to a point. Thunk each tooth as you're finished with it to remove the burr, otherwise the point will be hidden by the burr and you won't be able to tell whether it needs more filing.

File the teeth with long strokes without wobbling. Go at it as if you mean it; avoid timid jabs. By using side pressure on the file stroke, you can take more off the larger teeth (these require the removal of more metal), while easing up on the smaller ones.

Take the saw out of the vise, lay it on a flat surface and dress the teeth with a triangular file tipped up slightly so it is removing material on the set portion of the teeth only. This step evens the set by removing the burrs hanging off the side of the teeth and helps ensure a clean-cutting saw.

Take a look at your handiwork to see the results. Check the height of the teeth to see how uniform they are. If a few teeth are below the height of the other teeth on the blade, don't refile the saw until all teeth are the same height. The low teeth will come up to the correct height as the surrounding teeth are lowered by subsequent sharpenings. Hold the saw with the toe just a little to the side of your nose, and eyeball the row of teeth on that side. If they look like a nice, even picket fence, congratulate yourself. Then, with the saw toe in line with your nose, look down the teeth again. You should see a nice, clean V-groove formed by the alternating set of the teeth. Carefully place a fine sewing needle in the V. If it slides the length of the blade without falling off, you can drink with the masters.

The process I described above is open to variation. Each filer has his own style regarding tooth angle, set, where to start, where to finish and so forth. Filing techniques are as individual as fingerprints. Some saw filers put less slope on the gullet, some prefer none. Some put slightly more slope, in profile, on the front of the tooth and decrease the rear slope. After you get the hang of it, sharpening a saw becomes fast and easy. A first-class job can be done in about 20 minutes, providing the saw hasn't hit a nail or been damaged in any way. A damaged saw needs a complete overhaul, and this may take twice that amount of time. However, saws that are only "wood dull" can be sharpened two or three times without jointing or setting.

Sharpening ripsaws—You file a ripsaw differently than a crosscut saw, though the process of jointing and setting the teeth is the same. If you are right-handed, put the saw in the vise with the toe to your right and file from the toe to the handle. Move the file perpendicular to the long axis of the saw and hold it horizontally (if you have a vise that tips back 10°, hold the tip of the file down 10° to compensate for this). Unlike a crosscut saw, the teeth on a ripsaw have neither fleam nor sloping gullets. If you are so inclined, you can start at the toe and, with each stroke, file the front of one tooth and the back of another, whether it slopes toward you or away. You can also file a ripsaw like a crosscut by filing only the teeth sloping away from you, then reverse the file and repeat the process.

A ripsaw is given less set than a crosscut of corresponding points per inch. The profile of a ripsaw's teeth differs from a crosscut as well. To describe their profile, revert back to a perpendicular drawn along the saw's teeth. The front of the tooth coincides with the perpendicular, while the back of the tooth slopes at 60°.

Trouble-shooting a saw—If you find the saw binding, don't keep pushing or you'll put a kink in it. Keep a chunk of paraffin on hand to give the body—not the teeth—of your saw a rub. You can also use silicone spray. This lubrication may save your saw and your temper until you can put more set in the teeth.

If your saw rattles and wobbles in the kerf, it has too much set. Lay the sawblade on a flat surface and side dress the teeth with a three-corner file. I snapped off an old three-corner file to 5 in. long, because they are easier to hold with one hand like this. To break the file, hold it in a vise and then whack it with a hammer close to the vise jaws (wear eye protection while doing this). Break off the file's tang and tip. The teeth are given two or three gentle swipes with the shortened file canted with the set of the teeth, not held flat to the blade.

What saws are worth owning and sharpening? Since handsaws are likely to last a lifetime, it is worth taking the time to pick a good, new saw or repair an old one. I prefer the latter option, because the old saws are generally of better quality. Yet there are old saws that are of poor quality or so badly damaged that you'd best pass them over. Below are some of the criteria I use for judging a saw and some of the techniques I use to salvage a good old one. You can find plenty of old saws hanging in sheds, in barns and for sale at flea markets and auctions. Among the best of these, I feel, are the old Disstons. The saws of Henry Disston, the company's founder, will probably live forever. And they should. Despite the fact that they came in various grades, I've never met up with a bad, old Disston or seen a better saw, though I'm sure there are saws that are just as good. Best of all, old Disstons are still relatively plentiful. I suggest snatching them up before the antique tool collectors do.

The key to their quality lies in their combination of hardness and ductility—two characteristics often at odds with each other. Other saw manufacturers couldn't match Disston's Rockwell hardness of 52-54. "They didn't know the secret of how to roll a new saw sheet so the teeth would not break during setting at that hardness," Bill Disston, Henry's great grandson, once told me. That explains why many of the saws made by the competition have a Rockwell hardness of only 46-48.

Don't pass over a saw that has a moderate amount of rust on its blade. Often this can be sanded off with wet-or-dry sandpaper lubricated with mineral spirits. If the saw is badly pitted from rust, pass it by, because pitted teeth are likely to break off during setting and will never have a sharp, clean edge, even after filing.

Pass over stainless steel and chrome alloy saws. When these first appeared, they were well-received by forgetful carpenters who left their saws out overnight. That they wouldn't rust was the only thing they had going for them. After many attempts during my 10 years of commercial saw sharpening, I gave up on them. Their steel is simply too soft.

It's hard to say whether you should buy a saw with a kinked blade. You'll have to judge it for yourself. A really bad kink may be difficult or impossible to remove, while a moderate one can be removed in a few minutes. There are two kinds of kinks: the slow, gradual kind and the abrupt kind. To remove a gradual kink, bend the sawblade in the opposite direction of the kink and then let it spring back. An abrupt kink is very hard to get rid of because the metal has been stretched almost to the breaking point, but if you work carefully, even these kinks can be removed. I've had good luck using the following technique. First, open the jaws on a large machine vise wide enough to span the area of the kink. Lay the blade flat on the vise with the jaws spanning the kink. Lightly hammer the kinked portion of the blade, while gradually closing the vise jaws. This supports the blade while working toward the kink's center. This is hit last and has to be hammered a bit more than the other areas to stretch the metal far enough so the blade will pop back straight.

It's worth having a saw with a good handle, even if you have to make the handle yourself. A saw should hang comfortably from your hand. I wouldn't reject a good saw with a bad or damaged handle, I'd repair it. This makes sense, because many old saws have missing or damaged handles and many new saws have uncomfortable handles. The handle should position your arm so it puts as much power as possible behind the saw in each stroke. The perfect grip should feel like a natural extension of your arm. I prefer a grip that rakes forward slightly. A grip that cocks your grasp too far backward, or too far forward for that matter, makes a saw feel awkward and tiring to its user.

So there you have it, a lifetime of my father's experience passed along to me and now to you. The rest of it is just practice. □

Harold "Dynamite" Payson builds boats in South Thomaston, Me., and writes on saw sharpening and boat building. His book, Keeping the Cutting Edge, *is available for $7.95 (plus postage) from WoodenBoat, Box 78, Brooklin, Me. 04616; (800) 225-5205.*

Handsaws and how to use them

by Henry T. Kramer

I love handsaws. Sure, I use power saws most of the time. But every once in a while I grab a handsaw off the rack and save a lot of time and trouble. Yes, I know a power saw cuts a lot faster, but that's only part of the story. Sometimes the work is too big, too long or unsteady, and the power saw can't be used without risking damage or injury, or rigging up jigs, braces or heaven knows what. Another reason for handsawing is that I like to do it. A good, sharp saw, properly set, is a joy to use.

Traditionally, saws came in three sizes, measured along the teeth from heel to toe: ripsaws, 30 in. long; handsaws, 26 in. long; and panel saws, 16 in. to 24 in. long. The average saw today measures 26 in. long, though saws 16 in. to 22 in. long seem to be selling well—probably because their shortened length makes them less expensive.

There is no advantage to a shorter saw, however, except the paltry difference in price, which itself is a false economy. It takes more work to saw through a board with a short saw, so the few dollars saved will be of no advantage in the long run. A longer blade means fewer but longer strokes and fewer return strokes. Since you're not sawing lumber on the return stroke, it pays to saw as much lumber with as few return strokes as possible. Also, sawing with long, smooth strokes is more comfortable and more satisfying than sawing with short, choppy strokes.

Saw with one hand only, as using two hands will require an awkward position toward the board. The one exception is ripping thick stock, where you literally may find yourself standing on top of the stock.

Position yourself for maximum mechanical advantage when sawing. Your sawing arm and that shoulder should be in line with the cut. In most cases, you'll want to position yourself so you can see the line you are cutting to without looking over the saw-blade. Position the stock at a height you find comfortable and efficient—this will require some experimentation, depending on how tall you are and the kind of cut you're making. You can crosscut thin stock by clamping it to a typical 30-in.-tall workbench. Sawing thick stock requires considerably more force, however, and you may find a standard-height workbench is simply too high to allow you to get enough force behind the saw. A pair of short (24 in. tall, or so), sturdy sawhorses is a definite advantage with these cuts.

For crosscutting, hold the saw with its tooth line at 45°. Stand with your feet about shoulder-width apart and your forward foot pointing ahead. For fine cutting, make your mark with a knife on the face and edge of the board, but for rough work simply mark the board across its width with a pencil. Grip the board over the edge with your free hand and steady the saw when starting the cut by butting the thumb of that hand up to the blade. The saw should rest just slightly on the scrap side of the line—the more proficient you get, the closer you'll be able to saw to the line. Draw the saw back, putting light pressure on the saw to make it cut slightly. In softwood, using a sharp saw, it may take just one back stroke to get the saw started. In hardwoods, it may take three or four. Also, the coarser the saw's teeth, the more difficult it is to start the cut. Finally, watch your thumb, if the saw jumps out of the kerf in the beginning of the cut, you could get a nasty cut—don't underestimate the damage a saw can do just because it's powered by hand and not electricity.

Cut with long and smooth strokes using as much of the sawblade as possible. Be careful, though, that you don't draw the saw right out of the kerf on the return stroke. Western saws don't cut on the back stroke, so lift the saw slightly when drawing it back. It will take some practice before you can crosscut a board so it's square across the face and edge. A saw that is properly sharpened and set will easily saw to the line. A saw that wanders from the line, despite your best efforts, has too much set on the side it wanders to.

Though it's virtually impossible to correct a cut that has gone significantly awry, a small deviation can be corrected by flexing the handle toward the line and working the saw back after a few strokes. But if it looks like the saw is going to run off significantly, let it wander where it chooses rather than twist and jam the saw in an attempt to get it back on track. Support the board with your free hand when you get to the end of the cut. Don't saw as aggressively as you near the end, rather ease the saw out to reduce splintering.

There are a couple of different ways to crosscut a board. Some woodworkers dip the saw below 45° slightly while drawing it back to start it; others dispense with this. Once started, you can saw straight across the board without altering the pitch of the saw or you can provide a kerf for the saw to follow by sloping the saw down slightly, making a few cuts, and then resuming the

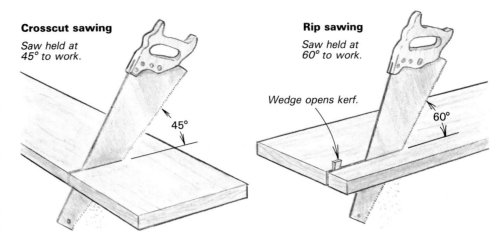

Crosscut sawing
Saw held at 45° to work.

45°

Rip sawing
Saw held at 60° to work.

Wedge opens kerf.

60°

45° sawing angle. Either method works, it just depends on which you like more.

A ripsaw is held at 60° while cutting, and it requires a lighter touch to get started because of its coarse teeth. Start a ripsaw by holding it nearly parallel to the face of the workpiece (about 5°), and very lightly push it forward so it just begins to nick the edge. The configuration of a ripsaw's teeth means that it has hardly any scoring effect pulling it backward, hence it has to be started on a forward stroke. Some older ripsaws have finer teeth at the toe to overcome this problem—I suggest you snatch up one of these if you find it. Bring the saw up to 60° after you get it started and saw as you would with a crosscut saw, using long, rhythmic strokes. Ripsaws have a tendency to jam in the kerf as the cut progresses and the kerf closes on the saw. Correct this by inserting a thin stick or wedge in the kerf, not enough to spread it significantly, but just enough to keep it open. You can also keep the kerf open by spreading a wooden parallel-jaw clamp over it and tightening it down.

Before sharpening or tuning the teeth of a new saw, remove the anti-rust coating it will almost certainly have. This coating is an effective rust inhibitor, but it reduces the effect of set on the saw's teeth and also creates a fair amount of drag. It's not easy to remove. You can remove it from the body of the saw with a sharp razor, rub it off with steel wool and lacquer thinner, acetone, or benzine (*not* "benzene," which is toxic). If all these methods fail, try using paint remover or brush cleaner. In any case, wear protective gloves and a respirator.

Remove a saw's handle and give the blade under the handle a good coating of grease to inhibit rust, then replace the handle.

Finally, set and sharpen the saw. The machine sharpening that saws receive at the factory is inadequate and often badly done. I lubricate the sawblade before I use it. I apply sparingly a thin coat of machine oil and rub it in well. Some woodworkers apply paste wax, others use paraffin. Regardless of which you use, don't let a residue of wax, sawdust and dirt build up on the blade. Remove this gunk every so often by lightly wiping the blade with steel wool and mineral spirits. Some don't use a lubricant on the grounds that it

may stain the work. I haven't found this to be a problem, because a sawn surface is always cleaned up with a plane or sanded smooth.

Don't toss handsaws in a drawer or on a pile where they can rub together and become dull. A wall rack or a rail with pins to hang saws on works well. If you carry them to the job site, make a seperate canvas sheath for each saw.

Because sharpening handsaws is more work than sharpening a chisel or a plane iron, it's tempting to use them dull. Don't do it. A dull handsaw will jam in the kerf and bend, and a bent handsaw is much more difficult to repair than a chipped chisel or plane iron. Take the time to sharpen a dull saw, you'll thank yourself for it while you're using it. You don't even have to use a handsaw to tell if it's dull; if the teeth tips reflect light as a line, then you know its time to refile it.

When using backsaws, you have to be careful. Given a chance, they'll "getcha," and you'll wind up with more of them than you ever thought you would. For a long time I never thought much about them, but I discovered I like their small size and fine teeth (you can get them with as many as 20 or more teeth per inch). Backsaws take their name from the rigid back or spine attached to the blade. The added weight of the back is a help, I've found, in keeping the saw on track, but its primary use is to make the blade more rigid to further reduce the tendency of the blade to wander during critical cuts.

A backsaw is an instrument used for fine joinery and not rapid cut-off work. I own half a dozen or so in 8-in., 10-in., and 12-in. sizes, each filed in crosscut and rip patterns. Backsaws come from the factory as crosscuts, and converting them to ripsaws is something you should try only after you become an experienced saw filer. Converting a crosscut to a ripsaw sounds radical at first, but the practice is more widespread than you might think, finding such advocates as Tage Frid, woodworking professor emeritus of the Rhode Island School of Design. A backsaw filed with rip teeth makes sense, since you are mostly ripping when you saw a tenon or a dovetail joint. □

Henry Kramer works wood in Somer-ville, N.J.

Sharpening Carving Tools
The essential steps for a keen edge

by Ben Bacon

Author Bacon lays a parting tool on the grinding wheel's tool rest and shapes its bevels by grinding one face, then the other. Depending on the hardness of the wood to be carved, he grinds a bevel angle between 22° and 30°, judging his progress by eye.

As a professional carver, I maintain a kit of a couple of hundred tools, and often find myself at the sharpening bench twenty times a day. I have to be fast at carving *and* sharpening. After all, I get paid to carve—not fiddle with my tools.

The techniques for sharpening carving gouges and chisels are very similar to those for sharpening other edge tools. First, grind the edge to the proper shape and bevel. Then, hone the bevel on successively finer benchstones to remove the grinding marks and to smooth the edge. The honing will raise a burr on the back of the bevel, which will fall off when the edge is honed on a slip stone. Finally, polish the tool's bevel by lightly stroking it on a leather strop loaded with jewelers' rouge. You can also polish the bevel using a rubberized abrasive wheel.

I'll explain this process in greater detail, but let me add here that sharpening carving tools presents unique difficulties. First, it's critical that you maintain the shape or definition of the tool's edge. The hallmark of good carving is crispness and clearly delineated lines where cuts intersect. You can't cut cleanly if you carve with tools that have had their corners rounded off by careless honing or polishing. If the entire edge of the tool isn't cutting, the intersection of cuts will be left rough and ragged.

Secondly, many carving tools have a curved edge. Sharpening straight-edge and skewed carving tools is a lot like sharpening chisels or plane irons, but you'll need to practice on tools with curved or multiple edges to gain sharpening proficiency. For this reason, I'll discuss sharpening V-shaped parting tools and gouges, although the same steps apply for all carving tools.

Grind the tool with a bevel angle between 22° and 30°. The harder the wood, the higher the angle. A low angle will give you a very sharp edge, but it will also be delicate and prone to chipping when forced into very hard wood, such as maple. It's better, therefore, to go with a steeper angle—one with more steel behind the edge—when carving hardwoods. As a general rule, you want to use the smallest angle possible. Only experience will teach you just how fine an angle you can get away with. In the beginning, though, it's better to play it safe.

I grind my sharpening tools on a 1000-grit horizontal waterwheel (available from Woodcraft Supply, 41 Atlantic Ave., Woburn, Mass. 01888). The water cools the edge as it's shaped, the horizontal wheel gives a flat and sturdy bevel, and the fine grit often lets me skip honing on a medium stone and go straight to a fine, hard Arkansas—the stone used in final honing.

You can also grind on a standard bench grinder, but this requires a much lighter touch, and honing takes three to four times as long. These wheels spin at a much higher RPM, so there's a greater risk of burning the tool. Quench the tool frequently and

From *Fine Woodworking* magazine (September 1987) 66:48-51

watch the cutting edge carefully for any change in the steel's color. If you see yellow, you can still save the tool's temper by quenching it immediately. A bronze color is borderline. But if you see black or blue discoloration, it's too late—you've overheated the edge.

Regardless of the type of wheel you're grinding with, be careful to maintain the shape of the carving tool's edge. I grind by eye and have achieved consistency in my grinding by practice. On the waterstone, I steady the tool by resting my hand on the tool rest. Then, I lay the back of the bevel against the wheel and tip it forward to achieve the correct angle. Check your progress every so often—the goal is to produce a single true, flat bevel right up to the cutting edge. With a dry grinding wheel, you would aim for a slightly concave bevel. Honing on a benchstone tends to round off the bevel, producing a blunt edge, so the object of both kinds of grinding is to produce a bevel fit for honing.

Grinding a V-shaped parting tool is reasonably simple: grind one bevel, then the other. If you're working with a grindstone as fine as the one I use, round off the point where the two bevels meet by gently rocking the tool back and forth. If you're using a bench grinder, then I suggest you do this on a benchstone where there's less risk of removing too much metal. Even with the waterstone, be careful not to remove too much material—the wheel removes metal quicker than you might think.

If you're not grinding on a very fine wheel, hone the parting tool on a medium India stone (a man-made stone). When honing large tools, you can push and pull the tool across the stone as you please, because the large bevel will give stability on the stone. But smaller, fine tools require a more deliberate touch: Push *or* pull the tool

along the stone, but lift the tool on the return stroke. Then, repeat the process. Hold the tool perpendicular to the long axis of the stone with one bevel flat against it; secondary bevels (small, second bevels right behind the cutting edge) are rarely used on carving tools. The bevel has been sharpened when marks from grinding have been removed, and when a small but even burr has been raised on the inside of the tool. You can see this burr on larger tools or those made of softer steel; on smaller tools, you can feel it with your fingertip. Gently hone the juncture where the two bevels meet by rotating the tool as you move it along the stone. This removes any burr that projects at the intersection of the bevels. The bottom right-hand photo on this page shows what to aim for. Move to a hard Arkansas benchstone and repeat the process, honing the outside bevels.

The next step is to remove the burr raised during honing by rubbing the tool's inside face on a medium slip stone, followed by a rubbing on a fine slip stone. Slip stones are made from the same material as whetstones: bonded, man-made abrasive crystals (such as India and Crystolon stones) or natural crystals (such as white and black hard Arkansas stones). They come in a variety of shapes, including round convex, round concave, triangular and conical. The type you use isn't as important as getting one that matches the shape of your carving tool as closely as possible. Slip stones are available through most major tool catalogs, especially those that sell or specialize in carving tools. On rare occasions, they also turn up in industrial-supply catalogs, so check these, too.

In removing the burr, the slip stone should be parallel to the long axis of the tool. Draw the tool back and forth until you

To hone a parting tool's bevel, lay one face flat on the benchstone and push or pull the tool along the stone. Lift the tool at the end of each stroke, and repeat the process. Note that the tool is held perpendicular to the length of the stone.

Above: Remove the burr that's raised in honing by inverting the parting tool over a slip stone and sliding it gently back and forth. Below: parting tools after sharpening, showing the rounded juncture where the two bevels meet (left), the inside corner, which is left sharp (center) and the bevel after polishing (right).

Photos: Robert Aberman

A gouge is ground similarly to a parting tool, but requires a little extra dexterity. Begin grinding by laying one corner of the bevel on the wheel (top, left) and spinning the tool slowly so the entire bevel is evenly ground. Next, hone the gouge's bevel by starting at one corner and moving the tool down the length of the stone, *maintaining the bevel's angle (above, left). Rotate the tool during each pass to hone the entire bevel. When done, a burr should be raised along the edge. To remove the burr, hold the slip stone on the bench, invert the gouge over it and rock the tool back and forth until the burr breaks off (above).*

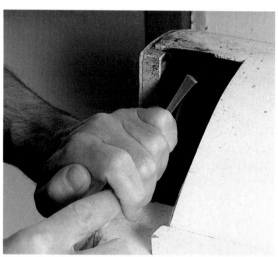

Polish the inside face of the gouge on a leather strop rubbed with jewelers' rouge. Flex the strop to match the curve of the gouge (above, left). An alternative to leather-strop polishing is to polish the tool on a rubberized wheel (above, center). The inside *face can be polished on the corner of the wheel, the bevel on the face of the wheel. Test a carving tool for sharpness by making parallel cross-grain cuts in a pine block (above, right). The ridges between cuts should be sharp with no tearout.*

see—or feel—that the burr is removed. If the burr proves stubborn and doesn't want to break off, you may have to go back and lightly dress the bevel again on the hard Arkansas benchstone.

A gouge is ground in a similar manner to a parting tool, but the job requires a little extra dexterity. Start grinding with the corner of the bevel against the grindstone. Keeping the bevel against the stone, spin the tool slowly so the entire bevel is evenly ground. It's a little tricky to maintain the bevel's angle as you do this, but—with practice—you'll get the hang of it.

Next, hone the gouge perpendicular to the long axis of a medium India (or hard Arkansas) stone. Place one corner of the curved bevel on the stone and push it down the length of the stone. Pivot the gouge slightly as you do this so the entire bevel is honed when you reach the end of the stone. Repeat these passes until the bevel is properly honed. An alternative is to place a corner of the bevel on the stone and push it along the

stone so that only a portion of the bevel is honed. This technique is useful for removing local high spots in the bevel, but it leaves a faceted edge, and the facets will have to be removed by using the previously mentioned honing technique.

Next, as with the parting tool, hone the inside of the gouge with a slip stone. If you're using a tapered slip stone, be careful not to move the tool up where the stone is wider than the tool's edge—you're sure to round over the cutting edge.

To maintain as much control as possible in sharpening most carving tools, I recommend that you place the slip stone on the bench and move the tool over the stone. With very small or complex carving tools, however, it's sometimes easier to move the stone over the tool.

After honing on the slip stone, polish the edge by stroking both the inside face and the bevel on a leather strop charged with jewelers' rouge. Polish the exterior surface of carving tools by laying the strop on the bench and moving the tool over it. For the inside of a gouge, I flex the leather to the curvature of the tool. For parting tools, I stroke the tool on the edge of the strop.

You can also polish the tool on a rubber wheel. Proceed carefully, however, as you can burn the tool on one of these wheels. The wheel must be moving away from you; otherwise, the carving tool will cut into it. You can polish the inside surface of flatter carving tools on the corner of the wheel. Polish the bevel in the same manner that you sharpened the tool, but go lightly to avoid rounding off the bevel.

I avoid giving carving tools their final polish on a cloth buffing wheel loaded with polishing compound. These wheels have a tendency to round off corners and round over the bevel behind the cutting edge. This changes the tool's cutting angle and causes the wood to exert more pressure on the tool as it's pushed into the cut. I can, however, see using these buffing wheels with sharpening tools that are used in large sculpture work. Here, great tool definition isn't essential and—because the tools take a greater pounding and have to be sharpened more frequently—you'll need a quick method of restoring the edge.

When sharpening is completed, test the sharpness of the carving tool by making parallel cuts across the grain in a piece of scrap pine. If the ridges between these cuts are sharp and free of tearout, the tool is sharp. If not, go back to the fine benchstone

and take the honing process from there. If the tool still isn't sharp, go back to the medium benchstone and try it again.

I use a lightweight oil as the lubricant in honing, and I clean metal residue from the sharpening stones every so often by brushing them off with gasoline or any fluid that will cut oil and dirt, such as lighter fluid. Obviously, it's important to use powerful solvent with care and to clean the stones outdoors or in a well-ventilated area.

Carving tools have a tendency to wear out the center of a benchstone, so I suggest you get a separate set of stones and reserve them just for these tools. In so doing, you'll preserve the flatness of your other stones so they can be used to hone larger edge tools that require flatness, such as plane irons.

I resharpen a carving tool after about 15 minutes of hard use. It takes me a minute to re-hone a simply shaped carving tool, and three or four minutes to completely regrind and rejuvenate the edge (usually done after about ten sharpenings). At the absolute most, I spend 20 minutes repairing a damaged tool.

Sharpening your carving tools might not be much fun, but once you get good at it, you become so quick that you can get back to the carving in short order. □

Ben Bacon, formerly a Virginian, now resides in London, where he earns his living in a carving shop.

Multi-wheel sharpening system

by Russell Orrell

You could spend a fortune on a bench grinder and numerous gadgets to keep your carving tools sharp, but I believe my homemade system of plywood discs, cloth buffing wheels and grindstones is even better. The system can sharpen all kinds of carving tools, plane irons and chisels. I built it with used materials for $30 (excluding the 1,000-grit waterstone); made from new parts, it would cost about $100.

The system is powered by a used two-speed (1,125 and 1,750 RPM) ½-HP motor salvaged from an evaporative cooler. These motors might be hard to come by if you live outside the warmer areas of the country, but check with your local motor shop anyway. If you can't find one, you'll have to use a motor with a different speed (a good motor source is Burden's Surplus Center, 1015 West O St., Box 82209, Lincoln, Neb. 68501-9973) and modify the pulley arrangement.

The motor is wired to a dual-switch three-pole wall switch used to control on/off and high/low speed. The motor's arbor runs a cloth buffing wheel and a 1½-in. pulley. From this pulley, a ½-in. by 38-in. V-belt runs to a 7-in. pulley that drives the gang-wheel assembly.

Mounted to the ⅝-in. axle running through the large pulley are a 1,000-grit

Homemade carving tool sharpener

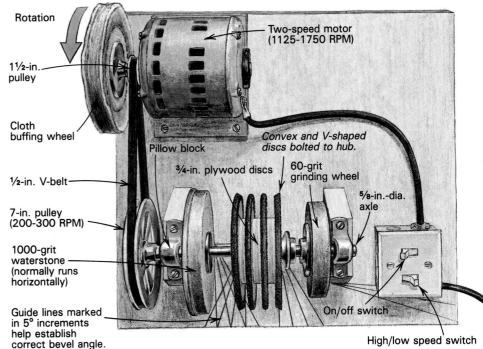

Rotation

Two-speed motor (1125-1750 RPM)

1½-in. pulley

Cloth buffing wheel

Pillow block

Convex and V-shaped discs bolted to hub.

¾-in. plywood discs

60-grit grinding wheel

⅝-in.-dia. axle

½-in. V-belt

7-in. pulley (200-300 RPM)

1000-grit waterstone (normally runs horizontally)

On/off switch

Guide lines marked in 5° increments help establish correct bevel angle.

High/low speed switch

Makita waterstone; four 7-in.-dia., ¼-in. plywood discs loaded with red rouge or emery compound; and a 60-grit grinding wheel. The discs and wheels turn at around 300 RPM at high speed and 200 RPM at low speed. The discs are separated by ¾-in. by 4½-in.-dia. plywood washers. Two discs have a 60° edge angle, and two have a rounded edge to match carving-tool profiles. Sight lines are located beneath the wheels to help me establish the bevel angle (I sharpen freehand). I

modified a hub from the scrapped evaporative cooler and ran two bolts through it to keep the discs and washers clamped together and fixed to the axle. I epoxied another hub to the 60-grit grinding wheel to fasten it to the axle. A V-belt pulley epoxied to the wheel would also have done the job. □

Russell Orrell is a professional woodcarver and carpenter who lives in Los Angeles, Calif.

Drawing: Michael Janos

Carving Benches

Woodcarving benches are as idiosyncratic as the carvers who use them. Carvers who work on pieces that are small enough to be handheld don't need much more than a table to hold their tools. Relief-panel carvers need solid, flat surfaces to anchor their work. Sculptors who work in-the-round not only need to secure their work, but must also be able to rotate the piece, or at least have space to work around it as they carve. And, depending on the person's height and the type of work being done, each carver tends to feel most comfortable working on pieces held at a certain angle or height.

It's no wonder that few carvers are satisfied with commercially available benches, and either customize their store-bought models or start from scratch and build specialized benches and clamping systems to solve their individual problems. Here are two such solutions—a heavy-duty sculptor's bench, which would also be good for many cabinetmaking operations, and a versatile shaving horse that combines a traditional design with a Chinese carving bench.

A carving/shaving bench

by E. D. Lyman

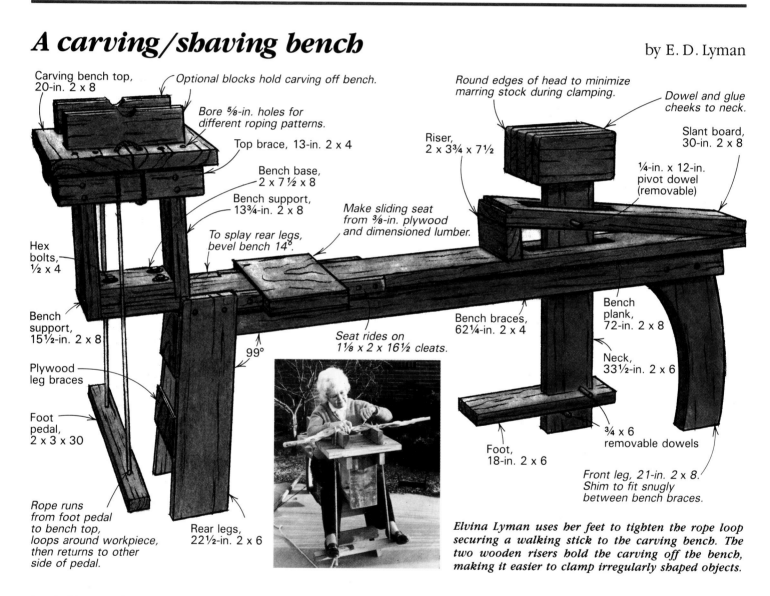

Carving bench top, 20-in. 2 x 8

Optional blocks hold carving off bench.

Bore ⅝-in. holes for different roping patterns.

Top brace, 13-in. 2 x 4

Bench base, 2 x 7½ x 8

Bench support, 13¾-in. 2 x 8

Make sliding seat from ⅜-in. plywood and dimensioned lumber.

To splay rear legs, bevel bench 14°.

Hex bolts, ½ x 4

Bench support, 15½-in. 2 x 8

Plywood leg braces

Foot pedal, 2 x 3 x 30

99°

Seat rides on 1⅛ x 2 x 16½ cleats.

Rope runs from foot pedal to bench top, loops around workpiece, then returns to other side of pedal.

Rear legs, 22½-in. 2 x 6

Round edges of head to minimize marring stock during clamping.

Dowel and glue cheeks to neck.

Riser, 2 x 3¾ x 7½

Slant board, 30-in. 2 x 8

¼-in. x 12-in. pivot dowel (removable)

Bench braces, 62¼-in. 2 x 4

Bench plank, 72-in. 2 x 8

Neck, 33½-in. 2 x 6

Foot, 18-in. 2 x 6

¾ x 6 removable dowels

Front leg, 21-in. 2 x 8. Shim to fit snugly between bench braces.

Elvina Lyman uses her feet to tighten the rope loop securing a walking stick to the carving bench. The two wooden risers hold the carving off the bench, making it easier to clamp irregularly shaped objects.

As a hobby, I make walking sticks from diamond willow and sumac. I needed a way to hold the stock securely while I shape it with a drawknife, as well as a place to carve the shaped sticks. To save space, and concentrate the messiest parts of my hobby in a single spot, I decided to build a bench combining the powerful clamping and quick release capabilities of two traditional designs—a dumbhead shaving horse and a Chinese carving bench.

In addition to creating a functional, attractive bench, I found the extra weight of the combination bench makes each of the devices more stable. I made the whole thing from scrap: oak for the head, neck and foot; pine for the rest of the horse and the carving bench. The head end of the horse is about 2 in. higher than the rear, which makes for easier, nearly horizontal shaving. The sliding seat provides great comfort, and I sometimes mount on a tractor seat for long stints. I also added more holes on the carving bench, so I could vary the roping patterns, and two notched risers, 2x4s with dowels that fit into the bench holes, to raise the work off the bench surface and give me more room for carving. □

E.D. Lyman is a physician and woodworker in Lincoln, Neb.

From *Fine Woodworking* magazine (January 1986) 56:58-59

Photo: E.D. Lyman

Cloutier secures the carving with a carvers' screw, above, then tips the bench, raising the piece to a comfortable work height, below.

Articulated sculptor's bench

by Richard Starr

The Canadian town of St.-Jean Port Joli is home to at least 100 professional carvers. One of the most accomplished is Pierre Cloutier, whose work appears in numerous big-city galleries under the name Pier Clout.

Cloutier works both in-the-round and in bas-relief. He specializes in life-size human forms and is widely recognized for his extraordinary ability to portray living flesh. His studio is clean, roomy and efficient. Huge windows provide west light that can be softened with white drapes. Storage cabinets are hidden behind large white panels. His tool rack, which is adjustable in height, can be moved anywhere in the room, as can his solid and versatile bench.

The bench's heavy T-shaped base is fastened with a threaded rod to one of the several keyed sockets that are cast in the shop's concrete floor. Once the base is attached to the socket, the bench can be rotated a full 360°, to take advantage of the natural lighting. Fitting over the base unit are two slotted tabs, which are, in turn, mortised into the benchtop.

A large Acme-thread vise screw pulls the tabs tightly against the base of the bench, and allows Cloutier to adjust the angle and height of his work surface. Cloutier grinds slight hollows on the inside surfaces of the tabs, so they'll grip the base better when the screw is tightened. Work can be held on the bench with a carvers' screw or bench dogs, or be clamped directly in the Record vise mounted at the end of the benchtop. □

Richard Starr teaches woodworking at Richmond Middle School in Hanover, N.H., and is the author of the book Woodworking with Kids *(The Taunton Press, 1982).*

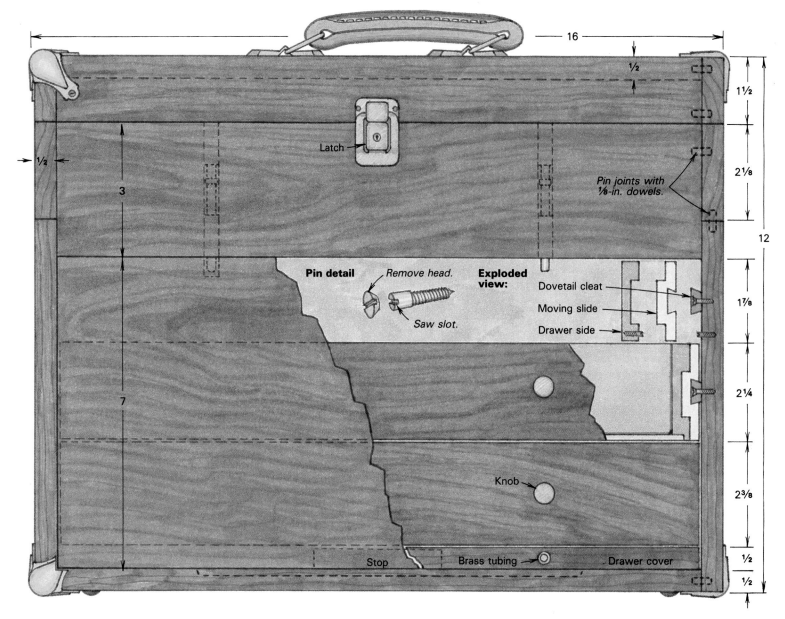

16

1/2

1 1/2

1/2

2 1/8

Latch

Pin joints with 1/8-in. dowels.

3

12

Pin detail   *Remove head.*   **Exploded view:**

Dovetail cleat

Moving slide

1 7/8

Saw slot.

Drawer side

7

2 1/4

Knob

2 3/8

Stop   Brass tubing   Drawer cover

1/2

1/2

Carvers' Chest
Drawers on moving slides

by Aaron C. Zeamer

I got the idea for this carvers' chest from a photo in the *Woodcraft* catalog. Their small tool chest seemed a good size to make as a gift for my woodcarving son. I modified the design somewhat by including a moving-slide drawer support, which allows the drawers to extend fully without falling out.

The chest is made to look as if the top compartment is a separate box that can be lifted off, but it is not—the horizontal-grain part of the sides is firmly doweled and glued to the lower part before the sides are cut to size. This is the sort of cross-grain construction that should be avoided on large woodworking proj-

ects, because seasonal wood movement can break such joints apart (wood shrinks and expands in width, but not in length). But this chest's sides are only 8 in. wide and it has held together fine for several years now. There is always some cross-grain joinery in any solid-wood box, and this design actually minimizes the more troublesome cross-grain joint between the back, which has horizontal grain, and the sides, which would otherwise be entirely vertical grain.

Two or three parts in the drawing may need some explanation. The drawers run on a moving slide which, in turn, runs on a dovetail cleat, as shown. The critical part of the system is the location of the pins, one in the drawer and one in the case side. When the drawer is pulled out, the pin in the drawer runs out to the end of the channel in the moving slide and hits the front stop. Then the pin pulls the slide out with the drawer to provide support. When the moving slide reaches full extension, it is stopped by the pin in the case side. When the drawer is returned, its lip pushes the moving slide back into the case.

Proper placement of the pins—in conjunction with the dimensioning of the moving slide's channel and stops—is necessary for the extension system to work properly. The drawing gives positions and dimensions that can act as a guide, but the pin locations are best marked after all the wooden parts are made. The pins should project far enough to engage the slide, but must not project so far as to foul each other as the drawer moves.

When the chest is fully closed, a wooden panel covers the draw-

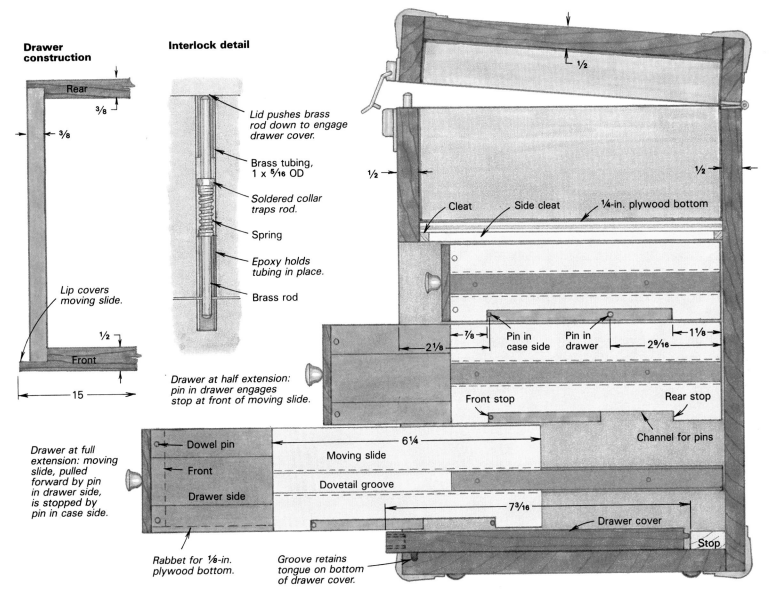

Drawer construction

Rear

3/8

3/8

Lip covers moving slide.

1/2

Front

15

Interlock detail

Lid pushes brass rod down to engage drawer cover.

Brass tubing, 1 x 5/16 OD

Soldered collar traps rod.

Spring

Epoxy holds tubing in place.

Brass rod

Drawer at half extension: pin in drawer engages stop at front of moving slide.

Drawer at full extension: moving slide, pulled forward by pin in drawer side, is stopped by pin in case side.

Dowel pin

Front

Drawer side

Rabbet for 1/8-in. plywood bottom.

Groove retains tongue on bottom of drawer cover.

Moving slide

Dovetail groove

6 1/4

7 3/16

Drawer cover

Stop

1/2

1/2

1/2

Cleat

Side cleat

1/4-in. plywood bottom

2 1/8

7/8

Pin in case side

Pin in drawer

2 9/16

1 1/8

Front stop

Rear stop

Channel for pins

ers; when the chest is in use, this drawer cover stows away beneath the bottom drawer, as shown in the drawing. The drawer cover is secured at the top by an interlock—a spring-tensioned brass rod—that is activated by the chest's lid. I obtained the parts at a local crafts shop, but the rod, springs, tubing and silver solder can be purchased by mail for about $15 from Small Parts, Box 381736, Miami, Fla. 33238. The bottom edge of the drawer cover is secured by a tongue and groove. Because the tongue is off-center toward the rear edge of the panel, the panel tips forward by gravity when the lid is opened and does not require a finger-grip.

Traditionally, chests like this are equipped with brass corner protectors. These, hinges and other hardware to suit are probably best bought locally. I lined the drawers of my son's chest with adhesive-backed felt, from Constantine, who also supplied the 1/8-in. basswood plywood for the drawer bottoms.

It might be of interest that even though I had a fairly complete shop in our home in Warrenton, Va., ninety percent of this chest was built in Clearwater, Fla., while my wife, Lois, and I were spending the winter in St. Petersburg. I had taken a three-month membership in a small woodworking shop, allowing me practically unlimited hours using their machinery and tools, which happened to be mostly Craftsman, as mine were at home. A migratory woodworker *can* have the best of both worlds. □

Aaron Zeamer now lives in Bradenton, Fla., year round. His son and the completed chest are in Germany.

The drawers, which will be lined with adhesive-backed felt, ride on moving slides that allow full extension. The drawer-cover panel stows away beneath the bottom drawer when the chest is in use.

Cam Clamp

by Dave Flager

Fig. 1: Cam clamp

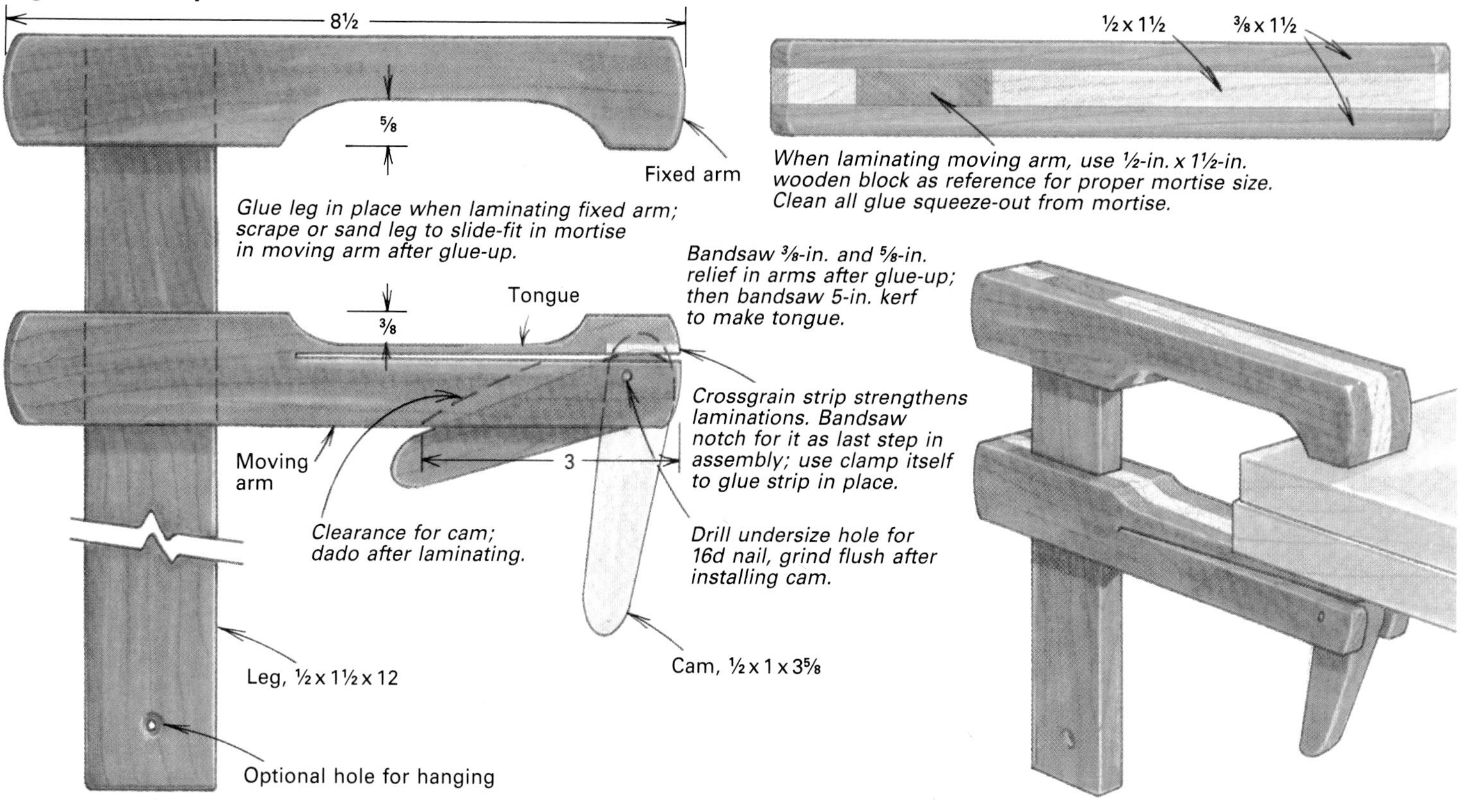

8½

⁵⁄₈

Fixed arm

Glue leg in place when laminating fixed arm; scrape or sand leg to slide-fit in mortise in moving arm after glue-up.

³⁄₈

Tongue

Moving arm

Clearance for cam; dado after laminating.

3

Leg, ½ x 1½ x 12

Optional hole for hanging

½ x 1½   ⅜ x 1½

When laminating moving arm, use ½-in. x 1½-in. wooden block as reference for proper mortise size. Clean all glue squeeze-out from mortise.

Bandsaw ⅜-in. and ⅝-in. relief in arms after glue-up; then bandsaw 5-in. kerf to make tongue.

Crossgrain strip strengthens laminations. Bandsaw notch for it as last step in assembly; use clamp itself to glue strip in place.

Drill undersize hole for 16d nail, grind flush after installing cam.

Cam, ½ x 1 x 3⅝

A while ago, I made a list of items that would improve the efficiency and earning power of my shop. More C-clamps came to mind, but these little tools are expensive and mostly they just hang around. They didn't seem to be a good investment for my limited cash resources. Thumbing through magazines, I saw a number of clever shopmade clamps, but they all required cash layout for hardware such as reverse-threaded rods and aluminum knobs. Spending money was something I wanted to avoid.

Then I came up with this all-wood cam clamp, which can be made from scraps that would otherwise be destined for the kindling pile. Best of all, the only metal needed is the shank of a 16d nail.

The design for the cam clamps is a budget version of the Klemmsia clamps seen in catalogs. Cam clamps are typically called instrumentmakers' clamps, but I've found them very useful in general cabinetmaking as well. In use, the fixed arm of the clamp is held against one side of the work to be clamped, and the moving arm is positioned against the other side. When the cam is tightened, the moving arm wedges itself in place on the leg, and the cam then bears against the flexible tongue to exert clamping force on the work. While cam clamps can't exert the bone-crushing force of a C-clamp, they are surprisingly powerful.

I've made several batches so far. By laminating the arms, I avoid having to cut precise square mortises in solid stock. The center layer of the laminations should be a hardwood, such as maple or cherry, to resist wear. The two outer laminations can be made from any knot-free, stable wood. I've used Philippine mahogany, alder and cedar with success.

The leg must be a slip fit in the mortise in the moving arm. One

way to achieve the necessary clearance is to make the center lamination in the moving arm a hair thicker than the leg and the other center laminations. Instead, to avoid confusion, I make all center laminations the same thickness. To allow clearance for the leg, I gauge the size of the through mortise in the moving arm by installing a ½-in. by 1½-in. wooden block while laminating. When this block is pushed out (before clamping the laminations tight), it produces enough lengthwise clearance for the leg, and I am able to achieve the necessary side clearances by scraping or sanding the leg after assembly. The drawing explains my work sequence, but feel free to devise your own.

When laminating my latest run of clamps, I used air-driven nails during glue-up. This sped the assembly time considerably, but didn't affect the cost. If you want to take the other approach, cam clamps can be made from beautiful exotic woods and inlaid with decorative brass or contrasting wood. Whatever your approach, a dozen or so cam clamps will find many uses in your shop. In fact, I've made a set of 10 clamps, 40 in. long, that I absolutely love. The only necessary change for the longer version is to make the cam itself capable of about twice the displacement of the short ones. The longer leg flexes under load, just like a steel bar clamp does, and you need the extra throw to compensate. Similarly, the looser fit of the moving arm on the leg, the more throw you will need on the cam. This is no problem, as you can drive out the nail whenever you need to adjust or replace the cam. ☐

Dave Flager is a renovator, custom cabinetmaker and guitarmaker. He lives in Placerville, Calif.

From *Fine Woodworking* magazine (July 1988) 71:71
Drawing: Bob La Pointe

Index

A

Adzes, elbow, about, 98-100
American Machine and Tool Co., Inc. (AMT),
  miter trimmer, reviewed, 95-97
Anderson Laboratories, Inc., tests chisels, 80-
  84
Angles, right, with trammel, 28-29
Art du Menuisier en Meubles, L', cited, 17
Art du Menuisier, L' (Roubo), quoted, 14, 15
Axes, sharpening, 108

B

Backsaws, rip teeth for, 115
Bacon, Ben, on sharpening, 116-19
Bahco Record Tools:
  ergonomic chisel, reviewed, 87
  planes of,
    discussed, 34, 37-38
    shoulder, reviewed, 50-53
Beech, American (*Fagus grandifolia*), for
  clamps, 74
Bench dogs:
  choosing, 9
  disassembling with, 12
  screw, 18, 20
  slots for, 12
  wooden, 16-17
Bench jacks, types of, 9
Bench screws, source for, 9, 12
Benchstones:
  diamond, 107
  discussed, 105-109
  vs. Japanese waterstones, 106
  slip, using, 117-19
Bertorelli, Paul, on squares, 69-73
Bits:
  auger, for endgrain, 78
  expansion, using, 79
Blackburn, Graham:
  on hollow and round planes, 58-60
  on wooden planes, 40-45
Blacksmithing:
  drop-hammers in, 83
  See also Steel.
Blandford, Percy, on marking tools, 28-29
Block planes, discussed, 37-39
Blomberg, Gregg, on adzes, 98-101
Bone, working, 61
Braces:
  joist, source for, 77
  old, buying, 77-78
  using, 78-79
  See also Dowel pointer. Hollow
    augers.
Brass:
  dovetails in, 46-47
  tablesaw blade for, 69
Buck Bros. chisels, manufacture of, 83
Buffers, rubber wheel, using, 119

C

Capet, Antoine, on shopmade sash clamps, 74-
  75
Carving:
  benches for, 120-21
  tool chest for, 122-53
  tools for, sharpening, 116-19
Chalklines, using, 28
Chisels:
  bevels for, 106-10
  double-skew, 86, 87
  ergonomic, reviewed, 87
  laboratory testing of, 80-84
  manufacture of, 83, 84
  sharpening, 116
  square-handled, 23
  tuning, 87
  types of, 85-87
  See also Slicks.

Clamps:
  cam, making, 124
  sash, making, 74-75
Clifton shoulder planes, reviewed, 52-53
Cloutier, Pierre, work by, 121
Compasses, large, improvised, 28-29
Cummins, Jim:
  on miter trimmers, 95-97
  on sharpening with diamonds, 107
Curves:
  large, compass for, 28-29
  marking gauge with, 25-26
  scraper finishing of, 68
  See also Trammels.

D

Darr, Bob, adze use of, 100-101
Dictionary of Tools (Salaman), cited, 60
Dill, Richard, tests squares, 72
Disassembly, bench dogs for, 12
Disston handsaws, about, 114
Dolan, Charles, on panel plane, 46-49
Dovetail a Drawer (Klausz), source for, 13
Dovetails:
  double-skew chisels for, 86
  in metal, 46-47
  paring chisels with, 86, 87
Dowel pointer, using, 79
Drawers:
  felt for, adhesive-backed, 123
  full-extension tool-chest, 122-23
  marking, 24, 25
  plastic, source for, 8
Drawknives:
  bevels for, 108
  sharpening, 92
  using, 91-92

E

Economaki, John, squares by, 69
End grain:
  bit for, 78
  chiseling flat, 89
Eze-Lap diamond plate, reviewed, 107

F

Felt, adhesive-backed, source for, 123
Files:
  chalk fill for, 49
  with sandpaper hooks, 71
  saw, 111-12
  as tool steel, 98
Fine Tool Journal, mentioned, 43
Finishes:
  penetrating-oil, 63
  turpentine, beeswax, and linseed oil,
    16
  See also Paints.
Flager, Dave, on cam clamps, 124
Footprint Tools:
  chisels of, tested, 80-84
  planes, discussed, 34-36, 37-38
Fraser, Maurice:
  on block planes, 37-39
  on shoulder planes, 50-53

G

Glaser, Jerry, on grinding wheels, 102-104
Gouges, sharpening, 116-19
Great Neck:
  chisels, discussed, 83
  planes, discussed, 33-34
Grinders, jointer-blade jig for, 106
Grinding:
  bevels for, 106-108
  process of, 106-108
  quenching during, cautions for, 100
  waterwheel for, 116, 118
Grizzly Imports:
  miter trimmer, reviewed, 95-97
  planes of, discussed, 36

H

Handsaws:
  anti-rust coating on, removing, 115
  hack, using, 49
  sharpening, 110-14, 115
  troubleshooting, 114
  using, 114-15
Hardware, interlock, parts for, 123
Hatchets, sharpening, 108
Hirsch chisels, tested, 80-84
Hold-fasts, 18th-Cent., 14, 15, 16
Holes:
  boring, with brace, 78-79
  undersize, enlarging, 79
Hollow augers, using, 79
Honing:
  of carving tools, 117-19
  rubber wheels for, 119
Horgan, Paul, on chisels, 84
Hornbeam, European (*Carpinus betulus*), for
  clamps, 74
Humidity, relative:
  effect on wood, 30
  measuring, with wooden hygrometer, 30-31
Hygrometer, wooden, making, 30-31

I

Iyoroi chisels, tested, 80-84

J

Jack planes:
  cheap vs. expensive, 33-36
  described, 41-42
  panel, making, 46-49
Jansson, Conny, designs chisel, 87
Japanese:
  chisels,
    tested, 80-84
    using, 19-20
  planes, using, 20
  saws, using, 21
  stone grits, comparing, 106
  woodworking,
    body mechanics in, 18-19
    chiseling in, 19-20
    workbench, 18-21
Jointer planes, described, 42
Jointers, saw, 112-13

K

Keeping the Cutting Edge (Payson), source
  for, 114
Klausz, Frank:
  Dovetail a Drawer, 13
  on marking gauge, 24-26
  reviews diamond spray, 107
  Wood Finishing, 13
  on workbenches, 8-13
Kramer, Henry T., on handsaws, 114-16

L

Landis, Scott, on 18th-Cent. workbench, 14-17
Langsner, Drew, on Japanese woodworking,
  18-21
Legs, marking gauge for, 25
Levine, Lew, makes squares, 72, 73
Lie-Nielsen, Tom, planes by, 38
Linseed oil, with beeswax and turpentine, 16
Lion miter trimmer, reviewed, 95-98
Lock, Jeff, on rabbet plane, 61-63
Locks, for drawer interlock, 123

If you enjoyed this book, you're going to love our magazine.

A year's subscription to *Fine Woodworking* brings you the kind of practical, hands-on information you found in this book and much more. In issue after issue, you'll find projects that teach new skills, demonstrations of tools and techniques, new design ideas, old-world traditions, shop tests, coverage of current woodworking events, and breathtaking examples of the woodworker's art for inspiration.

To try an issue, just fill out one of the attached subscription cards, or call us toll free at 1-800-888-8286. As always, we guarantee your satisfaction.

Subscribe Today!
6 issues for just $29

Taunton
MAGAZINES
for fellow enthusiasts

Taunton Direct, Inc.
63 South Main Street
P.O. Box 5506
Newtown, CT 06470-5506

Taunton
MAGAZINES
for fellow enthusiasts

NO POSTAGE
NECESSARY
IF MAILED
IN THE
UNITED STATES

BUSINESS REPLY MAIL
FIRST CLASS MAIL PERMIT NO.19 NEWTOWN, CT

POSTAGE WILL BE PAID BY ADDRESSEE

**Fine
WoodWorking**
63 SOUTH MAIN STREET
PO BOX 5506
NEWTOWN CT 06470-9971

Taunton
MAGAZINES
for fellow enthusiasts

NO POSTAGE
NECESSARY
IF MAILED
IN THE
UNITED STATES

BUSINESS REPLY MAIL
FIRST CLASS MAIL PERMIT NO.19 NEWTOWN, CT

POSTAGE WILL BE PAID BY ADDRESSEE

**Fine
WoodWorking**
63 SOUTH MAIN STREET
PO BOX 5506
NEWTOWN CT 06470-9971